-SOMERSETT-

-SOMERSETT-

Or Why and How

Benjamin Franklin

Orchestrated

The American Revolution

PHILLIP GOODRICH

PHILGOODRICHAUTHOR.COM

Published by Phillip Goodrich.

ISBN: 978-1-7349117-0-1

Editor: Allister Thompson

Cover design & interior formatting:
Mark Thomas / Coverness.com

To my grandmas, Hulda and Ida,
who taught me from an early age
the importance of doing my homework

Table of Contents

Author's Note

You are about to read the story of the inception of the American Revolution, as plotted by Benjamin Franklin over the course of about five to ten years. You will learn of his motivation, his colleagues, and the issues that made our nation a reality. Most of all, you will learn that this story is in fact quite true. I have added dialogue in order to give an appropriate framework as to how Franklin used current events to advance his cause (the dialogue is primarily within an "inner circle" of confederates, and the lines are preceded with the surname initial of the speaker, except with Franklin and Fothergill, where I had to supply the first *two* letters of the surname). Two major events, affected by his colleagues and acquaintances, brought the revolution from a vague dream to a reality. Both events were quite real, and the major players involved are presented as the public of that time would have known them. The intrigue is added by raising the question of who had the motive, the connections, and the ability to keep a disjointed group of American patriots focused on the goal. I have been careful to remain true to the political motivations of the characters presented and have used their correspondence and memoirs when possible to explain the events depicted. For those interested in further information, I would commend you to the bibliography, where all the threads involved in this story are elaborated. The currency of the day appears during the story. The

British pound, £, the French livre, ₶, and the American continental dollar, $, are the various currencies referenced. The exchange rate of the pound and livre are approximately 1 pound=23.4 livre. As to the continental dollar, well, think of it rather like Confederate money in about 1864 and you'll have a rough approximation.

I stumbled upon this story as a result of a now-misplaced book found on a bookstore (remember those?) close-out table about those stories of history that are compiled by trivia lovers, historians, and bibliophiles (guilty on all counts), in this case along the lines of "Stories You Never Heard (or Knew, or Were Taught, something like that) about the American Revolution." One of the many stories included in the anthology mentioned in passing the case of *Somersett v. Steuart* as a possible motive for revolution among slave-owners in the American British colonies. Having never once heard of this case during my upbringing, I pressed for more information, and the story rapidly unspooled. Seeking who might have had a motivation to use the case for political purposes pulled me into the Hutchinson letters, the second story I had never heard before. And there was a single unifying connection to both stories, again that I had never been taught. It was a connection that I believe America, 250 years after the fact, deserves and needs to know.

The story that we were taught growing up two hundred years after the American Revolution was always along the lines of: "a handful of men in Boston were upset over taxation by Parliament without representation and reacted by throwing a modest supply of tea into Boston Harbor. As a result, Great Britain called for more taxing of the colonies, and we went to war. And we won the war." But the war was waged by Americans under the leadership of a Virginian (how did *he* become embroiled in this?), and at least a dozen other Virginians, including four future presidents (Washington, Jefferson, Madison, and Monroe) rose to the forefront of the cause, while only one of the latter three (Monroe) was involved in the military. Some orator from Virginia named Patrick Henry gave a speech about "give me liberty or give me death." Some author from Boston named Thomas Paine wrote an article titled *Common Sense.* The American naval hero was a guy named John Paul Jones, but he didn't fight a single naval battle in the American colonies; he said, "I have not yet begun to fight," but even the teachers didn't know where he was fighting when he said this. Washington was a great military hero but won only *two* major battles (Trenton and Yorktown) over six years. He was fighting against the largest army and navy in the entire world. The greatest American military victory of the revolution took place in Saratoga, New York, while Washington was two hundred miles away. And all during the revolution, every American port was blockaded. There were no firearms factories in the colonies to provide weapons to Washington's army. This old guy that started libraries and the post office hung around like a semi-awake grandfather in a bunch of meetings. In summary, this story is a mess, and I never heard any coherent explanation for the many unanswered questions raised by these apparently random events. Herein lies your explanation, and you're welcome.

As for the spelling throughout this book, it frankly isn't my fault, or my editor's fault. Jefferson, for example, was a notoriously poor speller in his era, but frankly, no effort at standardized American spelling would occur until fifty years after our founding fathers took quill and ink to paper, by a lexicographer from Connecticut named Noah Webster (of dictionary fame). He is the father of the grammar police and forever codified American spelling. And so all our great American documents during the Revolutionary Era are repleat with mispellings. In various discussions of *Somersett*, the record shows variants in spelling. So we might just as well start with the title. "Somersett," "Sommersett," and "Somerset" appear in various references to the name of the slave in our story, including contemporaneous court citations from the eighteenth century. As the name was invented, there is no clearly correct spelling, and so I chose to use the spelling with two terminal "t"s. This decision was self-serving, and I will accept the charge: there are currently two novels in print that bear the title *Somerset*. I selfishly felt that this story was significant enough, and the individual was so pivotal to that story, that I needed the title to be distinctive while acknowledging the role of that court decision in the inception of our nation. So there it is.

After Chapter 13, you will find an "*Interlude*" inserted: this section explains the man, and the decision, behind the title of the book. It is placed in a reasonably chronologic location to the tale, but if the reader prefers, it could be read prior to Chapter 1 if my location proves too distracting to the narrative (the majority of the characters within the Interlude do not appear elsewhere in the narrative). I will leave that decision to you.

THIS REALLY HAPPENED

Prologue

They were not trying to create the greatest democratic republic the world has ever seen. They were simply trying to conceive boys. And not just any boys. Sons. Legitimate, primogenitary sons. And the situation had some urgency. The emperor of the Holy Roman Empire (in the words of Benjamin Franklin's French contemporary, Voltaire, it was "neither Holy, nor Roman, nor an Empire"), Leopold I of Austria, had succeeded in raising two sons who would be the heirs-apparent of his several thrones and kingdoms in central and eastern Europe.[1] But this was a vestige of the once powerful Habsburg dynasty, which had ruled in various parts of Europe over the previous three hundred years.

Unfortunately, the vicissitudes of history had insidiously laid claim to the majesty of the Habsburgs, and they were already barely a shadow of their previous greatness. Literal boatloads of riches too easily acquired from the New World, sexually transmitted diseases from the New World, and Protestants had, in that order, assailed the Habsburg family over the previous 250 years. The Spanish Habsburg rulers had made, and spent, untold fortunes arriving in the wake of the Columbian expeditions to the Caribbean in the late fifteenth and early sixteenth centuries, leaving them with a terrible credit rating and the inability to effectively secure financing for military purposes. (The Spanish

Habsburg line ended in 1700, and the Bourbons in the rise of the eighteenth century had inherited that debt with that crown.)

And the "French diseases" (or "Spanish diseases" or "Italian diseases," depending upon which nation one wished to disparage, referring to sexually transmitted illnesses) had taken a toll not only on the commoner, but on the ruling class as well, as we shall see shortly. Finally, the ascendancy of Protestantism, from northern Germany, Great Britain, Switzerland, Scandinavia, and the Low Countries, had seriously diminished the authority and influence of the Roman Catholic Church. And with the loss of influence of the church, the secular rulers of Europe felt less compunction about waging war on other "Christian nations."

For centuries throughout Europe, the Salian law of Clovis I, King of the Franks in 500 CE, had been the irrefutable law of the land. And one of its most significant tenets was absolute male primogeniture, or that women simply could not inherit crowns, or thrones, or scepters. They could inherit goods and limited amounts of land, but never an actual kingdom, or even a duchy. Male chauvinism was the supreme law. And several wars in Europe would be fought over this issue. If a king or emperor died without a son and heir, whose land was it? And who could determine the closest *male* relative? And who would ultimately respect that decision?

And so, in Vienna, in 1700, Leopold I, the emperor of the Holy Roman Empire, was in discussion with his sons, Joseph and Charles. The topic was that Joseph had thus far been unable to produce a son. Two beautiful, healthy little girls, yes; but his only son had died in infancy. Leopold, already having spent forty-five years in near-constant warfare in Europe, and coming to the close of his life, wanted assurance that his family would retain his hard-won claim to the thrones of Austria, Hungary, and many duchies and kingdoms throughout Eastern Europe. Joseph was of little help or reassurance; he was perpetually interested in music, hunting, and assuaging a vigorous libido upon various courtesans throughout Vienna.

Therefore, Leopold I proclaimed the Plan of Succession for his throne, making sure that it was widely disseminated and publicized throughout

Europe. The document decreed that his two granddaughters by Joseph would be eligible, in succession, to ascend the various thrones of Leopold, short of that of the Holy Roman Empire. Europe begrudgingly agreed—or at least expressed no opposition. In May 1705, Leopold died, and Joseph assumed the throne and arranged his election as emperor. Shortly thereafter, Joseph acquired a sexually transmitted disease from one of his courtesans and promptly shared it with his wife, whose fallopian tubes scarred shut.[2] Which guaranteed that Joseph would never produce a son. And so his wife was permanently sterilized by Joseph's prodigal life. In perhaps a stunning bit of karma, Joseph died in a smallpox epidemic eight years later, in 1711, precisely ten years and perhaps one pandemic before the Turkish inoculation might have spared his life. Such are the idiosyncrasies of history.

This left the throne of the Holy Roman Empire to the younger son, Charles (VI). Charles was more pragmatic and less prodigal, but no more successful at conceiving males. His one son died in infancy, and Charles subsequently became the father of three beautiful little girls. And no sooner was his first daughter, Maria Theresa, born than Charles renounced the "Plan of Succession" and replaced it with a "Pragmatic Sanction" (what did I tell you about Charles?), which proclaimed that *his* daughters, and not Joseph's, would be the legal heiresses of his many thrones and crowns, an "agnatic primogeniture."[3] A howling immediately arose throughout Europe, but after some coin changed hands, the rulers of the various nations of Europe reluctantly accepted this change in plans.

Twenty-seven years later, in 1740, King Charles VI finally died. With his death, several nations tied to the Pragmatic Sanction broke their ties with it and refused to acknowledge Maria Theresa as the rightful monarch of Austria.[4] This unleashed a war throughout Europe, known as the War of the Austrian Succession, which ultimately reached from Spain, to the Netherlands, to Turkey and Russia, before a sort of "treaty," more along the lines of a truce or armistice, was signed in Dresden, Germany in 1745. The final Treaty of Aix-la-Chapelle was signed in 1748, and by that time the French had carried the war to North America, with skirmishes and battles against the British, from Nova Scotia to New York. Despite the British seizure of Fort Louisbourg from the French, the treaty would restore Nova Scotia and Quebec to France, in exchange for Madras in India. But before that treaty was finally signed by all parties, colonists in British North America, from Massachusetts and New York, to Pennsylvania and Virginia, had faced French and Indigenous warriors who had threatened their properties and their very existence.

Chapter 1

The life of Benjamin Franklin is widely celebrated in American literature as one of the earliest exemplars of the "self-made man" that became part of the greater myth of the "American Dream." Born January 17, 1706, in colonial Boston as the youngest son of a middle-class tradesman named Josiah Franklin, young Benjamin would be apprenticed to his older brother, James, due to a lack of family funds to support his education. While Franklin may have had dreams of Harvard after his conclusion of studies at the Latin School in Boston, he would never attend university and would literally attain a wealth of knowledge through the "school of hard knocks." As an apprentice printer working for his brother, he showed a significant precocity in the written word, frequently penning anonymous editorials for the *Boston Courant* that James Franklin had founded and writing a series of observations under the pseudonym of "Silence Dogood."[5] The series of articles garnered immediate public interest and increased the circulation of the *Courant*, but the identity of the author could not remain long suppressed, and in the end, James was outspokenly displeased with his younger brother over this ruse. At the same time, brother James, like so many other publishers, was significantly political in a climate of political corruption rampant throughout Europe and her colonies. As a result, he did not suffer corruption in Massachusetts quietly, and his editorial stance quickly pushed him into the ranks of the opposition to local government.

Now, along with the political corruption pervading Europe, there was a simultaneous sense that achievement of a government position, *any* government position, was an opportunity to participate in the largesse of corruption and thereby make a better living than one's fellow man. So the ambitious man, the "clever" man, was often at mixed motivations, decrying this very source of potential social elevation. Those within government also learned how to maintain that lofty status against any rivals, and perhaps the key to maintenance of one's position was knowing how to deal with one's critics. The method of choice in the eighteenth century was to simply apply to the local sheriff or magistrate for a charge of libel against adverse publications. This charge would invariably culminate in the imprisonment of said critic, typically for several months, but in the case of the Crown or of nobility, it could be years at Newgate or the Tower in London. The latter sentences could commonly be tantamount to capital punishment, as the prisons of the day were cold, dark, and filled with the contagious denizens of the community. For the outspoken James Franklin, the publisher, editor, and columnist for the *Boston Courant,* his criticism of the royal governor of Massachusetts would result in a four-month prison sentence in Boston Gaol in 1722. During that time, he most assuredly wanted to maintain his print shop and the *Courant,* not only as his major source of income, but also as his only pathway out of the dreaded Boston Gaol. To this end, he enlisted the little brother he rather detested, Benjamin. James was no fool, and while he resented his brother his talent and his ability to "get on" with the public, he also recognized Benjamin as a gifted printer, writer, and perhaps most importantly, a hard worker. At the same time, he realized that an apprentice was not a proper person to operate a print shop and newspaper independently, and to this end, he arranged with Benjamin to give him a bogus "release" from his apprenticeship, while at the same time writing another apprenticeship commitment to be filed in the office of the shop. So James went to prison, and Benjamin, bearing the "release of apprenticeship" in his pocket, went to work as the newly minted owner, publisher, and editor of the *Boston Courant.*[6] He proudly changed the masthead of the *Courant* on February 11, 1723 to "Benjamin Franklin, publisher."

During James's short absence from the shop, Benjamin learned much about the careful management of local politics, whom to approach, and whom to avoid, whom to praise, and whom to criticize, who was a source of potential business for the shop, and who was a financial dead end. In all this, he was learning quickly the original meaning of politics: how to get along with everyone. This part of his education would serve him well in the next sixty-five years of his life. At the same time, his natural ability to engage strangers, combined with an incredible recall of persons with various talents and abilities, provided him a mental card file that would prove vital in his personal endeavors. When James returned that summer, he announced to Benjamin that it would once again be "business as usual" in the shop, and he would invoke the secret second apprentice agreement carefully stashed in his desk in order to put Benjamin back into his place. Benjamin was careful to keep the bogus apprenticeship release from his brother, and James never thought to ask him to relinquish that writ. Once again, James changed the masthead, and once again began treating Benjamin as a (much) younger brother and personal apprentice/servant. But now he had unwittingly provided Benjamin with a "get out of jail free" card. And Benjamin, learning the value of intrigue, even against his own family, was ready to use it.

In September of that same year, 1723, Benjamin quietly fled Boston and was soon on a packet ship for New York.[7] Arriving in New York with no letters of introduction, and hiding from detection as a fugitive, he sought out a print shop to try to attain a journeyman position. He entered the shop of William Bradford, late of Philadelphia but newly established in New York after a dispute with his former partner. Bradford advised him that he had no situations available but that his son Andrew, still in Philadelphia with his own shop, had recently lost his journeyman to death and might be open to young Franklin. After all, the writ produced by Franklin showed that he had completed his apprenticeship in Boston and was prepared to work.

And so Benjamin found a sloop headed to Philadelphia, and with virtually no funds remaining, boarded the vessel. No sooner had the vessel come into open sea than it foundered and took on water. The passengers, including Franklin, boarded a rowboat and took turns pulling for Amboy. From there, it would take him another five days of walking, riding, and taking ferries, before he finally arrived in Philadelphia. During this odyssey, he had realized that as a young man of seventeen, he was at the prime age to be "taken up" either by press gangs for the British navy, or by bounty hunters to be enslaved as an indentured servant, and therefore he had to constantly maintain an evasive demeanor.[8]

But he never lost the apprenticeship release, and once arrived in Philadelphia, happily presented it to Andrew Bradford. Andrew sadly informed Franklin that he had no positions available due to personal financial constraints. He did, however, direct Franklin to one Samuel Keimer, a young printer who had recently completed his apprenticeship in the Bradford family business. It was there that Franklin would finally achieve his position in Philadelphia as a journeyman printer. At that point in his life, he would also be introduced to the world of the Pennsylvania Quakers, through the eyes of a "French prophet," related to the Huguenots, one Andrew Benezet, with whom Franklin would cross paths almost hauntingly over the next fifty years.[9] For among the many spiritualists of Philadelphia outside of the mainstream Anglican church, Benezet was one of the firmest, albeit quietly and yet quite publicly, abolitionists in the colonies.

In retrospect, Samuel Keimer is probably to be pitied. The Benjamin Franklin that stood before him in his Philadelphia printing shop was a robust young man, not quite eighteen, physically larger than his peers, but attired more like an indentured servant or house slave than the journeyman he was presenting himself to be. Likely, William Bradford in New York had checked his credentials in only a cursory fashion, looking at a contemporary issue of the *Boston Courant* with the masthead showing his brother, James, as the editor and publisher, and therefore having absolutely no reason to suspect that Franklin was actually a fugitive apprentice. And so he looked simply like a newly minted free man that badly needed a job. Keimer needed the help.

It seemed ideal at face value, but little did Keimer realize that he was about to walk into the meat grinder that was young Benjamin Franklin at his most desperate and most ambitious.[10]

Within a year of joining Keimer, Franklin had made what he thought was a great contact in Sir William Keith, governor of Pennsylvania. Keith encouraged Franklin to 1) talk to his father, Josiah, in Boston about possible financial help in setting Benjamin up in business, and 2) travel to London to make some further key contacts to advance his career.[11] Franklin headed back home to Boston first, and then to London, with an eighteen-month hiatus from Philadelphia. Keith's "London contacts" amounted to nothing, but Franklin was able to secure positions in two different printing houses, Palmer's and then Watts's, both top-notch and far more skilled than any print shop in the colonies.[12] There, young Benjamin would learn how the best printing was done and what the finished product should look like. There he would also meet a printer, William Strahan, "Straney," who would become a lifelong friend through many trying times over the next sixty years. And there also he would learn how to print government documents and currency that were relatively counterfeit proof. The latter was a skill that would place young Franklin in high demand back in the colonies.

Returning to Philadelphia in the fall of 1726, Franklin first tried his hand in a general store, but his silent partner contracted typhoid within a couple months of opening and died.[13] Left without financial support, or even title to the business, Franklin went hat in hand back to the long-suffering Samuel Keimer and was soon working again as a partner. In that same year, the Governor's Council of the neighboring colony of New Jersey had approached Keimer with a proposal to print currency; Franklin was now perhaps the only printer in the middle Atlantic colonies who could provide plates complex enough to prevent counterfeiting, and soon the councilmen gravitated away from Keimer and toward Franklin.

In the meantime, Franklin had also contacted an apprentice in the shop, Hugh Meredith, in confidence, and the two concocted a scheme to open their own print shop, financed by Meredith's father.[14] In early 1728, Franklin and Meredith opened a print shop in direct competition against Keimer and against young Bradford. By fall of the following year, Keimer was bankrupt and out of business; he gathered up what meager resources he had left, sold the *Pennsylvania Gazette* name to Franklin and Meredith, and moved to Barbados, never to return. Meredith fell into drinking and shirking his duties at the new print shop, and Franklin promptly bought him, and his father, out of the business. Meredith returned to farming and maintained a close long-term friendship with Franklin; he simply didn't have "printer's ink in his veins." By 1730, Franklin was printing, publishing, and editing while running the local postal service out of his shop. Highly industrious by the standards of the day, Franklin also found commercial contracts gravitating to his shop.

Chapter 2

Thus began the Golden Age of Franklin's writing, editing and publishing. In 1732 he inaugurated *Poor Richard's Almanack*, his most lasting collection of proverbs and essays.[15] With homespun humor and piercing criticisms of the local political scene, Franklin rapidly gained a following throughout the British colonies and in London. During this time, he also entered a common-law marriage with Deborah Rogers, née Read, whose legitimate husband had disappeared to the Caribbean, never to return, but with a marriage never annulled.[16] Franklin also fathered a son out of wedlock with a woman forever unnamed but most assuredly *not* Deborah Read Rogers. This was William Franklin, of whom he would assume primary custody by the time the child was three years old. He would never reveal the identity of the mother; with some poetic justice, William would likewise father an illegitimate son a generation later, who would prove a valuable resource to grandpa Benjamin during the American Revolution, and who would likewise father an illegitimate son.

In this timeframe Franklin would also launch the "Junto," a semiformal philosophical club composed of a dozen close friends and dedicated to the debate of questions of politics, science, philosophy, and spirituality.[17] Meeting initially in a local tavern, they would ultimately lease a meeting house that allowed the Junto to create its own library, the first lending library in the American colonies. Further, efforts from the Junto would spearhead development of a fire company; an academy that would become the University of Pennsylvania; an intercolonial mail service; a local constabulary and militia; and encouragement of medical education, which Shippen and Morgan would develop into the first medical school in the colonies. Through the modest beginnings of the Junto, Philadelphia was quickly becoming the prime city in America, surpassing Boston and New York in its populism and progressivism. Franklin for his part was learning the rewards of hard labor, combined with intrigue, through valued contacts, to achieve his goals; it was a process that would serve him well in the next fifty years of his life.

Into Franklin's somewhat idyllic existence in Philadelphia in 1732 entered Thomas Penn, son of the founder of Pennsylvania, William Penn, to oversee the affairs of the colony. Thomas had resurrected the Penn family from the financial disarray of the father at the beginning of the eighteenth century, and through shrewd management of their resources, was finally pulling them out of the ashes. Much of the credit for this recovery must appropriately go to Thomas, who, while not the primary recipient of the estate (that would go to his older brother, John), mustered the younger brothers in particular and directed the financial conduct of the family. He was determined to avoid the errors of their father in being perhaps too lax, and too trusting, in the administration of the fledgling colony during the previous generation and would hold an iron fist on its administration in the ensuing forty years. And so it was to this end that he appeared in Philadelphia to take charge. He would remain over nine years and in that time would prove to be a most difficult personality to warm to or even approach. Extremely conscious of social status and societal stratification, he would converse with a very tight circle of persons within the colony and soon declared a "Council" or commission of administrators for the colony, including Governor Patrick Gordon, Isaac Norris (a personal friend of Franklin), James Logan, Samuel Preston, and Andrew Hamilton. He most assuredly could not be bothered by interaction with "the people" and conspicuously avoided Benjamin Franklin and others of the trade or mercantile class. The one descriptor objective observers would employ repeatedly in official interactions with Penn in those nine years was "cold."[18] There is no evidence in the residual papers, documents, and biographies over the two hundred fifty years since to contest that description. Such a personality was certain to conflict with the gregarious, curious, and robust personality of the colony's most famous printer.

Thomas Penn was focused on the larger picture in his colony and to that end seemed particularly interested in shoring up the definition of the borders, while at the same time encouraging immigration of industrious persons who would assure the net profit of the colony to the Penn coffers back home. To the former, he had assigned his younger brothers to maintain dialogue with Charles Calvert, Lord Baltimore, regarding the contested southern border between Pennsylvania and Maryland.[19] Penn had made no secret of the fact that he detested Roman Catholics generally, and Maryland, being the one Roman Catholic colony in America, with Baltimore as the seat of the archdiocese for all the colonies, was a perennial source of angst for Penn. At one point he had gone so far as to recommend prohibition of Roman Catholicism in Pennsylvania, but this effort was roundly condemned by the Quaker majority, who insisted on perpetual religious freedom throughout the colony. And so, if he was to be forced to share a common border with Maryland, he resigned himself to simply defining that border to "keep his enemies closer." Penn's personal religious practice was problematic throughout his long life; born a Quaker, of course, he never accepted or adopted the practices of the sect and instead gravitated back toward the Anglican church. Nonetheless, he never formally entered into communal fellowship with the Anglican confession and would die without benefit of sacraments.

As to the latter issue of encouraging immigration, Penn wanted to establish the definition of the borders and ownership of the land to the west of Philadelphia to open this area to settlers from northern Europe whom he felt would be industrious and agriculturally oriented. To this end of securing land, he opened a dialogue with the Indigenous peoples of Pennsylvania, basing his claims to the western lands upon the original treaty negotiated by his father back in 1686. Not surprisingly, the local chiefs disavowed any knowledge of this treaty and more or less left Thomas Penn to renegotiate the treaties *de novo*. Ultimately, the Indigenous tribes agreed to a "walking purchase" of land west of the Delaware River; i.e., they would sell the amount of land a man could walk due west from the Delaware River in a single day.[20] Whereupon Penn enlisted some apparently skilled local long-distance runners who were able to acquire up to a fifty-mile extension from the western bank of the Delaware River reaching deep into the "Indian lands" of the colony. The resentment felt by the chiefs over this athletic approach to a walking purchase, designed only to acquire the immediate western bank of the Delaware, would flare intermittently right up to the American Revolution.[21] And the locals, rather than Penn, would bear the brunt of this resentment.

Penn would otherwise occupy his time in Philadelphia with shoring up his proprietary interests in agriculture and industry, both of which provided a significant profit potential. In the environs of Germantown, Penn found settlers eager to establish an agronomy that would be self-sufficient and capable of providing surplus produce for export to the adjoining colonies and beyond. Penn was also supportive of light industry and manufacturing, although here British interests would intervene within the next twenty years to render production and exportation of iron and linen so duty laden as to become unprofitable. After nine years of negotiating borders and trade to his personal satisfaction, and with business concerns increasing in Great Britain, Penn departed by way of Boston in the fall of 1741 and would never return to America.[22] During his nine-year sojourn in Philadelphia, by intent or not, he and Benjamin Franklin would succeed in avoiding any personal interaction. This situation would change dramatically in the near future.

Chapter 3

I t was during Penn's return crossing to Great Britain that the War of Austrian Succession was really heating up. Although the first outbreak in Silesia had begun in 1740, not until 1743 would King George II become the last British monarch to lead an army in the field, when his Pragmatic Army (no, they were not unduly practical but rather an alliance of the Netherlands, Great Britain, and Russia, who all had supported Maria Theresa in her efforts to ascend the Austrian throne, via the "Pragmatic Sanction" of Charles VI, v.s.) roundly defeated a French army at Dettingen.[23] From that time forward, the British colonists in America would refer to this complicated European conflict as "King George's War." And because the British king had led an army against French forces, France immediately assumed any and all British subjects and landholders were fair game.

It would not take long for France to direct its collective gaze toward the St. Lawrence River and the scattered colonies to its south, especially the border colonies of Massachusetts (which at that time included Maine), New York, and Pennsylvania. While these colonies were far removed from the real estate of Europe, the overarching sentiment on both sides of the English Channel was that any conflict that diverted an army from Europe to North America could potentially, and significantly, change the military balance in their favor. And

Louis XV's France, ever on the brink of financial collapse, was perpetually looking for ways to avoid direct warfare against the British in Europe.

While in theory Spain was allied to France in King George's War, its threat to the British colonies was meager at best.[24] Forces from Havana would skirmish with Britain's West Florida forces at Pensacola, to little point, and Georgia at this time was a fledgling colony barely worth the effort to attack from St. Augustine into Savannah. Therefore, Philadelphia was not threatened by Spain, as Franklin was intimating in the press.[25] On the other hand, France was a real threat through the "Forks of the Ohio" and the Great Lakes portal from Canada. Both France and Great Britain were more than willing to approach alliances with the various Indigenous tribes in the area as well, and the frontier settlers were the most at risk.

Franklin was fully aware of the attacks on colonial soil by combined French and native American raiding parties, notably at Fort Saratoga/Schuylerville (New York) in 1745 and Fort Massachusetts/North Adams (Massachusetts) in 1746. Both were associated with significant loss of American life and property. And in 1746, French and Spanish ships were noted off the coast of the Delaware plantations, just outside the Delaware River. This placed them within a hundred miles of Philadelphia itself and was a significant source of discomfort for this relatively successful entrepreneur whose wealth was directly tied to the safety and well-being of his local community. So he decided to travel to Fort Saratoga and to evaluate first-hand the impact of the raid and pillage of Schuylerville. It is not at all clear what his motives may have been to take this step, but after walking through the burnt-out ruins of this village, Franklin realized how this could so easily be his beloved Philadelphia and how vulnerable his adopted hometown truly was.

When one looks at a map of the American eastern seaboard (and especially an eighteenth century version, when much of the specifics were different), one is immediately taken by a simple yet jarring fact: there is but one of the original thirteen colonies that has absolutely *no* direct access from the Atlantic. And that colony is Pennsylvania. While New Hampshire, New York, and Virginia have limited access directly, in correspondence with their size, they indeed have at least one oceanside port of entry. The only true port of entry for Pennsylvania was Philadelphia, one hundred miles above Delaware Bay. And this was no accident of geography. This was a colony founded by pacifists, the Society of Friends, known to one and all as "Quakers." As Quakers, they were opposed to war, truly to any display of aggression at any level. And they were therefore reluctant to defend themselves against hostilities. Thus, they sought a natural defense from the warring powers of European Crowns and knew that their best defense was literally hiding geographically from the foreign seafarers frequenting the American seaboard throughout the eighteenth century. The Delaware plantations had been offered to Pennsylvania colony on several occasions, as they had been to New Jersey. Ultimately, of course, they would become a separate colony, because Pennsylvania frankly did not *want* that ready access to the Atlantic, or more specifically *from* the Atlantic.

But in July 1747, the war finally came to Pennsylvania.[26] French raiders landed in southeastern Pennsylvania, along the coast of the Delaware River south of Philadelphia, terrorizing settlers in the area and pilfering from various plantations. The Philadelphia city council appealed to the Pennsylvania Assembly to organize a militia for defense. The response of the Assembly was swift: "In case of enemy attack from the Delaware River, local riverboat pilots are hereby instructed to tell the enemy that the port of Philadelphia has been closed" and refuse to pilot ships farther north on the river. Any failure to heed this order was to be considered a crime of treason on the part of the riverboat pilots. Then the Assembly summarily adjourned, having determined the problem solved.

Franklin was incensed! He had had previous dealings with the Penn family, who were the Proprietors of the colony but resided in Great Britain. And he had found them intransigent in wanting to spend any money on this colony founded by their father. This issue would prove no different. Not only were they unwilling to financially support the development of a "Home Guard," but they further forbade Franklin from starting one himself.[27] Frustrated by the lack of assistance from his British Proprietor, Franklin responded once again, as he had in the past, with the pen and the press.

First, he began running articles in his *Pennsylvania Gazette* outlining the theory of military defense in emergency situations, for his Quaker audience. And then, in a separate pamphlet, he fired off his own bombshell, "The Plain Truth."[28] In this treatise, signing himself as "A Tradesman of Philadelphia," Franklin laid out the basis for providing defense of Pennsylvania generally, and Philadelphia in particular, based on a home guard model of local volunteers. He pointed out that Great Britain was currently engaged in a war (King George's War, or the War of the Austrian Succession), which "rages over a great part of the known World." While perhaps overstating the threat from Spain, he appropriately noted the real threat from France, who of course relished any opportunity to fight against anyone considered British, even half a world away in the colonies of North America. He went on to point out that every other colony maintained a militia, except Pennsylvania. And then he carefully outlined how he proposed to form and finance a local militia. Volunteers could be solicited outside of the Quakers (in actuality, several Quakers also joined), and the enterprise could be readily funded through a Pennsylvania lottery. He went on to describe for his relatively naive audience what a lottery is and how it worked.

Now, Pennsylvania, along with Maryland and Delaware, were "proprietary colonies," which meant that they were owned in their entirety by a single individual or family in Great Britain. This further meant that the proprietor of the colony, living in Great Britain, was responsible for the financial needs of the colony, including those of administration and defense. Thomas Penn, son of the namesake founder, was pretty much by 1747 the sole proprietor of Pennsylvania (his sons and wife were also listed). Penn steadfastly refused to even consider Franklin's effort at self-financing a militia. Despite this, Franklin pressed on, and within two months over a thousand volunteers had signed on as "Associators," and through a lottery, Franklin had readily raised the finances to back them.[29] By March 1748, they were organized into brigades, with uniformed officers and with weaponry provided through Franklin's lottery by an arms dealer in London named David Barclay.

It was now Thomas Penn's turn to be incensed![30] In defying his direct order not to form a militia, Franklin had created a home guard now standing in the square in Philadelphia, pledged to defend Pennsylvania from any attack. Penn wrote, *This Association is founded on a Contempt of Government, and cannot end in anything but Anarchy and Confusion.* He felt that Franklin's initiative was treasonous to the Crown.

Fortunately for all concerned, as the War of the Austrian Succession died down in Europe, the passions of Penn and Franklin died down with it, and most of the Associators had gone home by the summer of 1748.[31] But the animus between Franklin and Penn would intensify further for the next quarter century.

Chapter 4

The uneasy "peace" of the conclusion of the War of the Austrian Succession would not be very durable in Franklin's neighborhood. Having Indigenous people, and the British, and the French, living in such proximity to one another in one of the most beautiful settings in all North America simply invited discord and violence. The primary tinder box for the ensuing thirty-five years would be the confluence of the Allegheny and Monongahela Rivers, known in colonial times as the Forks of the Ohio, and to the world today as Pittsburgh. But in the years after 1748, the French would press their claim to this area from the north and the west, while the Brits would pursue the same from the east and the south. To this end, in 1754, Governor Robert Dinwiddie of Virginia would send out a small force under the direction of a twenty-two-year-old major from Alexandria named George Washington who knew the area well.[32] And Dinwiddie took this initiative without so much as a note to the House of Burgesses in Williamsburg, or to Parliament, or to the Crown. It seems that this group of advance British troops had been sent to the Forks of the Ohio to press the claim of Virginia on this land by building a fort. The French, having none of it, had arrived with a force of about five hundred trappers and native Americans to tell them to stand down and return to whence they had come. And the much smaller British group did precisely that. The French, seeing the strategic advantage, and beauty, of the Forks of the Ohio, stayed on and proceeded to build Fort Duquesne. There they would maintain occupation of western Pennsylvania.

Governor Dinwiddie was likewise having none of it.[33] His twenty-two-year-old major, a young son of a planter family from tidewater Virginia, was recommissioned a lieutenant colonel. And off he went, with rather ambiguous orders to reestablish British presence at the Forks of the Ohio and to engage any resistance to that presence. This same George Washington had participated in a surveying expedition of the northwest portion of Virginia and knew the land reasonably well. Fortuitously, a young Mingo warrior, Tanacharison, who had sided with the British cause against the French, a decision not terribly popular with the Iroquois nation in the area (Mingo: *treachery, deceit*, from the Algonquin), brought a raiding party and joined with Washington. Now, Washington had been told that Fort Duquesne was defended by a force of perhaps five hundred, and he was able to round up only about 150 Virginians to ride with him, along with the native group. Therefore, rather than taking on Fort Duquesne, where his force would be badly outnumbered, he chose to build a smaller fort thirty-five miles south of Fort Duquesne, which he named "Fort Necessity." The French, yet again, were having none of it and sent a group of about forty French soldiers to clear the Brits out. The reports vary as to how this confrontation went down, but in the end the French officer in charge had been shot and scalped, the French soldiers were taken into custody, and Washington would write to his older brother, *I heard bullets whistle, and there was something charming in the sound.* Both sides would take notice of the behavior of this young officer under duress of battle. Later that same year, the French returned with a force of about nine hundred, and Washington was forced to surrender.[34] In the aftermath of his surrender of "Fort Necessity" to the French, he was stripped of his command and subsequently in a fit of pique resigned his commission.

This Seven Years' War, known today in Europe as "World War Zero," was complicated in its causes, but everyone agreed that the British and French had started it in their colonies in North America (where it would be forever known as the "French and Indian War"). Before it was over, it would reach to India and to Sweden and embroil all the major powers of Europe in yet another more or less meaningless turmoil, which ultimately would settle almost nothing (the changes in real estate in the "Treaty of Paris" would be massively undone after the American Revolution and its own "Treaty of Paris"). During the fighting in Europe, the British decided to send a force of British Regulars (actually Irish conscripts) under the command of a self-confident and self-important, if over the hill general named Edward Braddock, a career military man from the age of fifteen, now sixty. And Braddock understood that his task was to get the French, once and for all, out of Fort Duquesne, and essentially out of the British colonies.

So Braddock and his troops landed in Alexandria, Virginia in 1755 and there were met by a volunteer officer, the same George Washington, once more a lieutenant colonel in the colonial army of the "Old Dominion."[35] Braddock sized him up and immediately welcomed him into his service. The regulars then marched to Frederick, Maryland, to seek provisions, wagons, and horses. And there the expedition to relieve Fort Duquesne ground to a halt. After requisitioning 150 wagons to carry arms, provisions, and men to western Pennsylvania, the response was twenty-five dilapidated wagons in various states of disrepair. Braddock was ready to return to Great Britain.

But who would appear, at that moment as by Divine Providence, but Benjamin Franklin, sent by the Pennsylvania Assembly to provide what support Braddock needed to cleanse Pennsylvania of the enemy. Braddock, exasperated, explained his dilemma, and Franklin responded, "You would have been better served to have landed in Pennsylvania, where every farmer has a second wagon in excellent repair and would be at your service."

Franklin, out of political correctness, avoided mentioning the fact that Thomas Penn, proprietor of Pennsylvania, had refused to provide financial support for Braddock's foray. Braddock brightened; Franklin almost always had that impact on new acquaintances. After agreeing to the rental terms, Franklin and his son William set out to obtain provisions and returned with 150 wagons and 259 horses, two weeks after advertising the request.[36] Braddock brought his army to Philadelphia to show Franklin his appreciation and to assemble the train for the journey through Pennsylvania.

The Assembly had assured Franklin of adequate funding for the endeavor, and Braddock also assured him that the Crown was willing to provide repayment and insurance for any lost wagons. With that assurance, Franklin reached into his own purse for supplemental immediate funding for food and horses. In conversation, Braddock assured Franklin, "Duquesne should only take three or four days, and then we are to proceed to Niagara, and then to Frontenac, if the season will allow. Which I assume it will, as there are no impediments to my marching to Niagara."

Over the brief time spent with Braddock, Franklin noted that he treated the native Americans in his train poorly, refused the advice and suggestions of locals, confiscated the African slaves of the Pennsylvania farmers, and even tended to minimize Franklin's concerns regarding the potential for "Indian ambuscades" between Philadelphia and Fort Duquesne. As the train departed west, Franklin waved but shook his head. *He has too much self-confidence, too high an opinion of his Irish troops, and too mean an opinion of French American militia and native Americans in combat*, Franklin thought to himself.[37] He would never see Braddock alive again.

It would take Braddock's army two months to cross the Pennsylvania wilderness of forest and mountains, but they received no "Indian ambuscades," and Braddock was beginning to think that even the purportedly sage Benjamin Franklin was overly timid and ill-informed. But after a challenging ford of the Monongahela River, the army was greeted by a frontal assault of French and native American scouts and skirmishers. Initially, the fight went well for the British regulars, but then they fell prey to a method of fighting that would plague the British army for the next twenty years in America: guerrilla warfare. The Canadiens and their Iroquois allies rallied and took to fighting from heavy forest cover, and the mounted British officers were no match. One by one, the officers were cut down, and the British troops scattered, fleeing back to the river, and into the face of their own rear guard coming forward. Chaos ensued. It was at this point that Braddock was hit with a shot that would prove fatal, and his adjutant was killed instantly. A disorderly retreat followed, with the Iroquois and Canadiens in pursuit.

Into the breach rode a surviving officer, clad in blue jacket and buckskin, calling out commands, not in panic but in orderly directions.[38] He managed to align the retreating regulars into a phalanx and called for a fusillade of shots. Reload. Fire. Reload. Fire. And strangely, the chaos broke, and the Canadiens and Iroquois headed for forest cover. The officer called for recovery and evacuation of the wounded, while keeping covering volleys ongoing, and brought out the surviving troops in an orderly retreat to the river. From there, he was able to provide a more organized fording of the river, bringing all casualties along. Braddock was among the wounded. The officer finally paused and took stock: he was already on his third horse of the day, and he noted *four* fresh holes in his blue jacket, from ball or blade. He was, of course, that same George Washington, now aged twenty-four.

Braddock at that point was already semiconscious and fading from pain and blood loss. "Who would have thought this could happen?" was his only response. "At least we will know better what to do next time." Then he was gone. Upon return to Philadelphia, the ragged army also took stock: two-thirds of the army were casualties, with more than one-third dead. Three-fourths of the officers were dead. It would be recognized as one of the worst defeats in British military history to that point. In the subsequent requisite inquiry in London, much would be made of the lack of financial support provided by the proprietary family of Pennsylvania. Meanwhile, in Philadelphia in the fallout from this debacle, the Pennsylvania Assembly was left with compensating the locals for their loss of equipment and horses and voted a tax on land, including the extensive land holding of the Penn family, to provide the funds. The Penn family, safely ensconced in Great Britain, promptly vetoed the tax and assured the colonists that there would be *no* assessment of revenue on Penn proprietary lands, then or ever.[39] As in the aftermath of the "Associators" controversy of 1747, Franklin was furious with Penn, but this time Thomas Penn had overplayed his hand by refusing financial support to defend his own colony.[40] The British ministry was made aware of the Penn intransigence and its potential impact upon the Braddock expedition and was notably displeased.

Franklin was also extremely disturbed by the outcome of the Braddock expedition, but at the same time he realized that there were lessons to be learned. The French had demonstrated that a force of British regulars could be defeated by guerrilla warfare, and George Washington had shown incredible resilience during a setback and retreat. He never left the battlefield, faced enemy fire with incredible poise, and provided moral support to his forces at a time when a lesser leader might have excoriated them. He was resolute, determined and fearless...*special.* Mature beyond his years, Washington had already learned how to lose a battle without losing an army or losing a colony. Franklin took note.

In the winter of 1756, the Assembly, at the insistence of the governor of Pennsylvania, Robert Hunter Morris, asked Franklin to organize a state militia to protect the farmers in the northwestern part of the state. To this end, they voted a tax (*without* Penn family support, of course) of £55,000.[41] Franklin decided to use this money to build protective forts in the area, starting at Bethlehem. He took his son, William, as his aide-de-camp. Ultimately, they would build three forts and raise a militia force of about 1,200 men, supported by artillery. Upon his return to Philadelphia, he would be saluted with cannon and musket fire. This celebration was duly reported by the governor to Thomas Penn. Now it was *Penn's* turn to be disturbed, and he promptly reported Franklin's insubordination to the Privy Council of the King, back in Westminster.

During this time the Canadien and Iroquois threats toward Massachusetts, New York, Pennsylvania, and Virginia had forced the hands of the Board of Trade in London, and they ordered a colonial congress to assemble in Albany, New York in 1754.[42] This was to be attended by delegates representing all British colonies in North America, to discuss mutual defense from French incursions into British lands. Franklin, selected as a delegate from Pennsylvania, was most optimistic, opining that if the Iroquois were capable of uniting their six nations as a single force, it should be far easier for British subjects of ten or twelve colonies to accomplish the same. He formulated his own design to present at the Congress, which he styled "The Albany Plan of Union," and then lobbied his fellow delegates from Pennsylvania, as well as friends from Virginia and New York. At the congress, Franklin made a motion that a committee be formed to prepare and receive plans for the union of the colonies, primarily for mutual defense. And he made sure he was named a member of the committee. It would take nearly a month, but ultimately Franklin spearheaded a concept of establishing a national congress, with representatives from each colony elected by their own assemblies and overseen by a "president-general" appointed by the Crown. It would be a federation of colonies, with central oversight. It would be a *nation*. One of his most ardent supporters was a shipping merchant from Boston named Thomas Hutchinson. A delegation from London had been sent by the Board of Trade to participate in the proceedings. One of the representatives from London was a studious young man named Thomas Pownall, the acting lieutenant governor of New Jersey.[43] During the Albany Congress, Franklin and Pownall would engage in an ongoing dialogue about the pros and cons of intercolonial defense and the financial responsibility, both from Great Britain and her colonies, in securing the necessary materiel and provisions for an army in the field.[44] Together they would finalize the document known as the Albany Plan of Union, based upon Franklin's draft, and a lifelong friendship was started.

Franklin lobbied hard for the Albany Plan of Union in the press, both at home in Philadelphia, and in New York and Boston. The Massachusetts governor argued that the Crown should appoint the federal congress and establish the taxation rate on the colonies to support the congress, but Franklin countered that "it is an undoubted right of Englishmen not to be taxed but by their own consent given through their representatives."[45] In this opinion he was advancing his fervent belief that the voters of the American colonies shared the absolutely identical political status of the landed gentry voters of Great Britain.[46] To this, the House of Lords would ultimately, within the safe confines of Westminster, respond with gales of laughter. Ultimately, despite the enthusiasm of the delegates, no colonial assembly would approve the plan. And worse, when the plan was transmitted to Parliament and the Crown, *both* were roundly critical and dismissive. Turned aside at every audience for his defense initiative, Franklin feared daily for the safety of his beloved Philadelphia and felt helpless to defend it.

In his anger and frustration over the intransigence of Thomas Penn, Franklin resolved to take his grievances directly to Penn in a face-to-face confrontation and had the Pennsylvania assembly name him as "Agent for the affairs of the colony of Pennsylvania" in London. For his part, Franklin was willing to offer one final effort at conciliation with Penn, but failing that, he planned on moving forward with an appeal to Parliament, and perhaps to the Crown itself, to persuade them to assume the rule of the colony of Pennsylvania.[47] He was quite sure that if Penn forced him to publicly enumerate the deficiencies in the proprietary rule of Pennsylvania, the Crown would be willing to step in and take over.[48] He was quite wrong.

Chapter 5

Three categories of colony (or "province") were recognized by the British government in British North America in the eighteenth century: provincial, proprietary, and chartered. The chartered colonies had arisen early in the colonial history of Great Britain, by stock companies seeking fortunes in the "new world." By the eighteenth century, these included Rhode Island and Providence Plantation, Warwick, and Connecticut. The charter of Massachusetts having been revoked in 1683, Massachusetts was, at the beginning of the eighteenth century, a provincial colony. The charter colonies had a provincial governor selected by the stockholders and an assembly elected by the colonists. All laws passed by the assembly were subject to review by the governor, and if he approved, they were subject to review by the British Board of Trade and the Privy Council of the Crown (more on these below).

The provincial colonies were Massachusetts, New York, New Hampshire, Virginia, North and South Carolina, and Georgia. These were also referred to as "Crown colonies" because they were under the direct control of the British monarchy. Administration of the provincial/Crown colonies was through a governor appointed by the ruling monarch, and the governor in many of the colonies also had a council selected by that governor (more or less a "staff" or "cabinet"). The assembly (such as the "House of Burgesses" in Virginia) were elected by the colonists. All laws passed by the assembly had to be submitted to the governor for approval and were then reviewed by the Privy Council in Westminster.

The proprietary colonies were Pennsylvania, Delaware, Maryland, and in the beginning of the eighteenth century, New Jersey. (New Jersey reverted to be a provincial colony in 1702.) The proprietary colonies were owned by a single British family, who also oversaw their administrations. This was accomplished by a governor hired by the family and given a "performance bond" (a stipend, the renewal of which was dependent upon the governor's ability to provide a steady income to the proprietor). The governor again frequently employed a council of his selection. The assembly was elected by the colonists, and laws passed by the assembly were subject to review not only by the governor but also by the proprietor, the Board of Trade, and the Privy Council.

The British government, based in Westminster/London, consisted of the ruling monarch and Parliament. Parliament had two "houses," or chambers, much like the United States Congress. But unlike our United States Congress, the two houses of Parliament were the House of Lords and the House of Commons. The seats in Commons were elected by British citizens with voting rights, and a handful were controlled by the Crown or by various departments of the government. The House of Lords was filled by British nobility, landholders who held hereditary seats in the house, some dating back to the "Conquest" (1066 CE). The monarch had a Privy Council of trusted advisors, at that time staffed by nobility who held key posts in the government, key clergy (e.g., archbishops), and other key figures such as royal family members or politicians not currently holding elected office. The Board of Trade was a subcommittee of the Privy Council and was charged with all trading endeavors, including administration of the British colonies. To facilitate this administrative duty, the Board of Trade employed a panel of career bureaucrats, designated "secretaries" and led by the "First Secretary of the Board of Trade," an executive director of a sort. Parliament had no direct oversight in respect to the British colonies; this would be a lesson that American patriots seemed unable to comprehend, despite repeated remonstrances to the contrary by various British political leaders. As of 1628, with the Petition of Right, Parliament gained sole authority to levy new taxes, and this was their only governing role over the American colonies. This relationship between Parliament and the colonies would be tested by Parliament against Massachusetts in response to the "Boston Tea Party" in 1774 with the passage of the "Intolerable Acts," as we shall see.

In 1757, Franklin was back in London for the first time since his teen years as a journeyman printer, now accompanied by his son William and two household slaves.[49] He was hosted by Peter Collinson and Dr. John Fothergill, Quakers who were members of the Royal Society, a gathering of amateur and professional scientists who met to discuss their research. With their support, Franklin found lodging and offices for his household group at the home of one Mrs. Margaret Stevenson, a middle-aged widow living in Craven Street.[50] Here Franklin would find a "home away from home" for the next eighteen years, and an abiding platonic relationship with his landlady and her pretty young daughter, Polly. In this time frame, Fothergill and Collinson would regularly conduct Franklin to meetings of the Royal Society for scientific and political discourse.[51] In one such meeting, Franklin advised them that he had come to try to wrest Pennsylvania from the fist of Thomas Penn, if necessary, by lobbying Parliament. Fothergill, ever a peacemaking Quaker, urged Franklin to talk with Penn first and assured him that Penn would acquiesce when he learned of the seriousness of the Assembly in their grievances against the proprietors.[52] So Franklin, dubious over the enterprise but at the same time out of deference to his British hosts, approached Thomas Penn. Penn promptly postponed their conference for two weeks, requesting a formal list of grievances to be presented in writing at a time when Penn's brother, Richard, would be available. So two weeks later, with Richard Penn in attendance, Franklin sat down with the man he hated most in the world.[53] Franklin presented a written list of grievances, curtly titled "Heads of Complaints." Penn scanned the list briefly, thanked Franklin brusquely for his time and trouble, and told him a response would be forthcoming. He then summarily dismissed Franklin and took the list to his personal solicitor, pointing out to him Franklin's lack of understanding the appropriate format for petitions to his proprietor.

Penn likely relished the delay over the ensuing months, leaving Franklin twisting in the wind, wondering when to expect a response. Franklin, for his part, insisted on another meeting in January 1758 with Penn to talk about the efforts by the Pennsylvania assembly to establish a formal trade agreement with the Indigenous tribes on the Pennsylvania frontier.[54] At that meeting, Franklin advised Penn that the Assembly had established a method of appointing commissioners to mediate trade.[55] Penn replied that the Assembly had no such authority to do this. To which Franklin retorted that indeed they did, as a representative body much like Parliament that could regulate trade in Great Britain. Penn laughed and told Franklin that only the proprietors could appoint any commissioners in Pennsylvania for *any* purpose. Franklin pointed out the royal charter signed by Penn's *own father*, William Penn, established that the Pennsylvania Assembly "shall have all the Power and Privileges of an Assembly according to the Rights of the Freeborn Subjects of England, and as is usual in any of the British Plantations in America."

Here Penn responded in a way that would forever rupture his relationship with Franklin. "My father had *no right* to grant that privilege to the settlers of the colony. The only source of those powers is the Crown, and if the settlers of Pennsylvania were told otherwise, they were quite misled. The Royal Charter is a public document, so therefore they would have been afforded ample opportunity to review it. If they did not understand this, it is their own fault." And then he laughed in Franklin's face and bid him good day.

Franklin's subsequent response to this episode would cement the schism, describing Penn's delivery as "a kind of triumphant laughing Insolence, such as a low Jockey might do when a Purchaser complained that He had cheated him in a Horse."[56] The "low Jockey" reference, meaning a "dirty conniving cheat," would come back in various forms over the next thirty years in reference to the relationship between these two.[57]

In November 1758, the response to the "Heads of Complaints" finally arrived. Penn's solicitor, Ferdinando John Paris, advised Franklin that the grievances were inappropriately submitted, groundless, some of them offensive, and therefore Thomas Penn would no longer offer his good faith in conference with Franklin. Paris had verbally torn up the document and thrown the pieces into Franklin's face. Further, in closing, Paris had advised him that he would no longer be recognized by the proprietors as the lawful agent from Pennsylvania (in essence, Franklin was summarily fired from his post).

At this point, Franklin was ready to move on to his original plan while in London: pursuing the freeing of Pennsylvania from the clutches of the Penn family. And to this end, he resorted to the advice of his circle of friends, which he had styled the "Club of Honest Whigs." Meeting every other week in a coffee house outside St. Paul's Cathedral, the group would include Joseph Priestley, Peter Collinson, John Fothergill, David Barclay, Thomas and John Pownall, William Strahan, and perhaps ten others, over the years.[58] Fothergill would also serve Franklin as his personal physician in London, and through his contacts in government, he afforded him access to many political leaders. Franklin was anxious to use these new contacts to press his concerns about the governance of Pennsylvania with Parliament, or so he thought.

Chapter 6

T homas Pownall was born in August 1722, the oldest son of William and Sara Pownall of Lincoln, England. Two years later, his brother John was born (sometimes mistakenly cited as the older of the two), and a total of six other siblings would be born into this marriage. Tragically, William, apparently never in good health, died in 1735 at age forty-two, leaving his widow to raise eight young children alone, with only a modest landholding in Lincoln for income. Thomas was educated at the local grammar school and prepared for matriculation at Cambridge University in 1740. With the aid of a scholarship (and thereby designated a "pensioner"), he graduated with a bachelor's degree in 1743 and returned to Lincoln to oversee the family's modest estate. John at age seventeen headed to London and quite miraculously, through family connections, was able to achieve a position as a clerk for the Board of Trade. The two brothers would prove inseparable in the coming decades, as John's work ethic provided opportunities to develop for his older brother. Ultimately, John would become the first secretary of the Board of Trade and thereby achieve tenure in his situation as a London bureaucrat. From that position, he was able to secure for Thomas a clerkship at…the Board of Trade.[59]

While serving the drudgery of a clerkship at the Board of Trade, Thomas was receiving a tremendous practical education in the administration of the British colonies in America. So when the position of secretary to Sir Danvers Osborne, newly appointed royal governor of New York, was advertised, he leapt at it as an opportunity to see these colonies. Thus it was that he found himself sailing into New York harbor on October 6, 1753, eager to see all that that city had to offer an ambitious young Englishman.[60] Then, at the close of the inaugural celebration of the new Governor Osborne, on the night of October 11, the old man strolled into the garden of his private residence and quietly hanged himself. This of course left young Thomas as secretary to… no one, and the lieutenant governor, James de Lancey, quickly slipped into the role of governor. De Lancey and Pownall then notified the Board of Trade in London, seeking a solution as to what Thomas was to do. In the interim of waiting for transmission of a message by sea, as well as a seaborne response, Thomas decided to see the colonies first-hand.[61]

The first city he chose to visit was Philadelphia, carrying letters of introduction to Richard Peters, proprietary secretary to Thomas Penn, as well as to Governor Andrew Hamilton, Speaker of the Assembly Isaac Norris, John Penn, Thomas's nephew and proprietary presence in the colony, and…Benjamin Franklin. From these he was introduced to the Philadelphia brahmins and feted at numerous dinners and parties. His interest in the "electrical demonstrations" endeared him both to Franklin and Lewis Evans, another pioneer "electrician," as they became known. And during conversations with these men, Pownall was indoctrinated into the nuances of colonial administration, colonial frustrations, and administrative shortcomings. Pownall quickly realized that this information would be invaluable as he sought further positions in colonial government through the Board of Trade. From there he traveled to Alexandria, Annapolis, New York again, New Haven, Providence, and, of course, Boston. He met Governor William Shirley of Massachusetts, who promptly offered him a position in the administration of that colony. During that time, he also received an education regarding the problems of colonial defense against the Iroquois nation and France. Pownall came to the realization that the best defense would be a united colonial effort to allow flexibility of the meager resources at hand, to position the colonies for their best protection in times of attack. He referred to this concept as a "flying military," a highly mobile mounted regiment that could quickly respond to an enemy assault anywhere from northern New York to western Virginia (this approach was becoming popular throughout European nations in that era, where the forces were more typically styled "dragoons").

As fate would have it, in an effort to achieve a defense agreement among the various colonies, the Board of Trade had debriefed Governor Osborne about calling a congress of colonies to a central location and had designated Albany, New York for this purpose. Unfortunately, with the governor's untimely and ghastly demise, the role of announcing this congress would devolve to de Lancey and Pownall, who together sent word to all colonies to send delegations to Albany for June 14, 1754. The stated purpose of this congress was to formulate an intercolonial plan for the defense of the British colonies against all enemies foreign and domestic, but implicitly the Iroquois and French. This fortuitous event afforded Thomas the opportunity to meet a multitude of colonial leaders, from Thomas Hutchinson of Massachusetts, former speaker of their assembly, to William Johnson, the largest landholder of western Massachusetts and northern New York in North America. Furthermore, he was able to meet with Mohawk, Mohican, and Oneida leaders from the "Six Nations" and realized that these were not "innocent savages" but were rather wily traders, prone to changing sides between Great Britain and France based solely on the highest bidder at the moment. What he was *not* able to do was establish an acceptable defense plan for the colonies, since his submitted plan, modified in conjunction with Franklin's, was rejected by not only the Board of Trade in London but also by *every* colonial assembly, including New York and Pennsylvania. Stung temporarily by this setback, Thomas retreated to Philadelphia with Franklin, where they subsequently launched a tour of the western country in early 1755.

Misfortune followed them in 1755 as the French and Indian allies decided to move on the "Forks of the Ohio" to lay claim to that land. And Pownall and Franklin quickly returned to Philadelphia. The Braddock disaster soon followed, after Pownall had left to return to New York seeking a response from the Board of Trade. Fortuitously for Pownall, his other Philadelphia friend, Lewis Evans, who along with being an "electrician" was one of the most noted cartographers in the colonies, had just produced a map of the "Northwest Territories" comprising what is now Michigan, Ohio, Indiana, and Illinois, complete with commentaries.[62] Pownall added his own comments, and the result was most advantageous and well-received by the Board of Trade and thereby the Privy Council. In return, Pownall learned that he had been appointed lieutenant governor for New Jersey.[63] This was also accompanied by the news of the Braddock disaster. In subsequent strategic meetings between New England, New York, and New Jersey, Pownall would serve as New Jersey representative. He was by now well-acquainted with the principals involved, including de Lancey, Johnson, and Shirley, but was much chagrined to find that New York and Massachusetts were at extreme odds over strategies dealing with the Iroquois nations. Johnson seemed to have the better understanding, and with Pownall's input, he submitted plans for dealing with the Iroquois Nations to the Board of Trade.[64] At the same time, Shirley spoke of dramatically different strategies for dealing with the French and Indian "menace."

Pownall's presentation in London, supported by the first secretary of the Board of Trade (his brother John), greatly impressed the Privy Council. In the aftermath, Shirley was recalled as military leader in the colonies and replaced by John Campbell, Earl Loudoun, at the order of Lord Halifax. In return, Loudoun named his secretary: Thomas Pownall![65] And with this appointment, Pownall was able to pass notice to Franklin that it had taken no less than *two years* for the Privy Council and Parliament to provide him an official status following the suicide of Osborne. Although somewhat sluggish even for Parliament, this action clearly demonstrated to Franklin the deliberately slow reactions that the British government applied to information received from colonial sources. It would prove an extremely vital piece of information in Franklin's, and Pownall's, future plans and activities.

With his star rising to new levels yearly, Pownall suddenly found himself a "man in demand." And who should come calling? The Penn family! Frustrated with the perceived lack of leadership by their governor, Robert Hunter

Morris, they sought an affirmation from Pownall to be the next governor of Pennsylvania.[66] But Pownall for his part saw greater glory aside Lord Loudoun and asked the Penns for a yearly stipend of £7,000! Likely he was never serious about this demand and knew full well that it was egregious by half. But it gave him the satisfaction of publicly refusing their much reduced counteroffer, discounting the Penn family's proprietary cheapness and essentially poking them in the political eye on behalf of his new friend, Benjamin Franklin, scoring one for the Franklin side over the Penn side. And just at this point, with war against the French and Indians ongoing, the proprietary side was in no position to retaliate against Pownall and simply had to let the slight go. All through 1756, the proprietary supporters and Franklin supporters were at odds, with Pownall clearly in Franklin's corner. Governor de Lancey of New York now expressed concern regarding the aims of Pownall, who appeared to have the appointment of governor to *any* state between New Hampshire and South Carolina at his beck and call. And the presence of John Pownall at the Board of Trade only strengthened this impression.

The military campaign of 1757 in America would prove disastrous politically for all concerned. In the van of the disaster was a change in British government featuring the ascendancy of William Pitt as *de facto* prime minister, with a falling away of some of Loudoun's support and the entry of totally new faces in the roles of military and financial administration. Pownall had been sent by Loudoun back to London to assist with the prosecution of Shirley for misappropriation of funds for the military campaign of 1756 and gross mismanagement of the military. Shirley, for his part, was rallying a defense in the House of Commons, blaming Johnson for the huge expenditure of supplying the western forces in New York. Only after Pownall, speaking in the Commons, explained confidently and thoroughly how difficult it was to deliver supplies through the uncharted lake country of upstate New York, did Loudoun's side prevail.[67] Shirley was never court-martialed but lost his governor's seat in Massachusetts, and four years later he would be assigned to the administrative chair of the Bahamas, a clear demotion in status.

For his part, Thomas Pownall was thereupon appointed the replacement royal governor of Massachusetts and assumed that post at the end of 1757.[68] His meteoric rise in British North America was now complete, and perhaps no one in Great Britain was quite as amazed by this as Thomas Pownall. He was thirty-five years old.

But amid the heady atmosphere of his ascendancy, personal storm clouds were rising, sent aloft by none other than Lord Loudoun. James Campbell, Earl Loudoun was a proud Scot and a career military leader. As such, he was used to giving commands and having them obeyed without passion or prejudice and would brook no other response. So when the raid on Fort William Henry (North Adams) in extreme northwest Massachusetts took place, and Pownall was forced as governor to beg for troops, provisions, and transport from the Massachusetts assembly, Loudoun took extreme issue and accused Pownall of excessive timidity.[69] Pownall took the stance that a colonial governor had to work *with* the local government, "leading them, not *driving* them." Loudoun was unconvinced and unrelenting. He believed that in order to prevail in this war, the military had the right to simply take whatever men, transport, ammunition, and food were necessary for success, and the colonies simply had to provide them without complaint or hesitation. Pownall found this stance untenable and said so—loudly. The ultimate confrontation devolved around Loudoun's demand for quartering (housing) British soldiers in the houses of the colonists in Boston and the surrounding towns. Pownall's stance was that the military had to request permission to do this; Loudoun said that the military could *demand* the full use of any house it needed. This confrontation would fester in Boston for the next twenty years between many other persons on both sides of the argument.

The year 1758 saw no improvement in the relationship between Governor Pownall and Lord Loudoun. They had, to a point, agreed to disagree, but at the same time, by virtue of their quite unequal status in a society for which social stratum was the basis of authority, Pownall was at a clear disadvantage. As the campaign of 1758 began, Pitt's British government suddenly approved a substantial financial contribution to the war effort, which would obviate the need for an increased revenue levy. But the levy of manpower was more problematic, and in the end Pownall was forced to use impressment to fill the ranks of a local Massachusetts militia promised to Lord Loudoun. Enforcement of the impressment was supervised by Pownall's new lieutenant governor, one Thomas Hutchinson, the mercantilist friend (at that time) of Benjamin Franklin. As the campaign progressed, Pownall focused his attention and military leadership on Maine. It is important to this issue to recall that Maine, prior to 1821, was a part of Massachusetts as a single colony, separated at the Atlantic coast by a small port area around Portsmouth, New Hampshire. Maine was, other than the most southern portion of its seashore, disputed land, with the French in Quebec claiming much of the northern coast along with almost all of inland Maine. Pownall's forces would withstand, and ultimately defeat, a siege set by the French and native tribes at Fort Kennebec, without loss of a man. In the aftermath, Pownall returned to Boston, but his British forces moved on to Louisbourg, Nova Scotia, capturing that stronghold.

By 1759, the Brits were ready to move on Quebec in an all-out effort to drive the French out of North America.[70] Pownall's military support both for upstate New York and northern Maine was considered integral to the ultimate success of this endeavor. He focused the 1759 campaign upon securing Maine for the Massachusetts people, an effort that would prove critical after the American revolution in arguing for Maine as part of the American mainland. Fort Pownall would be established on the Penobscot River near present-day Bangor. By the close of the year, the British had forced the French back to the city of Quebec, and France's hold in North America was slipping away. Pownall was hailed a hero upon his return to Boston. That winter, Pownall would petition the Board of Trade for two goals: a well-deserved stint for rest-and-recreation in Great Britain, and the governorship of French Canada.[71] The Board of Trade would approve the former and award him the governorship of South Carolina. Pownall accepted with little true reluctance and planned to head homeward.

In the wake of Pownall's departure from America, he began writing his masterwork *The Administration of the Colonies,* which would pass through five editions over the ensuing seventeen years.[72] Pownall laid out in this treatise his theories in providing the best oversight of the issues unique to colonial British America, from dealing with tax levies, to defense against Indigenous peoples, to optimum governance by the colonies themselves. Through this work, Pownall would find himself the resident expert on America, both by the Board of Trade and by Parliament. It would serve him, and Franklin, well.

᪖

Chapter 7

So it was that in 1759 John Hanbury of Virginia and John Fothergill, as a well-connected London physician, arranged an audience for Franklin with Lord Carteret, Second Earl Granville, head of the King's Privy Council, an extended type of cabinet that had the ear of the king.[73] When Franklin started in with how his rights as a British citizen to the defense of his home and estate, and equal taxation under the law, were being illegally suppressed by Thomas Penn, Carteret stopped him in mid-sentence with a hand held to Franklin's face. "You Americans have the wrong idea of the nature of your constitution. The laws given by the Crown, or the Proprietors, or the holding company, are the law of the land. And your assemblies, and your citizens have no right to ignore or violate them."[74]

Franklin was gob smacked. No one had ever asserted this concept, not this bluntly, and certainly not from a source as close to the Crown as Carteret. Franklin's understanding was that the provincial assembly was to write laws and submit them to the Crown, and once approved, *that* became the law of the land. Carteret reiterated that Franklin was woefully misinformed, and that the *king* was their legislative assembly, and he most assuredly was not subject to review or rejection. This was the first inkling for Franklin that lobbying was going to be difficult. (Fothergill would later gently point out to him that

Carteret was, after all, the brother-in-law of Thomas Penn and likely resented Franklin attempting to circumvent Penn's authority).

A showdown between the attorneys of Penn and Franklin was subsequently arranged at the Cockpit of Whitehall Palace in London to address the state of taxation of private citizens v. the proprietor of Pennsylvania.[75] Not surprisingly, this failed to establish any compromise between the two principals. But in the aftermath, one member of the Privy Council pulled Franklin aside into an empty office and asked specifically how Penn had come to have caused such furor and why he had failed to support the Braddock expedition. Franklin, a bit off-guard, advised him that Penn would not allow proprietary lands to be subjected to general land-taxes in Pennsylvania.

"Could your taxes be levied at a rate that would not injure the Penn estates?" the gentleman asked.

Franklin replied in the affirmative.

"Well then, you both can have no objection to entering into an engagement to secure that point!"

To which Franklin agreed. As they departed the Cockpit, Franklin turned to John Pownall and asked, "Who was that man?"

John laughed and replied, "That, Benjamin, is Lord Mansfield, Chief Justice of the Court of King's Bench."

Franklin marked well the face and the accommodating temperament. Subsequently, the first secretary and clerk for the Privy Council, John Pownall, would draw up articles of taxation for Pennsylvania, assessing all proprietary holdings at a base rate of 3s per £100, with the imprimatur of Franklin and Mansfield. The result would be the *Supply Act* of 1759, as voted and approved by Parliament. Thomas Penn had finally, unwittingly, entered into the financial support of Pennsylvania.

But despite this modest success under the directive of Mansfield, Franklin had been educated by Lord Carteret that the American colonists remained clearly "second-class citizens" in the eyes of Westminster.[76] Franklin had tried, in his list titled "Heads of Complaint," to recall the benevolence of Penn's father, the legendary William Penn, who recruited colonists with an assurance that they would have an assembly with powers similar to those of Parliament in London, in terms of self-governance. And now Franklin had been advised that the colonials by eighteenth century British law were ruled by the Crown directly, were therefore "second-class citizens," and were not free to lobby Parliament for grievances. Franklin was simply wasting his time in his effort in London to assert this concept of colonial representation. Penn had won.

Or had he? At this point, Franklin retreated to his lodgings in Mrs. Stevenson's house and further retreated into his thoughts. He tried to sort through how he might lobby the Crown to assume the administration of Pennsylvania and realized that that road went through Carteret, Penn's brother-in-law. Perhaps he could lobby Parliament directly? No, the charters were not issued by Parliament but by the Crown. Penn's proprietary hold on Pennsylvania appeared ironclad. And therefore Franklin's fortune, and the issue of his family's safety against the Canadiens, Iroquois, and who knows who else, was directly tied to his worst enemy in the world. But then a realization came over him, and a smile came to his face. If he could not convince Great Britain to wrest Pennsylvania from Thomas Penn, well, perhaps *he* would have to wrest it from Penn himself. But how?

Franklin was at the turning point of his entire life, and in desperation, he began concocting a plan that would free the American colonies from their British oppressors and allow them to formulate a system of government based on the concepts of the brightest political scientists of the age. During this time, he remained in consultation with the Pownalls, and with Fothergill, but betrayed nothing of his plan to them. Later in 1759, with a letter of introduction from his friend and Scottish native William Strahan, Franklin took a side trip to Edinburgh.[77] He was met there with great enthusiasm by the faculty of the University of Edinburgh, who were taken not only with his discussions of electrical experimentation, but his political discussions as well. Franklin for his part took advantage of the knowledge of this prodigious faculty and first made the acquaintance of David Hume, at that time custodian of the Advocates' Library of the University of Edinburgh.[78] Franklin was impressed by Hume's command of the philosophies of Hobbes, Locke, and

Montesquieu, among others, and heard from him an erudition and clarity of philosophical thought the equal of which he had never previously known. He pressed Hume for a standing invitation to return for future meetings to discuss these ideas on the philosophy of revolution. Curious to find this philosophical man of letters at work in a legal library, Franklin learned that Hume's cousin, Henry Home (Henry had maintained the original spelling of the family name, pronounced "H-you-m," but David, after long-standing frustration at correcting the pronunciation, took the expedient of changing the spelling), by that time chief justice of the Scottish royal courts, had secured that position for him. Franklin was subsequently introduced to Henry Home, Lord Kames, with whom he would maintain an ongoing correspondence. Home had recognized the academic gifts of his young cousin, as well as those of Adam Smith, and had gathered them into the Edinburgh University family of philosophers that would lead the British "Age of Enlightenment" throughout the remainder of the eighteenth century.

Since the inception of the Junto in 1727, Franklin had drifted into amateur discussions of philosophy through a series of questions posed on a monthly basis to his various members.[79] From early straightforward questions such as "Hath any body attacked your reputation lately? And what can the Junto do toward securing it?" and "Have you lately heard any member's character attacked, and how have you defended it?" subsequent questions shifted more toward "Have you lately observed any defect in the laws of your country of which it would be proper to move the legislature for an amendment? Or do you know of any beneficial law that is wanting?" and even policy issues, such as "Does the Importation of [Slaves] increase or advance the Wealth of our Country?" and philosophical concepts like "Can a Man arrive at Perfection in this Life as some Believe; or is it impossible as others believe?"

Over the years, with changes in the membership rolls of the Junto, the philosophical discussions would sometimes be silly and trivial but occasionally would move into the works of political scientists of the previous hundred years. This would of necessity force the membership into reading and reviewing Thomas Hobbes and John Locke, arguing similarities and differences and delving into discussions about basic human motivations and behaviors. And the more that various members studied philosophy, the deeper the discussions devolved. By Franklin's arrival in Edinburgh in 1759, he felt comfortable in debating with David Hume (no less!) the processes that incite a man, and a group, to foment revolution. Hypothetically, of course.

For Hume, the debates regarding war and revolution devolved from a sense of progressive passion based on the perception of ongoing wrongs directed toward a governed people, who in turn lacked redress of grievances.[80] Franklin mostly listened to, and questioned, this most profound philosopher of the human condition.

Fr: "How do a people conclude that their appropriate resolution is a revolution against their rulers?"

H: "Dr. Franklin, the answer lies in their passion for change and the ongoing ability to fuel the passion of a people to act. In the absence of a burning passion, the will of the people will falter, and they will lapse into toleration of the injustice."

Fr: "And how does one keep that passion aflame?"

H: "The revolutionary must discover that which invokes the deepest passions of the downtrodden against their government, and that open wound must be provoked again and again. If the legitimacy of their resistance against their government can be affirmed, it will pervade their sensitivities toward their government. This requires a single protagonist throughout the process, to maintain that provocation, a protagonist who through personal affront understands the essence of the conflict and can iterate it to the people. Only then will the fire of revolution continue to burn brightly."

Franklin returned to Philadelphia in 1762, his political mission to London a total disaster.[81] But oddly, on the surface Franklin remained undeterred and was almost ebullient.[82] Even his colonial friends were confused, but Franklin's trip had been personally rewarding to a dramatic degree. He had made the acquaintance of scores of influential people in Great Britain who would be invaluable to him in the coming years. And perhaps equally or more importantly, they had met *him*. This almost mythical figure from the far-off kingdom of Philadelphia had dazzled audiences from London to Edinburgh with his erudition, his scientific curiosity, and his wit. If a "man on the street" poll could have been taken in Europe in 1762, asking people to name any person born in the British American colonies, of all the people who could have come up with but a single name, over ninety-five percent of the time it would have been "Benjamin Franklin." And now European politicians, merchants, men of science and letters, and women everywhere, understood why. Some would react with cynicism, some with envy, some with admiration, but *all* reacted with wonder. And yet throughout his absence from his home in Philadelphia, he had maintained his "under the surface" influence there as well, and upon his return, his friends coalesced behind him in support. Then during his welcome home, new problems arose from the Pennsylvania frontier.

Chapter 8

At the close of the French and Indian War, the Treaty of Paris in 1763 called for France to renounce not only Quebec but also all claims to land between the Appalachians and the Mississippi River (present-day Michigan, Indiana, Ohio, and Illinois).[83] The Canadiens promptly withdrew, leaving not only a leadership vacuum but also a massive group of Indigenous peoples who were terrified of the ramifications of this treaty from faraway Europe: the French were their allies, and the British were their extremely violent enemies. What would happen to the tribes now? Into this vacuum appeared a leader, Pontiac, who promptly initiated a "war" against settlers in this area the British called the "Northwest Territory." The British, now realizing that the Penn family would provide *no* response, sought their only available military detachment, a company of two regiments that were in Cuba under the command of one Major Henri Bouquet, a veteran of the Seven Years' War and a Swiss "soldier of fortune" in the employ of the British army.[84] He brought his depleted army to Philadelphia and proceeded to march them toward Fort Pitt, along with a detachment of five hundred Pennsylvania and Virginia volunteers, more eager than able.[85] Past Fort Ligonier, but not yet to Fort Pitt, the British were attacked by a combined group of Delaware, Shawnee, Mingos, and Mohicans in an area known as Bushy Run for the steep creek ravine at the far end. The Brits fell into line and managed to hold off the attack with multiple fusillades, and the natives dropped back to regroup. In the meantime, the Brits formed a square of wagons, gear, and sentries around their wounded, and prepared for the second attack. Once again, the native combined group attacked into the British line and once again was repulsed. At this point, the devastation of Braddock was called to mind by many of the regulars, but Bouquet, an experienced infantry officer, had a different idea.[86]

He called back over half his force to the sides of the ravine and had them quickly and quietly scale the sides into position. He then dropped back his supplies and his wounded to a point above the blind end of the ravine. And then proceeded to execute the Hastings strategy with his remaining force: attacking the natives full force, this group pushed forward through the ravine firing their muskets at will into the Canadien front until receiving return fire. Immediately they retreated in a purposeful helter-skelter fashion, breaking ranks and running through woods and brush, directly back through the ravine, with the natives in hot pursuit. Only after all had reached the terminus of the ravine did the command to "fire!" come from Bouquet. And in the withering fusillades from the two sides of the ravine by experienced British marksmen, the native warriors were trapped. Over forty warrior chiefs perished that afternoon, and the natives were left in full flight. It was a very risky strategy, difficult to execute in real time in the heat of battle, but as old as the Conquest and devastatingly effective when correctly applied. And Bouquet had pulled it off perfectly.

In the aftermath, Bouquet's army was in no condition to pursue but secured supplies in order to relieve Fort Pitt.[87] They arrived four days later without further attack and replenished the stores at the fort. The surviving Indigenous warriors of the "Bushy Run" defeat told their chiefs of the British major who had killed so many of their cohort. Thus alarmed, the tribes evacuated the environs of Fort Pitt and retreated into Ohio. Ultimately, they would retreat as far as Sandusky and Presque-Île. Then winter came, and all forces stood down. Bouquet returned to Philadelphia, where he made the acquaintance of their famous postmaster and electrician, Benjamin Franklin.[88] Franklin was already excited, as was much of the populace, over the heroic defeat of the

Indigenous tribes by Major Bouquet and pressed him for stories. Bouquet, for his part, was equally impressed with Franklin and enquired about his educational background. A somewhat self-conscious Franklin admitted that he was almost completely "self-taught," but Bouquet was even more impressed by this fact, marveling at Franklin's inventive ability and general erudition in conversation. Franklin asked the same of Bouquet and was surprised to hear that Bouquet, in pursuit of a career as a European mercenary, had taken classes in military science at Utrecht, where he had learned theories of skirmish and war strategies, as well as mathematics. Franklin was fascinated. He wanted to know more about this mathematics instructor, and Bouquet regaled him with stories of Professeur Koenig of Utrecht, who had once argued physics and mathematics with Euler. Franklin pressed Bouquet at that point for a letter of introduction, that he might correspond with this learned mathematics instructor. Bouquet was happy to oblige.

Meanwhile John Penn, son of Richard and nephew of Thomas, arrived in October 1763 as the newly appointed proprietary governor of Pennsylvania. An indifferent and inexperienced leader, John was hoping that his term of office would be uneventful.[89] He needn't have waited long to be disabused of this hope. In December, a gang of frontier settlers decided that they had had their fill of Indigenous persons raiding their villages, stealing crops and livestock, and generally making life miserable. Thus they made it their sworn objective to totally eradicate the tribes from western Pennsylvania. On December 14, they broke into an Indian home in Conestoga Manor and killed six women and children.[90] Then in Lancaster, two weeks later, they killed thirteen more. The Christian Indians uprooted and fled to Philadelphia, seeking asylum. The gang of settlers followed in hot pursuit. John Penn responded by condemning the group, now referred to as the "Paxton Boys," after the town where the uprising had started. Penn requested a "Riot Act" from the assembly, which was quickly passed and signed into law by John Penn. With the Indians safely sheltered in Philadelphia, the citizens formed a makeshift militia and waited.

On the night of February 4, 1764, Penn was advised by a rural messenger that over fifty Paxton Boys were in the outskirts of Philadelphia, heavily armed, and looking for the Indians *and* John Penn![91] Penn, not knowing where to turn, pounded on the door of…Benjamin Franklin, at 1:00 a.m., awakening him and asking him for help. Franklin, recalling his treatment in London at the hands of the father and uncle of this young man, smirked and invited him in. For his part, Franklin took the diplomatic high road and assumed the role of mediator and counselor, and when a group of perhaps twenty armed westerners arrived near dawn, he faced them down and swore to listen to their grievances, release them uncharged to their homes, and meet with them in Germantown within forty-eight hours. The gang, exhausted from their travel, finally stood down, shouldered their rifles, and headed home. If Franklin had any illusions about a grateful John Penn, they were quickly dashed. The assembly agreed to an emergency session to discuss the terms of peace with the Paxtons and invited Penn to preside. Penn promptly refused, saying it would be "unbecoming the Honor and Dignity of the Government" for him to meet with the assembly. From Franklin's coign of vantage, this was the second generation of oppressive conceit in the proprietors.

But at least the assembly was seeing first-hand what Franklin had already known: the Penns were simply an intolerable group, and "all Hopes of Happiness under a Proprietary Government were at an end."[92] Franklin wondered in an editorial whether "were there another mob to come against him, [Penn] probably could not find a dozen men to protect him." This set the stage for an ugly 1764 election year in Philadelphia. All seats in the assembly were at stake, and Franklin had raised the stakes further with a "Petition to the Crown to revoke the Pennsylvania Colonial Charter in favor of conversion to a Crown Colony" appearing as a ballot initiative.[93] The campaign was mudslinging at its worst, and Franklin, perhaps the best-known person in America, had the most skeletons lurking. Penn's political alliance lost no time resurrecting old issues, and old stories, including the illegitimacy of Franklin's son William, as well as Franklin's common-law marriage. In the end, it was more or less a draw: Franklin was turned out of the assembly for the first time since 1741, but his petition was approved, with Franklin himself designated to bear it to Parliament and to the Crown. The Penns did everything they could devise to try to reverse or suppress the outcome of the vote, but in the end Franklin was headed back to London.

As winter waned and spring approached, a refreshed British army in Philadelphia regrouped, resupplied, and headed back toward Fort Pitt, led by now-brevet Brigadier General Bouquet. It seems that His Majesty, George III, was also quite taken by the miraculous victory of Bouquet at Bushy Run, in an area and setting where Braddock had failed so miserably eight short years before. Thus, he had precipitously named Bouquet a brigadier general.[94] Bouquet hoped to find the Indigenous tribes in a more settled and compliant mood, and in that he was not disappointed. The Delaware and Shawnee were ready to sue for peace, and Bouquet set the harsh but inevitable terms: putting down the tomahawk (in this case, actually "throwing the tomahawk into the air" rather than "burying the hatchet"; Bouquet wished to symbolize returning the tomahawk back to God/Nature as a permanent laying down of weapons), and returning all European persons and African slaves taken by every tribe during the entire French and Indian Wars (in some cases involving persons who had lived with their captors for close to ten years!). The Shawnee balked initially at this; many of the young women had married into the tribes, and there were many children born from these "marriages" who knew no other lifestyle. But Bouquet was resolute on this issue, for better or worse, and ultimately, fearing reprisals from this savage European leader, the Indigenous people returned *all* European persons and African slaves, over two hundred people, with a large reunion on Market Street in Philadelphia. Bouquet was hailed in Philadelphia, London, and Havana as a great war hero and was awarded command of the entire British forces for the southern British Colonies in North America. In late 1764, he took command of the forces headquartered in Pensacola, in what was known at that time as "West Florida," a British colony since the close of King George's War. In the summer of 1765, he contracted yellow fever and died ten days later.

Franklin, during the last days of October 1764, wrote to Professeur Koenig in Utrecht, advising him that he was sailing from Philadelphia to London as the "Agent of Pennsylvania" to the Crown and would be able to travel to continental Europe in the spring of 1765, where he hoped they would be able to meet to discuss the mathematics of electricity as it was then understood. What Franklin, and Bouquet, did not know was that Johann Samuel Koenig of Utrecht had died in 1757, during the time of the Seven Years' War.

Chapter 9

On November 7, Franklin boarded a packet ship for London, crossing the Atlantic in near-record time and arriving by December 10.[95] He headed directly to Craven Street, where he was greeted enthusiastically by the Honest Whigs and Mrs. Stevenson. For his part, Franklin sensed a curious feeling of being "back home." He was becoming, emotionally, exactly what he had wished the British ministers to understand politically: a British citizen. And this "British citizen" was faced almost immediately with an idea from George Grenville to recover the costs of the French and Indian War from the colonies.[96] He needed Franklin's input on how the colonists would receive a "Stamp Tax" on printed materials, including legal documents, newspapers, and even playing cards. Franklin blundered badly on this assessment, advising Grenville that while duties and tariffs were expected and tolerated by the colonies, an "internal tax" (i.e., a duty placed on items produced *and* sold in the colonies, and not tied directly to Great Britain in any way) would cause a furor throughout the colonies. In the latter, he was quite correct, but his opinion on the "duties and tariffs" could not have been more wrong.[97] Boston and New York were simply not interested in *any* taxes that the colonies would be forced to send to Great Britain, and Franklin was daily identifying more with London than with Philadelphia, Boston, or New York.

Through 1765, Franklin met with the Club of Honest Whigs, seeking advice and contacts with Parliament and the Crown. He spoke repeatedly of the petition to multiple politicians and colleagues. His colleagues were supportive, but the political authorities of British government were most assuredly not. The Board of Trade tabled the petition, and their newly retained first secretary, John Pownall, later pulled Franklin aside and assured him that it would *never* come to a vote, as revocation of a Royal Charter at the request of colonists was clearly antithetical to the Crown. In 1768, Wills Hill, Lord Hillsborough was appointed Secretary to the Colonies of North America, and Franklin took his petition directly to him. Hillsborough listened patiently and promised to take the issue to the Crown. In August, Hillsborough quietly but firmly advised Franklin that the Crown would not consider the change, as it was not in the interest of the empire.[98] And this in essence ended the effort to convince the Crown to assume control of Pennsylvania.

Franklin and his colleagues were visibly depressed over this turn of events.[99] And in the Club, one of his most long-standing British advisers and friends, Thomas Pownall, engaged Franklin in a prolonged discussion about his designs on the administration and defense of Pennsylvania. Pownall had been in a unique position to observe multiple colonial administrations from both the British side and the colonists' side and had formulated well-reasoned approaches to the resolution of multiple issues. In Great Britain, he had published *The Administration of the British Colonies* as a guideline for dealing with the colonies, then already in its fourth edition, and as a result was considered a recognized expert in the mediation between the two. Franklin, for his part, remained focused on Pennsylvania and the Penns. It was clear to Pownall that Thomas Penn had become a Franklinian obsession and that Franklin would think more clearly if his horizons were expanded.

So Pownall questioned Franklin about the other British colonies.[100] What did Franklin understand about his native Boston in the past three years? The *Stamp Act* had hit them severely, and Franklin had testified before Parliament in 1766 as to the state of affairs in Philadelphia, while extrapolating to New York and Boston. But he hadn't visited Boston in years. Franklin had made to

Parliament under sworn testimony in 1766 a statement that Bostonians would have considered ridiculous: "American colonists recognize the right to place *external duties* on products imported into the colonies, but oppose *internal taxation* on any basis within the various British colonies." The Bostonians, on the contrary, were stridently opposed to *all* taxation, internal or external. What did Franklin understand about South Carolina? Was he aware that Charleston, South Carolina was the leader in the slave trade in the entire western world? Clearly he was not. Pownall encouraged him to educate himself by reading articles, newspapers, and treatises published throughout the colonies.

Franklin felt that Pennsylvania should be permitted to negotiate a unique relationship with Great Britain that would result in their obtaining financial and military security on a permanent basis, while allowing them the autonomy to create their own system of laws and revenues. Pownall felt that this was quite impossible, since there was no clear pathway in British government to establish such a relationship with a single colony. He challenged Franklin to provide a coherent counterargument. Pownall recalled to Franklin their discussions twelve years previously, during the Albany Congress, when it was Pownall who had convinced Franklin of the necessity of combining the resources of Massachusetts, New York, Pennsylvania, and Virginia in a single joint defensive effort. By 1766, at least in Great Britain, the consensus of the Privy Council was that the British American colonies were to be treated as a unit.[101]

So, during this time, Franklin was coming over to Pownall's reasoning on the relationship of the colonies to Great Britain. The colonies would have to be considered as a single unit to achieve a meaningful hope of independence. But save Pownall and Fothergill, in confidential discussion, he would never admit to this. They realized that they were starting to drift into discussions that were best kept very quiet; Franklin, for his part, had already arrived. He knew what had to be done. The next step was to formulate the plan.

Fomentation of revolution has never been a straightforward exercise in Western civilization. Franklin and Pownall were silently forewarned by all the initiatives and false starts of the past and realized that simply kindling an uprising against British authority would culminate in bloodshed throughout the colonies, to no useful purpose. No, they needed to carefully consider not only how to *start* a revolution, but just as importantly how to maintain the revolutionary passion through the process of privation, and in the end a precise vision of how the culmination would look. Hume had provided a "rough draft" for maintaining revolutionary zeal through the difficult times between initiation and success. From that foundation, Pownall and Franklin read feverishly through the essays of the theorists on "nation-building" of the previous century, starting with Lord Francis Bacon and including Hobbes, Locke, and Montesquieu. They read the new essays of Jean-Jacques Rousseau from France. And they realized that in all these philosophers, there was simply no "blueprint," no clear pathway for their proposition. So they would need to write one. Hume and Franklin had discussed the basis of revolution during Franklin's visit to Edinburgh eight years previously but had never brought it down to the "brass tacks" of America and Great Britain. Franklin had feared, at the time, that any discussion of specifics would have been greeted at best with stony silence from Hume, and at worst with horror and notification of the British ministry. Wisely, he had kept his counsel throughout those conversations.

From the perspective of Pownall, the British colonies from the St. Lawrence River to the Florida Keys had to be considered and accepted as a unified concept.[102] Based upon that concept, they deserved better oversight and more professional management than that afforded by the British government, and specifically by the corrupt British ministry through its Board of Trade. His brother John was in agreement generally with this impression, and was ever frustrated, as First Secretary of the Board of Trade, by the frequent changes in government, and thereby the changes in policy toward the colonies. Without a unifying philosophy of governance of the colonies, John advised his brother, there can only be chaotic and aimless rules and regulations applied, here to Boston, there to New York, yet another to Philadelphia. Lord Halifax had advised the Pownall brothers as early as 1751 that reform of the colonial governance would be essential to their long-term administration. But from the Whigs of London came *no* reform, and Lord Chesterfield in 1766 would write, *if we have no secretary of state with full and undisputed powers for America, in a few years we may as well have no America.* Pownall and Franklin absolutely assented in this impression.

The years between 1760 and 1765 would prove extremely disillusioning to Thomas Pownall. He had requested relief from his assignment as governor of South Carolina, which was readily granted. Instead, he was assigned for military procurement of materiel in Germany and sent to Hanover.[103] While he would make contacts with arms manufacturers in Prussia and the Palatine, he felt that he was working in a position of demotion at the behest of the Privy Council of Westminster. There he would languish for two years, until the close of the Seven Years' War, and upon his return to London, and to Lincoln, he made a profound realization. No matter what he did, or aspired to, in London he simply could not attain any of the advancement he had enjoyed in America. It became glaringly obvious in that timeframe that in the sclerotic, corrupt, entitlement world of London, advancement by a mere commoner was impossible; he, like his brother John, was simply a tool of the nobility and would never be more than that. He longed for the days of advancement he had enjoyed in the colonies but was destined never to return there.

In 1764 he was introduced to Harriet Fawkener, widow of Lord Everard Fawkener, and was immediately infatuated.[104] By this time, his brother John had married and already had three children, which may well have moved Thomas to pursue the lifestyle of home and family. The following year, Thomas and Harriet, Lady Fawkener, were married, and he found himself the stepfather of four. Further, she was related to the Churchill and Walpole families and was anxious for her new husband to press his ambitions upon the nobility in a fresh and more prominent way. They took a town home in Albemarle Street, London, and Lady Fawkener became a social doyenne in London society. She was delighted that her husband knew the great Benjamin Franklin on a personal basis and took pride in showing off both Franklin and her husband to visitors like William Samuel Johnson and Horace Walpole. By 1767, she had convinced her husband to run for Parliament. Suddenly, Thomas Pownall was back! It would be in the late-evening discussions at Albemarle Street, over cigars and brandy, that the conversations between Franklin and Pownall would gradually move toward a better administration of the American colonies and how to achieve that. It was in this timeframe that George Grenville would school both Franklin and Pownall about the correct relationship between the Crown, Parliament, and the colonies. And Pownall would continue to press Grenville and Rockingham to remain more open-minded about colonial representation in London and about the issue of Parliamentary levy of colonial taxes. After their government failed, he would approach William Pitt, now Lord Chatham, with similar issues.

Chapter 10

Pownall had originally been of a mind that the individual American colonies, through their charters, were owed unquestioned loyalty by Parliament, as British citizens *in absentia*. But as leaders like Grenville challenged this stance, Pownall gradually came to realize that "federation" of the colonies would be essential to their ability to sue for justice from the Crown and the British constitution.[105] In this regard, he was well ahead of Franklin, and in the ensuing three years of intensive discussion, Franklin would gradually come around to Pownall's way of thinking about American rights and America's relationship with the mother country.

Pownall had lived the experience of royal governor and had seen the inconsistent application of this role in the colonies: some governors (he modestly excluded himself, but his administration in Massachusetts was the exemplar) had established strong relationships with the assembly of their colony, and with the "people" (an eighteenth century euphemism for "the rabble"), and worked as an impartial conduit of governance between the colony and the ministry in London. But other governors (in this Franklin could readily nod in assent) seemed interested only in personal gain, personal wealth, extraction of resources from the colony, and aggrandizement of their sponsor, either the proprietor or the Crown. There was simply no clear oversight, no unified administration, no… And here Franklin could interject, "No national government!" At that response, Pownall could smile and nod. Dr. Franklin was coming to understand the larger picture and was therefore ready to address the common, clear, and sole solution.[106]

In 1765, Pownall would publish a new edition of *The Administration of the Colonies* at a pivotal time in both British and American history.[107] The treatise was dedicated to George Grenville in an overly optimistic hope that it would inspire an overhaul of the governance described in the publication. At that time, the British military had maintained a presence in the colonies despite the peace treaty of Paris of 1763, which had officially ended the French and Indian War. Pownall raised the question of the mission of the ongoing military presence in the colonies moving forward. The governor-general and military commander of the British army in the colonies, Thomas Gage, was incensed by Pownall's publication, and felt that the undercurrent of federalism throughout the book invited revolution against British military authority.[108]

During discussions about the "colonial dilemma," the Club of Honest Whigs, through the input of Pownall and Franklin, had hit upon one key issue in the colonies, especially in the north, including Massachusetts, New York, and Pennsylvania: there was, simply, no money. Oh, there was most assuredly a flow of commerce, which at that time was reasonably brisk. Fortunes were being made by merchants who managed the shipping to Great Britain: Allen in Philadelphia, Livingston in New York, Hutchinson in Boston. But there was simply a chronic lack of currency and coin.[109] It was Franklin who would propose a stopgap measure to Grenville and Lord Rockingham: a system of Parliamentary-issued "notes" (along the lines of a promissory note or formal "IOU") that could be exchanged on the streets and in the shops of all the British colonies by the middle and lower classes, which the recipients of said notes could exchange with banks or receivers at a six percent interest, payable directly to the Crown.[110] It would solve the currency shortage and at the same time provide a rudimentary sales tax that could obviate the need for both internal and external taxation of the colonies. Franklin thought it made perfect sense. But Lord Rockingham thought otherwise. And then Great Britain experienced yet another change of government and change in the ministry. Now it was William Pitt, Lord Chatham, in 1766, who would summarily reject Franklin's idea. Great Britain remained adamant regarding the ability of Parliament to raise funds from the colonies by taxation, and colonial representation was, and would remain, immaterial.

In frustration regarding British intransigence over the colonial administration, Pownall would finally publish yet another edition of *The Administration of the Colonies,* in 1768, which contained language sufficiently inflammatory to draw some attention in the halls of Westminster.[111] Franklin and Pownall had witnessed the colonial resistance to the *Stamp Act,* its subsequent abolition, and then the passage of the *Townshend Acts,* all of which seemed to simply stress the colonials further. Otis in Boston and Dickinson in Philadelphia were circulating pamphlets fueling the colonial frenzy against Great Britain. The response in both Houses of Parliament appeared to be little more than a tired yawn. Pownall proposed an imperial federation, a commonwealth, much like the union with Scotland and Northern Ireland in 1707 that had first changed the national name from "England" to "Great Britain." Parliament would remain the law of the British empire, but there would be representation in Commons for the various colonies of North America. And then Pownall fired a stormy threat: "The whole train of events, the whole course of business, must perpetually bring forward into practice, and necessarily in the end, into establishment—*either an American or a British union.* There is no alternative; the only consideration which remains to every good man, who loves the peace and liberties of mankind, is whether the one or the other shall be forced into existence, by the violence of the parties, and at the hazard of events."[112]

Pownall felt quite strongly that the maintenance of a British regular military presence in Massachusetts and New York badly interfered with British-American relations, since it put continual pressure upon the colonists to house and equip the British military and to support their annual campaigns against France. It was expensive, disruptive, and violent. It was, quite simply, a "public relations disaster." Thomas Gage now felt that Pownall had gone too far with his criticism of British colonial policy generally, and with military policy specifically, and found Pownall inappropriately opinionated, if not downright disloyal.[113] It would prove a stumbling block for Pownall's London career for the ensuing fifteen years, and the whispering in publick houses and homes of Tory partisans about Thomas Pownall would commence.

The overarching reception of Pownall's inflammatory edition of 1768 was yet again one of ennui.[114] There were occasional eyebrows raised about the fomenting of revolution, but these were definitely in the minority. Edmund Burke, a friend of both Pownall and Franklin, would speak out publicly against the treatise, taking the position that Parliament, for better or worse, rightly or wrongly, remained the supreme arbitrator of government in Great Britain, and it was unreasonable to compare the American colonies to Scotland or Ireland politically. (One is encouraged to remember that Burke was a representative in Parliament from Ireland.) It was simply outrageous to conceive that the colonies were worthy of seats in Commons. Franklin would, interestingly, take the public stance that the colonies were as yet individual states, colonies administered separately under the oversight of the Board of Trade; this was a ruse, as Franklin had, by 1769, agreed to, and embraced, Pownall's concept of a federation in the British colonies.[115] One of the more insightful analyses of Pownall's work came from a clergyman in colonial Boston, Andrew Eliot. Writing to Thomas Hollis in 1769, he opined that *Governor Pownal's (sic) book is curious, and contains many valuable thoughts. No man has had greater advantages to know the state of the colonies than that gentleman.* But then he somewhat mysteriously continues: *Certain it is, that he is carrying on a secret correspondence with some leading men...in the other colonies.*[116] Indeed.

A curious book had appeared in London in 1769 under an anonymous author (later shown to be a collaboration by William Knox and Lord Grenville) entitled *The Controversy between Great Britain and Her Colonies Reviewed*, which asserted the absolute sovereignty of the Crown over the colonies, but then went on to assert that Parliament held the authority to serve as a kind of agent over the colonies to convey the will of the Crown.[117] This latter assertion was extraordinarily fresh, and the basis, through the abrogation by William and Mary of their sovereignty over the Colonies, was perhaps too great an overreach. To that end appeared just a few months later a treatise entitled *Remarks on the review of The Controversy between Great Britain and Her Colonies,* presented anonymously as well. It was a calm, logically sound if not clearly presented refutation of Knox and Grenville. Subsequent London circles would attribute the piece to one Edward Bancroft. In reality, he had been provided counsel and financial impetus from two insiders: Thomas Pownall and Benjamin Franklin. They now had enlisted a young protégé. Excited at the response in the press, and in the publick houses to the *Remarks* from the pen of Bancroft, Franklin and Pownall quickly realized that they had hit upon a new method of fomenting interest in a cause: the use of acolytes to spread their message.[118] It was an approach that would serve them well in the ensuing fifteen years.

Chapter 11

hile Franklin had spoken to Parliament about the problems with the *Stamp Act* in 1766, it would fall to Pownall to take up the cause of the colonies against the *Townshend Acts* in Parliament, first taking on the issue of the *Quartering Act*, requiring involuntary civilian housing of British soldiers in New York and Boston in 1767, and then taking on the concept of the *Extradition Act* which called for extradition/change of venue for colonists to London in 1769.[119] Unlike Franklin, Pownall was a seated member of Parliament, and his words carried perhaps greater gravitas than those of his friend, testifying in 1766. Nonetheless, the quartering act survived Pownall's attack.

In 1769, Pownall would speak more frankly, and more furiously, against the very idea that colonists could be transported to London for trial.[120] He attached this *Act* to the furor in the colonies over the seizure of Alexander Hamilton's trade ship *Liberty* in Boston Harbor the previous year and wondered why Parliament insisted on fueling the fires of dissent in the cities of the colonies. He went on to point out that the constant appearance of British soldiers in full regalia, carrying weapons and drilling in the streets of Boston and New York, left the colonists with an ongoing impression of military confrontation and threat of warfare. "The sword is indeed not drawn—but the hand is upon it. The word for action is not yet given, but mischief is on tiptoe" While once again, Pownall failed to carry the vote, he was now perceived in America, and in Westminster, as a colonial partisan in Parliament.

The murmuring now started in earnest in London: Pownall was not to be trusted.[121] While he maintained a correspondence with Massachusetts Governor Sir Francis Bernard and Lieutenant Governor Thomas Hutchinson in Boston, he now noted that his own mail was being clumsily molested with amateurish attempts at resealing letters addressed to him in confidence.[122] He advised Franklin that the situation was deteriorating relatively rapidly as 1770 opened. At that time, Pownall was in congress with the Parliamentary Whigs who were inclined toward the British colonies in North America, including Burke, Savile, and Dowdeswell, along with sixty others, attempting to establish a policy that would recognize colonial grievances as well as Parliamentary supremacy. This would culminate in Burke's *Thought on the Causes of the Present Discontents,* which appeared early in 1770. It was an attempt to find some middle ground between the ideas of Pownall and the strongly held precepts of the Crown. Pownall was dubious and feared that the efforts were little more than a Burke campaign effort at reelection.

And with yet another change in British government, Pownall found himself in discourse with the new minister, Lord North, a moderate who would maintain his role in Westminster through the majority of the American Revolution.[123] Lord North expressed to Pownall his opposition to the more severe parts of the *Townshend Acts,* including the *Quartering Act* and the *Extradition Act.* But North was adamant that a tax on tea should remain as a symbol of Parliament's supremacy over all colonial affairs. Pownall was unimpressed and vowed to challenge this tax. The date for the Parliamentary debate was set for March 5, 1770, a date that would live perpetually in infamy in Boston. Pownall railed against the tax during the day, but in the end North would prevail. And that evening on the other side of the Atlantic, in front of the Boston State House, the Bostonian "people" would gather, menacing a British sentry until a snowball was thrown his way, someone yelled "fire," and a line of British sentries would comply with what they construed as an order. Five Boston civilians lay dead in the snow. In the aftermath of the Boston massacre, as it would forever be known, the colonists would look with disdain at the potential culpability of their Royal governor.

Thomas Hutchinson was born in Boston, Massachusetts colony, September 9, 1711, only five years after Benjamin Franklin. Although born in proximity in Boston (indeed, they may well have seen one another during their childhood), through the vagaries of history their lives could not have been much more discordant. Unlike Franklin's father Josiah, who was a middle-class tradesman, the father of Thomas Hutchinson, also named Thomas Hutchinson, was a "Boston blueblood" from a family who traced their lineage back to the earliest days of that city. Although a fourth son, Thomas received ample family financial support and thereby matriculated at Harvard College at age twelve. He graduated four years later, in 1727, and immediately entered the mercantile business. In this he simply had "the golden touch." From a business standpoint, everything he did seemed to work.[124] He married well, and when his sister-in-law likewise married well, he found himself a part of the Oliver throng of Massachusetts and New Hampshire, yet another blueblood family of New England. It was then that he launched his political career in 1737. Elected to the provincial Massachusetts assembly, the "General Court," he took the position that the use of bills of credit (along the lines of "promissory notes") issued in the business sector as a type of primitive currency was ill-advised, since they could not be adjusted for inflation.[125] This was unpopular enough with the people that he was voted out in 1739. He managed to regain his seat in 1742 and held it until 1749; during that time came the assault on Fort Louisbourg in Nova Scotia, during the King George's War, by Loudoun and Pownall. In appreciation for this victory, the Crown rewarded Massachusetts colony with £180,000 in gold and silver specie. Hutchinson forced the buyout of all promissory notes in the colony by this windfall, and the people howled, having rather hoped for distribution of this money to the people. But once accomplished, the sudden influx of specie in the shops and publick houses stabilized the economy remarkably well. Hutchinson's stance was validated, his political opponents were simultaneously impressed and silenced, and his popularity as a Loyalist rose accordingly.[126]

Voted out of the assembly in 1749, he was immediately tapped for the Governor's Council. He would prove instrumental in arguing the colonial boundaries with New York, Connecticut, Rhode Island, and New Hampshire that exist to this day. In 1754, he would be designated as representative to the Albany Congress, and there he would officially meet Dr. Benjamin Franklin. While they would agree completely with a need for unified colonial defense, their thoughts on colonial currency, and the use of Crown-supported "promissory notes" as a surrogate, could not have been at greater variance. Hutchinson the merchant was focused on the impact of inflation upon promissory notes, while Franklin the populist was focused upon the political displeasure of taxation without representation as a substitute for taxation through promissory notes. In the end, they would simply agree to disagree and departed Albany in friendship. It wouldn't last.

In 1758, he was appointed lieutenant governor under the governorship of Thomas Pownall. This would prove a disastrous coalition (not unlike the vice-presidency of Jefferson under Adams, where Jefferson finally grew weary of Adams's steadfast ignoring of his presence in cabinet sessions and simply went home, forty years hence) since the two were politically polar opposites: Pownall was pure populist, and Hutchinson was, as noted, absolutely loyal to the Crown. The following year, Pownall, growing weary of the constant intrigue, resigned his commission as governor and returned to London. Hutchinson was ready to step smoothly into the power vacuum, but it was not to be. In 1760, Sir Francis Bernard took the reins as colonial governor and began a shakeup of the administration. Hutchinson requested appointment to be chief justice of the Massachusetts Superior Court of Judicature (essentially the state supreme court), and this was granted. At that point came a unified roar of protest from the populist side of the Massachusetts bar. Hutchinson was not licensed to the bar, had no legal training, and had never sat as a jurist. Outraged, James Otis and John Adams led the protest (Adams, as we shall see, was never far from outrage).[127]

In 1763, John Pownall, first secretary of the Board of Trade, advised Bernard and Hutchinson that Parliament had received the final bill for the Seven Years'

War in the colonies and was collectively angered regarding the sum. As a result, they felt justified in enacting a tax to force the colonies to pay for what they felt was their own defense (the fact that the colonists had virtually no role in instigating this war and had borne the majority of the financial and personal cost of this war in North America was deemed immaterial). The solution that Parliament proposed was a "Stamp Tax," where stamps would be sold by the Crown, which would have to be applied to *every printed product sold in, or exported from, all British colonies in North America*. Massachusetts considered sending Hutchinson personally to London to convey the anger of the colonists over what they felt was a totally unjust "Crown shakedown" of the colonists, and the phrase "taxation without representation" quickly became a calling card for the populists.[128] Interestingly, Hutchinson also adopted this stance, fearing the inflammation of the colonists while he and Bernard sat right in the midst of the ensuing crossfire.

And so Hutchinson and Bernard began a vigorous correspondence with all members of Parliament about how bad this idea was; in this they were joined by the strange bedfellows of Otis and John Adams. But then the old confrontations rekindled. Hutchinson and the populists argued heatedly over the wording of the protests to Parliament. In the end, Hutchinson would use his trump card as loyalist lieutenant governor, and the wording of the Massachusetts colony protest of the *Stamp Act* was perceived, not only in Massachusetts, but throughout the British colonies of North America, as, well... lame.[129] From then on, the publications of James Otis and a relative newcomer to the protests, Samuel Adams, would portray Thomas Hutchinson as a hired mouthpiece of the Crown. He would never be able to surmount that perception.

Parliament did indeed pass the *Stamp Act* over the protests of the Whigs of Parliament and over the protests of the populists (who now styled themselves as "Patriots") of Massachusetts and proceeded to name Thomas Hutchinson's brother-in-law, Andrew Oliver (who had brought Hutchinson into the Oliver family fold by marriage) collector of the stamp tax. This naturally brought more howls from the Boston rabble, and ultimately, mobs descended upon the home of first Oliver, and then Hutchinson, trashing the interiors but not torching them. Hutchinson and his family, having narrowly escaped personal harm, withdrew to Milton, Massachusetts.[130] Due in large part to the testimony of Franklin in Parliament against the *Stamp Act*, and the widespread protest by the "Patriots" throughout the British colonies via the shutdown of American exports of raw materials to Great Britain, the *Act* was repealed by 1767.[131] In its place, the British passed the *Townshend Acts*, primarily as a show of Parliamentary dominance over the colonies. And at that point, fearing for his personal safety, Sir Francis Bernard arranged his recall as Massachusetts governor and returned to Great Britain. On August 1, 1769, Hutchinson assumed the role of temporary governor of Massachusetts, which he would hold until the appointment was made permanent in 1771. He was thus the temporary governor at the time of the Boston Massacre and would have the trial of the British sentries that fired those shots in March of 1770 delayed for six months.[132] John Adams, outraged over the call from the Patriots for the immediate execution of all soldiers involved in the altercation, famously defended the British soldiers in this case, and only two would be convicted, and those two would subsequently have their sentences suspended.

The "Boston Massacre" would have a peculiar impact in the colonies, and in London. In Parliament, in May, Pownall demanded an investigation and review of the very presence of the British military in the colonies during what was supposed to be "peace time." Supported by Burke, Savile, Barre, and Beckford, a bill for a military inquest would fail in the vote. Now Pownall reached the nadir of his hopes for peace in his beloved American colonies. He wrote out of the depths of his despair to the Boston Committee of Safety, "the whole tenor of my correspondence with my friends in America, and of my advice to those [in London] who would give me the hearing, has been trying to form some line of reconciliation and reunion, and from time to time as the cases change to advise each party by conceding somewhat to take such ground as might meet that line. But I find that I have been the dupe of my own good wishes. The great men here despise my advice, and I see enough both in the ignorance and in the bad temper of men never more to advise any thing."[133]

Chapter 12

By 1771, Franklin was quite disheartened by the failure of all his lobbying efforts in London over the previous fifteen years; he had literally achieved nothing to further his plan to separate his "Pennsilvania [sic]" from the hated Penn family.[134] And he now felt that this left him only the obvious option: total schism, and independence, perhaps for Pennsylvania, but more likely for all the colonies as a political unit. Having had this discussion in confidence with Thomas Pownall over several weeks, he now proposed an "inner circle" of confidants, sworn to secrecy and to the ultimate aim of freeing Pennsylvania from the bondage of the Penns. Pownall swore to aid Franklin as much as he could. Franklin then proposed the other two members of the circle for Pownall's approbation: John Fothergill and David Barclay.

P: "Interesting choices, Dr. Franklin. Any explanation to support their membership in our little circle?"

Fr: "While we are of a voice in much of our thoughts, I perceive occasional divergences in our means and our ends. To this end, I feel that a duet is perhaps not the ideal basis for our endeavor, and that a third, and even a fourth, voice might provide a mediation, and even a sense of reason when we drift into more radical concepts of politics. To this end, I believe that Dr. Fothergill is a most trustworthy Friend who is also a voice of reason in this endeavor. He literally has the pulse of all London, and knows better than any, how the common man is likely to react to any initiatives on our part toward schism."[135]

P: "And Mr. Barclay?"

Fr: "He is clearly a man of financial genius and knows the American colonies perhaps better than any other individual in London outside of ourselves.[136] He too is a trustworthy Friend and has shown a past willingness to provide arms for the colonists despite his devout Quaker beliefs. He is, in short, a most invaluable resource of the means of revolution in terms of ordinance and capital, perhaps the best in Great Britain. I have a great deal of respect and personal affection for both of these men, and if they will accede to our design, I believe they will serve us well. Alternatively, if they do *not* accede to our plan, I am confident that they, more than anyone else of whom I am acquainted here in London, will be highly unlikely to betray our confidence to the British authorities. And circumspection here, Thomas, will be critical to our very being!"

P: "Your latter point is well taken, Dr. Franklin, and had not occurred to me. I believe your intent is well-reasoned, but I fear your plot is but half baked. I would encourage you to approach Dr. Fothergill and Mr. Barclay promptly, so that we can reason them out on your design. Only if they agree to assist us will I deem it prudent to press forward."[137]

And Franklin, with a heavy heart, agreed. He realized in that moment that he was losing control of his personal vendetta against the Penns and that solicitation of outside assistance was also an invitation to alternative designs or even betrayal. He had drawn Pownall into deeper water at this point and would need to be very circumspect moving forward, to ensure that any other confederates in the plot could be trusted to scrupulous loyalty.

Within two short weeks, Pownall, Franklin, Fothergill, and Barclay had gathered on a Tuesday evening in the private study of Fothergill. His study in Harpur Street was to be a familiar gathering point for the group, because with Fothergill's impossibly busy schedule of private patient calls throughout London, meeting with him was fully dependent upon a willingness for the other three to call upon him.[138] Fothergill simply never had a spare moment in his schedule and wasted little time with the luxuries of life such as eating and sleeping.[139] His comfortable home in Harpur Street was a showpiece in Bloomsbury and would provide Franklin a personal comfort that exceeded his own lodgings in Craven Street with Mrs. Stevenson. And Fothergill was perpetually the polite host, providing victuals and libations and comfortable and confidential accommodations for the group.

Pownall spoke first that evening. "Dr. Franklin and I have asked to meet with you here this evening on a serious matter of great personal importance to Dr. Franklin. But in order to proceed with this discussion, I must first beg your indulgence in agreeing to maintain strict confidence on this topic. It cannot go beyond this room."

Fothergill and Barclay exchanged puzzled looks. What secret topic could they be walking into?

Fothergill had a genuine affection for Pownall, but when he looked across the room, he realized that Pownall was not nearly the intellectual or analytical equal of the other three men present, including himself. Pownall was outgoing and entertaining when he was comfortable with his company, but more enthusiastic and boisterous than insightful. In short, he was more delightful dullard than profound philosopher. And as Franklin's own personal physician, Fothergill knew the topic could not be related to Franklin's somewhat tenuous health status; after all, he would have been aware of any serious issue long ahead of Pownall. So what was it?

Barclay spoke: "I can assure thee, Thomas, that any words from thy mouth shall never depart from this room."

Pownall knew, of course, that there was no point in insisting on any kind of sworn oath or promise from his two Quaker Friends; they were both extremely devout in their beliefs, and their word was their law. Fothergill echoed, "I can promise thee the same, Thomas. Pray, proceed with trust."

Pownall then outlined for the group the history of Franklin's distress with the behavior of Thomas Penn dating all the way back to King George's War, and through the Seven Years' War as well, and Penn's personal ridicule of Franklin, as well as the delay in providing a negative response to his well-reasoned

"Heads of Complaint." He went on to describe the petitions that Franklin had made to the Privy Council, which rejected him, and then the passage of the *Supply Act* of 1759 which, while attempting to satisfy Franklin's lobbying effort to establish taxation of the Penn holdings in their colony, had not provided any personal appeasement for him. Franklin interjected at this point that the *Supply Act* did nothing more than allow a base tax on proprietary lands but did not require any behavior on the part of the proprietors to reinvest in the defense, education, or well-being of the citizens of Pennsylvania. He then shared his personal experience with Parliament and with the Privy Council, over the past five years, in attempting peaceful resolution of the issues of Pennsylvania specifically, and of the North American British colonies generally.

Frustrated by this steadfast refusal to afford any autonomy to the Pennsylvania Assembly, on the part of the Crown, Parliament, or the proprietors themselves, Franklin was proposing a separation of Pennsylvania from the Charter, and thereby, from the empire, to be recognized as a free and independent state.[140] And there Pownall paused. After a silence, Fothergill spoke first.

Fo: "And how is this 'separation' to be accomplished?"

Fr: "By whatever means are necessary to secure independence for the people of Pennsylvania."

Fo: "And art thou then proposing violent disruption of the empire?"

Fr: "It need not be violent, but the goal would have to ensure the recognition of Pennsylvania as a part of the empire independent of absentee taxation, willful subjugation, and abridgment of freedoms as citizens of a free and independent state."[141]

B: "But hast thou attempted discourse with the Crown and the Proprietors, to no avail?"

Fr: "Well, yes. That, my dear David, is the basis of my frustration in this matter.[142] We colonists have little or no leverage with the government of Westminster. We can beseech or demand fair treatment, but currently I see no effort on the part of the Proprietors or the Crown, or our Parliament, to accede to these petitions."

B: "Dr. Fothergill and I are of the Society of Friends, as thou art well aware.

And as Friends, we will perpetually seek a peaceable resolution to all disputes. But we cannot take up arms in support of a civil opposition to our political foundations, no matter how egregious or corrupt they might be. I do not propose to speak for the doctor; he is fully capable of doing that himself. What I propose to thee is simply this: as long as thou dost seek the Peaceful way first, in every crossroads on thy path to independence, and will continue to seek first the peaceful resolution of all thy disputes, I will support thee to the fullest extent of my abilities."

Fr: "Thank you, David. I deeply appreciate your devotion in this circumstance."

Fothergill sighed. "I, too, Dr. Franklin, will support thee, if thou but follow the Peaceful solution wherever possible, on thy life's journey to freedom. And would ask only that thou continue to pursue freedom for *all*, in all thy ways."[143]

And here was a twist that neither Franklin nor Pownall had foreseen: a social contract that all four understood was to bind Franklin in perpetuity to abolition of slavery. Fothergill was, at heart, an ardent abolitionist, and the issue was foremost in his thoughts. While he hated no man, he could barely countenance the slave traders of Great Britain and the slave owners of America. Now it was Franklin's turn as a slave owner to breathe deeply.

Fr: "When my path to freedom is assured, I will initiate the process to clear the way for others."

Fothergill smiled, the tension broke, and then all four shook hands and began to embrace. It was the first step into the modern era of world history.

$\mathcal{C}\mathcal{D}$

Chapter 13

Through the remainder of 1771, in ongoing meetings, primarily at Harpur Street, but occasionally in Craven Street, in Albemarle Street (the Fawkener home of Pownall), and even in Cheapside at Barclay's London home, discussions about the North American colonies continued. Franklin and Pownall were almost of one voice, but Barclay was slow to concede to their objectives. Ever skeptical of the ability of this modest group to hatch such a scheme on the scale required, Barclay would ask infinite questions: had they thought about how to keep the revolutionary spirit alive in the colonies *in absentia*? How could they maintain a supply of food, clothing, and ammunition for the colonial army in the field? How could they ship supplies through the British blockade? Who would fund such a folly? How could they solicit funds from other nations when they lacked diplomatic credentials and truly lacked even recognition as an independent state? Had they identified a military leader capable of success against the British? Were this Washington to die or be taken up in battle, who would replace him? Were Franklin to die, would the revolution end? The harder the questions from Barclay, the more focused Pownall and Franklin had to become. And it was, little by little, forcing them to formulate concrete answers rather than vague dreams. Barclay would prove unrelenting.[144] He advised the circle that he had already abandoned the linen-draping industry in the American colonies as being economically unsound. To him, it appeared that the idyllic economy of the British North American colonies was deteriorating steadily. While he was yet procuring and shipping guns and ammunition to the colonies, he would not countenance persistence of this enterprise in the face of revolution against the Crown. Who would replace Barclay and Bevans in arming a rebellion?

Fothergill would serve primarily as a sounding board and the voice of impartiality. He was thoughtful and readily assumed the role of the outsider (which, to a large degree, he truly was), listening to both sides of a debate response and then pointing out the strengths and weaknesses on either side.[145] He felt that, throughout, his primary role was maintenance of the health of the principal architect of the plan. Indeed, Franklin had passed his sixty-fifth year in early 1771, and his health was challenged by poor circulation in his legs, poor vision, and gout, made manifest in excruciating pain at times in his joints, and in bladder stones. With Fothergill at hand through that year, Franklin would maintain remarkable health during this endless series of meetings; Fothergill oversaw his activities, and his diet, much to Franklin's chagrin and frustration. It forced Dr. Franklin to sneak out at times from the oversight of both Fothergill and Mrs. Stevenson to indulge in drink and rich foods. And then the attacks of gout would ensue, and Franklin would realize, as if he did not already know, that Dr. Fothergill was correct. Hume had told him that there had to be one protagonist who would continually keep the inclination of the people focused on the objective. Franklin *had* to be that protagonist. He could cavort at will and end the dream of liberty for Philadelphia, or he could behave and live out the one goal that had kept him focused for the past thirty years. Through the year, Barclay and Fothergill, with Pownall's support, would keep Franklin in that unrelenting focus that would see the revolution through.

At the close of 1771, Franklin journeyed once again for a visit with the doyens of the English Enlightenment in Edinburgh, including Lord Kames, David Hume, and Adam Smith, at their insistence.[146] In that rarefied atmosphere of philosophers, it would have been a difficult invitation to refuse. Franklin's views had always been received with great respect and careful regard by this most esteemed audience, and this visit would prove no different. But Franklin was a very different person from the one that a far younger David Hume had met in 1759. Franklin now spoke in strict confidence, but with much greater candor with his Scottish colleagues and friends.[147] And the topic at hand was less philosophical and more conspiratory: frank revolution appeared to be the final and now essential solution to the corrupt governance by Great Britain over the American colonies. Here Franklin would find a less enthusiastic audience, roundly discouraging his initiative in this regard. Their fears were carefully enumerated but generally well-founded: regardless of success or failure, there would be extensive loss of life and property on both sides of the Atlantic. The ultimate expenditure in capital and human life could well prove crippling to both sides. Failure would almost certainly culminate in the ignominious end of Franklin, Pownall, Fothergill, Washington, both Adamses, and perhaps many others, by execution at the Tower. No, while they swore never to betray the inner circle, they vociferously, to a man, implored Franklin to pursue this no further.

In January 1772, Franklin returned from Scotland in a more serious and subdued humor. He immediately sought out Thomas Pownall, specifically advising him *not* to bring his brother John along; and Dr. Fothergill, specifically advising him *not* to invite Barclay. They met at Fothergill's home, the familiar locus for their assembly. And there Dr. Franklin laid out the specifics of his plan: a revolution involving *all* the mainland British colonies in North America. The entire program was predicated on one essential element: the legal manumission of at least one individual slave in either the colonies or Great Britain. From that event, provocative letters would go to all the Virginia plantation owners: Washington, Mason, Jefferson, Madison, Henry, Lee, Monroe, Wythe, Harrison, Carter, Randolph, and several others. Henry Laurens of Charleston, South Carolina would also be contacted, along with other South Carolina plantation owners. At the same time, Samuel Adams would have to be convinced that revolution was expressly *not* about preservation of the condition of African slavery. Political support would have to be enlisted from Patrick Henry in the south and from the Adamses in the north. And then Franklin would have to solicit financial aid from continental Europe, probably France, the Netherlands, or Spain, to sustain an army in the field. All the colonial friends of Parliament would have to be unified in their support. Pownall would be enlisted to aid in this effort.

Fothergill expressed his skepticism about the entire scheme and secretly hoped his friend Granville Sharp would be unsuccessful in his efforts in London to free a slave. (Fothergill to this point had scrupulously avoided introducing Sharp and his manumission initiative, perhaps in the hope of peaceful resolution of the differences between the colonies and the Crown. Franklin was at that time almost certainly *unaware* of the efforts of Sharp and Mansfield, v.i.). Pownall was skeptical about the expressed necessity of involving Samuel and John Adams in the effort, fearing that they would betray Franklin and the others to the British and solicit reconciliation with Parliament. The Boston Massacre had been something of a "wake-up call" to the Adamses, and John had retreated into his law practice while Samuel had tempered his rhetoric dramatically.[148] The deaths of five of their fellow citizens had brought home to the Adams cousins the potential consequences of their persistent calls for revolution. And finally, Pownall knew that without significant financial support from Great Britain's enemies, the plan simply would implode from bankruptcy of the military. He asked, "Do you have any idea, Dr. Franklin, how much capital it would require to support a standing army during a prolonged war?"

Franklin had to admit that he had only a vague idea and redirected the question to Pownall. Pownall replied, "I could only guess. But we have an expert in our midst, and I would suggest that we reach out to him, moving forward."

Franklin hesitated. "I am naturally reluctant to allow our plan of action too many members, for fear of spoiling the entire intrigue."

Pownall responded, "I don't think you should object to the inclusion of Barclay, as he is already part of our inner circle and has agreed to our stipulations about these meetings."

Pownall and Fothergill rose at that point, and Fothergill spoke. "At least afford myself and David the opportunity to think about these things. What thou art proposing is troubling at least and may constitute treason against the Crown. Failure would prove fatal for many people, present company included." And without another word, Pownall and Franklin departed.

Franklin then set out with his private preparations for the possible manumission of a British slave. In February 1772, he prepared letters to all the prominent plantation owners (who were *de facto* slave owners) in both Virginia and South Carolina, simply pointing out that the Court of King's Bench had freed a British slave, and allowing them individually to reach their own natural conclusions of the impact, or potential impact, of that decision being applied in widespread fashion across the empire.[149] He wrote an especially impassioned letter to Henry Laurens, advising him of the potentially devastating impact that abolition of slavery would create for him and for his family. As per Franklin's habit, each letter concluded with "Please burn this after reading." He then addressed and sealed each, individually. Now, he needed a reliable and trustworthy mechanism of delivery, pending the actual manumission. To this end, Pownall and Fothergill would serve well. Fothergill was handed a mail parcel, already sealed, with instructions to send it to Anthony Benezet in Philadelphia, "Quaker to Quaker," packaged in the form of yet another packet of their endless tracts against some social ill or another and therefore highly likely to pass through the post without suspicion. Inside the parcel was a note from Franklin instructing his friend Benezet to forward all the enclosed letters, intact within the parcel, to Pownall's personal friend, John Hancock, in Boston, upon a signal from Franklin in London. Hancock, through postmaster Alexander Colden in New York, was instructed by separate correspondence from Pownall that he would one day be in receipt of over twenty letters to various gentry of Virginia and South Carolina and to see that they were securely and reliably delivered through his associate postmasters in Portsmouth, Virginia, and in Charleston, South Carolina. Hancock would be advised that the future of American liberty lay in that correspondence. Benezet was simply advised that the letters would encourage the slave owners that manumission was now an established fact in Great Britain, and that if they so desired, they should be able at that point to pursue voluntary manumission of their own slaves without legal interference. And Benezet was further advised that he would be alerted by publication of Franklin's response in the London press, to the manumission of the first slave. *Watch for my employment of 'Quaker pronouns' in my editorials in the* London Chronicle. *This will be your signal to mail the letters to Hancock.* In this carefully constructed, albeit nefarious project, Franklin's specific goal was to keep Benezet free from any suspicion of complicity, while taking full advantage of Benezet's rather unique ability to convey secure postage throughout the British world.

Henry Laurens would be a key source of potential political support for the inner circle due to his unique relationship to the African slavery trade. He was born March 6, 1724, in Charleston, South Carolina, the eldest son (he had two older sisters) of John Laurens, a saddler who would be highly successful in Charleston. Henry was sent by his father to London when he was twenty years old to study business. There he met Richard Oswald, who would become a business partner and lifelong friend.[150] John Laurens died three years later, and Henry inherited extensive real estate in the Charleston area. He married in 1750 and set up business with George Austin in Charleston, working in association with Richard Oswald, who was posted at Bunce Island.[151] Laurens was involved in the "farm and home" trade, selling implements such as clothes washers, dishwashers, friers, roasters, refrigerators, vegetable steamers, hair clippers, shavers, fans and heaters, and for the out of doors, lawn mowers, weed trimmers, planters, reapers, corn pickers, driers, milkers, and threshers. But unlike the implements of the twenty-first century, all Henry's farm and home implements were made of flesh and blood, much like his customers.[152] At the same time, unlike many of his customers, most of his implements were clad in very dark skin.[153] And Laurens was a highly successful dealer in farm and home equipment. Charleston became the foremost trading center for human beings in all North American by 1760, and the single largest and most financially successful supplier was Austin & Laurens. Henry would serve in the South Carolina Assembly beginning in 1757, while still maintaining his "business" in Charleston. In 1772, Franklin acknowledged Henry's status in British colonial affairs by having him nominated to the American Philosophical

Society of Philadelphia. Laurens would thus initiate a brisk correspondence with Franklin, then living in London. Henry was much inclined to seek conciliatory relations with Great Britain and considered himself a loyal subject of George III until later that same year, when he received a confidential piece of correspondence from Franklin in London that related specifically to his career and his family's future. It would be no overstatement to assert that the *Somersett* decision rattled Laurens to his very being.[154] This threatened his career, his financial support of his family, and perhaps even their lives, like no other potential business reversal. Thereafter, he would inexplicably, to all the businessmen in Charleston who *thought* they knew him, become a staunch American patriot.

Interlude: Somersett

Interlude: Chapter 1

He was born sometime in 1740 in Sierra Leone, the son of servants indentured to a tribal king, and was named Tombo Susu, the "surname" taken from his parents' ancestral group.[155] Tombo would demonstrate precocity, speaking his local Bantu language by age two and assisting in household chores by age four. At that point, he was sent to the rice fields of Sierra Leone to learn the system of sowing, tending, and harvesting the rice crop that was a staple in the local diet. Every summer, white men speaking an unknown language would come and point out a few people, who would then be bartered out and never seen again. Most of these were young girls and boys, and the men seemed to have an eye for the strongest and brightest. Tombo was no exception. At age eight he was bartered to the white men, who took him to the harbor town of Serra Leoa, and there they loaded him, with hundreds of other young persons of both sexes, on the slave-trading ship *William*, headed for Barbados. At the sight of a crew of white sailors, the locals spread the word that these were cannibals and that their cargo was to serve as meals at sea. Generalized crying ensued as the ship weighed anchor and left Africa behind.

The people in the hold of the ship were kept in shackles and below decks. They were given a bowl of grain soaked in water twice each day, and anyone found not to be eating, for any reason, was beaten with a short whip. The flooring below decks was grated to allow for urine and feces to drip through to the ballast but made an extremely uncomfortable base for a bed. Over the course of the seven weeks' crossing, about one third of these captives would die. These dead would be brought out of the hold and dispatched overboard. Generally, there was an eerie quiet below decks, as all wondered about the fate of the dead and wondered who was next. When motion stopped at seven weeks (due to anchoring at Barbados), the bulkhead hatches were thrown open and the "cargo" was unloaded onto the decks. There were already many whites on board, and as the slaves came out, they were prodded and pawed, examining head, teeth, body, musculature, and much chattering went back and forth with the captain. Many of the slaves would be marked with a leather thong and paper tag around the neck, and all were then taken down the gangplank. They were headed for the auction block. The slave traders of the Caribbean knew quality, and this young African boy had quality. They would purchase him and take him to Jamaica, to the sugar plantations, for "seasoning," a euphemism for enduring the yellow fever season. If he could survive yellow fever, learn pidgin English, the rudiments of the slavery rules, and the rudiments of the sugar industry, he might be a good bet to go to the plantations in the northern British colonies, where they paid top dollar.

On August 1, 1749, the *William* dropped anchor off the Chesapeake port of Norfolk, Virginia, and off-loaded cargo from the Caribbean, including a group of perhaps a dozen slaves who spoke rudimentary English.[156] The slaves were taken to the auction block in town. Charles Steuart, a twenty-four-year-old clerk, purchased Tombo Susu for fifteen guineas, a preemptive price for a child of this age, and took him home. Tombo was destined to be a personal servant to Steuart and as such was expected to learn a reasonably extensive vocabulary, basic domestic skills like cooking and laundry, and some skills related to Steuart's line of work. It seems Steuart was a mercantile exchange agent in Norfolk, which included trading of slaves. In his role, Steuart was professional and businesslike, with an eye for unusually gifted slaves, and treated Tombo well. Over time, he delegated more and more responsibility to his servant as

Tombo matured and learned the business of being a clerk in Norfolk. This freed Steuart for the more complex expectations and obligations of trading with the various ship captains and plantation owners who frequented his business office. One of his best customers by 1760 was George Washington, who had leased Mount Vernon from his own widowed sister-in-law (and would assume ownership two years later upon her death). Washington was always in the market for good workers for his plantation, and it became almost a standing joke in Steuart's office, as Washington would invariably ask, "How much do you want for Tombo?"

Steuart would laugh and respond, "Tombo's not for sale." And the exchange became so commonplace among ships' captains and plantation owners when they frequented Steuart's office that Tombo himself quickly learned the response, "Tombo not for sale," sparing Steuart from even looking up from his ledgers and always bringing a laugh.

In 1760, colonial Governor Francis Fauquier named Steuart "Receiver General" for Virginia at Norfolk, and in that role, Steuart was charged with providing for the well-being of all ships landing at Norfolk or Portsmouth, Virginia, and their passengers. As fate would have it, in 1762 a Spanish privateer was caught in a late-season storm, and the main spar was cracked.[157] The ship, the *Don Pedro Bermudez*, limped into the Elizabeth River, where a local gang of street toughs prepared to board her and plunder her cargo and seize the passengers, including one noblewoman from Havana, Cuba. A local ran to Steuart's house, raising the alarm. Steuart took up two muskets, loaded them, called Tombo (who was now twenty-one years old, muscular, and large for a typical slave), and, following a pause where their eyes met, handed Tombo a musket and told him to follow. The significance of this gesture was not lost on either man; it was highly unusual to arm a slave voluntarily and signified an incredible degree of trust. When they arrived at the *Don Pedro Bermudez*, the gang, armed with staves and torches, was calling out to the crew to surrender. Steuart leaped onto the bow of the ship and bade the gang stand down. Then he heard a pistol cock. He fired his musket into the air, and then he and Tombo immediately exchanged muskets. He again bade the gang disperse and then aimed his loaded musket at the leader. The torches were lowered, two or three cursed Steuart and pushed Tombo, but then they slowly walked away. Steuart, heart beating fast, reloaded the spent musket, and he and Tombo stood guard the remainder of the night. The following day, the spar was replaced and the ship set sail.

Thereafter, the degree of trust between the two men increased dramatically, and Steuart styled his young manservant "Somersett," feeling it sounded much more dignified than "Tombo." And they became inseparable on business trips up and down the Atlantic seaboard. They were known from Boston to Savannah, and Somersett was dressed in accordance with his status, including breeches and silk stockings. On a trip to London in 1763, Steuart was surprised to learn that the "*Don Pedro Bermudez* affair," as the press had styled it, had preceded him, and that His Majesty King George III, no less, was quite impressed by the care and concern that Steuart and Somersett had afforded the ship of an ally and its helpless passengers. The king invited an audience, for which both men of course had to have a new outfit. Steuart sat for a portrait for the occasion (still held by the Colonial Williamsburg Foundation), and in recognition of Steuart's valor, George Grenville, chancellor of the exchequer, named him surveyor-general for customs for the entire Atlantic seaboard from Quebec to Virginia. Two years later, he would rise to receiver general for North America, one of the most powerful (and well-compensated) Crown posts in the British colonies.

Unfortunately, while Steuart was accruing these prestigious posts in Norfolk, the British colonies were reeling under the severe taxation of the *Stamp Act*, and then the *Townshend Acts*, and by all descriptions, Steuart remained as dutiful as ever to the Crown, enforcing the collection of these taxes throughout the colonies. This rendered him, and Somersett, far less popular than they had been merely five years previously. In that setting, Steuart decided that he needed to relocate to Boston to more effectively administer the hated taxes, despite the increased danger of mob terrorism. Perhaps he trusted the British military presence in Boston for protection. Perhaps he felt that a mercantile colony like Massachusetts was a safer area to administer mercantile decisions than a Crown colony like Virginia. For whatever reason, he and his personal slave Somersett moved to Boston in 1765. By 1769, Steuart, withstanding the chronic anger of the colonists over taxation, living in constant fear of personal violence, and growing exhausted over the unending explanation of duties and assessments, was feeling chronically ill and requested from the Privy Council permission to come to London for recuperative purposes, perhaps distant from the likes of Samuel and John Adams and the persistent rabble of Boston.[158] The request was granted.

Steuart and Somersett arrived in London in November 1769 and established residence in Cheapside, parish St. Marylebone (or "Marleybone" as the locals called it), and Somersett continued as Steuart's personal aide and servant, doing the marketing and cleaning, supervising the laundry and hired transport, and generally acting as a "gentleman's gentleman" for his master. During this time, Somersett would be free to walk through the neighborhoods of the largest city (excepting Beijing) on Earth interacting with people of every ethnic and economic stratum. In the streets, he would be subjected to the idle talk and criticism from free Black people, who would chide him about his status as an American slave: "You tink you so well-off, because you wear silk and velvet? You not well-off. You not free. We free. We want eat, we eat. We need pee, we pee. We need shit, we shit. We no ask no massah notting."

Somersett was not alone in his status by any means. There were, at that time in Great Britain, at least ten thousand slaves working on farms, in factories, and in the cities as servants. But only a few were as "well-off" as Somersett. He was accorded an allowance and a wardrobe by Steuart and was not required to wear any neck chain or neck plate, as so many city slaves wore. Generally, when he considered the garb, the housing, and the diet of the "freemen" he regarded in the streets of East London and Southwark, he had to think his life wasn't all that bad. And yet, he wasn't...free. One afternoon, at the encouragement of white abolitionists in London, Somerset stepped into St. Andrew's Cathedral, where he was baptized as "James Somersett." This would be his legal and common name for the remainder of his life.

On about October 1, 1771, Somersett didn't come back to the house in

Cheapside. By the following day, Steuart realized that either he was a victim of foul play or that he had simply fled. And sounded an alarm. The authorities advised him to place an advertisement in the local newspapers and to post broadsheets on Tower Hill and other popular meeting sites. Steuart provided a description of Somersett and offered an unusually high reward of two guineas for his capture. While it might seem that Somersett could be hard to find, in actuality, Black Africans had few places where they could go without discovery. Even were he to change to a "freedman's wardrobe," (actually dressing *down*, dramatically, into discarded rags, in Somersett's case) there simply weren't enough Blacks in London at that time to allow him to disappear into a crowd. And two guineas was about two to four weeks' wages for a day laborer, so there was plenty of inducement to find him.

On Tuesday, November 26, 1771, professional bounty hunters came to the Steuart residence, announced that they had Somersett and requested what Steuart wanted done with him.[159] At this point Steuart became enraged.

"Haven't I provided for him? Haven't I given him a better life than he ever would have had in Africa? Haven't I protected him?"

In his rage, he told the bounty hunters to take him to the wharves and load him onto a "slaver" for the Caribbean. This, for a domestic servant like Somersett, would have been tantamount to a death sentence, working menial hard labor on the sugar plantations in the heat of Jamaica or Barbados. So Somersett was clapped into shackles and placed in the hold of the ship *Ann and Mary* under the authority of Captain John Knowles. But his situation was not hopeless—not yet. And by never actually receiving Somersett into his custody after capture, Steuart had, unbeknownst to him, committed a serious legal error.

In 1679, the British Parliament had approved the *Habeas Corpus Act*, which stipulated that no one could be held in custody for over seventy-two hours without being charged with a crime before a magistrate.[160] While originally designed to stop the arrest of political enemies of the Crown and allowing them to rot in the Tower of London, the abolitionist activists of London had seized upon this authority as an effective tool against the slave hunters. With the available funding of some wealthy and sympathetic London widows, they became accustomed to filing writs on a regular basis. The fervent hope was that someday, somehow, some bounty hunter and/or some owner was going to make a mistake filing a claim, or filing a court brief, and a slave was going to have to be freed.

The biggest shaker and mover in this entire effort was none other than Benjamin Franklin's sole hope for his plan in London, Granville Sharp, who had pledged his time, his money, and his legal talent to the sole purpose of identifying such a case. He had informants all through the London docks, watching for captured slaves being loaded onto ships. And so, on November 27, 1771, Elizabeth Cade petitioned a *writ of habeas corpus* at the Court of King's Bench, Middle Chamber, under the auspices of William Murray, First Earl Mansfield.[161] Mansfield looked at the writ, exhaled with cheeks puffed out through pursed lips and thought, *Here we go again.* He filed the official case as *England, the King [Rex] v. James Sommersett (sic), a Negro,* but even then, and ever after, it would become known as *Somersett v. Steuart,* the "king" in eighteenth century Great Britain being a surrogate for the plaintiff. In answering the writ, John Knowles dutifully presented Somersett, designated "James Somerset," before Lord Mansfield on December 9, at Serjeants' Inn, insofar as the Court of King's Bench, Westminster Hall, was already adjourned from Michaelmas term.

"Are you James Somersett?" asked Mansfield.

"Yes, sir, I am," Somersett replied.

Mansfield then looked to Knowles. "Thank you, you are discharged." And then said to Somersett, "Hearing is set for January 24, 1772, with a surety bond from Elizabeth Cade for one hundred forty pounds." And he gaveled the case adjourned for the following month.

On January 13, Somersett knocked on the door of The Jewry, the London residence of Granville Sharp.

Interlude: Chapter 2

I n order to understand the relationship between Franklin and the abolitionists, we must first introduce Anthony Benezet and then Granville Sharp. Anthony Benezet was born January 31, 1713, in St. Quentin, France, the son of French Huguenot parents.[162] Victims of persecution from the Roman Catholic court of Louis XIV, they fled initially to Rotterdam, but by 1715 they were living in an enclave of Huguenot refugees in London. Benezet likely attended a Quaker school in London, where, in 1726, a young Voltaire would make his acquaintance, and where Benezet would, between 1726 and 1731, become a Quaker. In 1731, Benezet, with his parents, would emigrate to Philadelphia, where Anthony would quickly learn to identify Quaker worship with the practices of the Huguenots of his youth. During this time, there would be an extensive "second migration" of Quakers to Pennsylvania, including printer Samuel Keimer, from France. Keimer would set up a print shop in Philadelphia and would ultimately employ a young runaway apprentice printer named…Benjamin Franklin.

One by one, the Benezet family, in the 1740s, forsook the Quaker church for the Moravians.[163] In 1743, Count Zinzendorf himself, on a rare visit to North America, would stay in the Benezet home. Anthony, however, never gave up his Quaker ties and remained a lifelong member of that church. During the 1740s, his father would attempt to establish a free school for the poor in Philadelphia; among the trustees of that school were the Reverend George Whitefield and Benjamin Franklin. From that time on, Franklin's and Benezet's paths would cross frequently.[164] Philadelphia was, by 1750, the largest English-speaking city in the colonies, and among its population were perhaps as many as a thousand African slaves.

Slavery had come to Philadelphia in 1684 aboard the ship *Isabella* out of Bristol, England.[165] One hundred and fifty slaves would be auctioned for farming and building houses. By 1705, one of every fifteen houses in Philadelphia owned slaves, including many Quaker families. In 1700, Philadelphia voted "Black Codes," which stated that Blacks could not be on the streets after 9:00 p.m., could not congregate in groups of more than four, and had to stay within a ten-mile radius of their owners. That same year, a "sales tax" was applied to slaves; while originally meant to be a fundraiser for the local government, this would in time be manipulated to price slaves out of the Philadelphia market, creating a *de facto* abolition throughout much of the colony. In the first half of the eighteenth century, the Quakers were dealing amid the slave trade; by 1775, the Quaker Meeting called for abolition of slave-owning by Quakers in Pennsylvania. Thereafter, Quaker ownership of slaves dropped dramatically.

Benezet would spend his adulthood in Philadelphia as an ardent abolitionist, one of the first well-known abolitionists in the colonies.[166] He married in 1736, and the marriage produced two children who both died in infancy. He and his wife became vegetarians and were frequently observing feeding the stray animals in their neighborhood, including dogs and rats. He was noted to be small and frail, incredibly studious, and held a personal library of over two hundred volumes. He would derive most of his income during his adult life as a teacher, writer, and proofreader, being too frail for manual trades or agriculture.

By 1750, he was tutoring Black slaves in his home, teaching reading and arithmetic.[167] In 1770, the Quakers started a free school for Blacks in Philadelphia, and Benezet would assume personal responsibility for demonstrating to white critics throughout the colonies that Blacks were every bit as capable of learning as their white counterparts. This simple issue and simple fact, which had been challenged for centuries, would be a massive step toward ultimate emancipation of slaves throughout America.[168]

In the mid to late 1750s, on the heels of the French and Indian War, Benezet would also reach out to the Indigenous peoples of America.[169] It was at that time that the Quakers generally decided that they were retiring from secular politics due to the mistreatment of Africans and native Americans. And during this time, and into the 1760s and onward, toward the American Revolution, Benezet would become a more and more outspoken champion against warfare.

Anthony Benezet often spoke to Franklin when bringing proofs for broadsheets and pamphlets about the horrors of slavery and the wicked treatment of Indigenous peoples.[170] And while Benezet was not a wealthy man, he was always prompt in paying for the publishing costs of these tracts. For Franklin, this was a most endearing trait. And like so many other Philadelphians, Franklin cultivated a deep respect for this quiet little man who had never met a stranger, nor an inferior. Franklin was by this time the postmaster-general for Philadelphia and indeed the deputy postmaster-general of all British colonies in North America under the direct supervision of Lord le Despencer, the Lord Postmaster of the British Empire. In this role he would often occasion the mailings of Benezet. And Benezet maintained a significant correspondence with abolitionists and other social reformers throughout the colonies and Europe. Franklin noted that the posts of Anthony Benezet were clearly written, clean, and correctly compensated. Likewise, the correspondence Benezet received was never tainted, or unsealed, or otherwise molested. He was, in short, the perfect postal patron, and correspondence addressed to or emanating from Benezet was apparently universally sacrosanct.

Granville Sharp was born November 10, 1735, in Durham, England, the ninth son of Archdeacon Thomas Sharp of Northumberland.[171] Four of his older brothers would survive to adulthood, leaving Granville, as fifth son, very little funding for higher education. As a result, he was apprenticed to a linen draper, despite his clear aptitude for language and mathematics. His master died within three years of the beginning of his apprenticeship, and Granville moved to the residence of his master's father-in-law, where he would serve out his final four years as an apprentice. In 1757 he joined the Worshipful Company of Fishmongers in London (despite the grandiose name, this guild was primarily associated with real estate management and leasing).[172] He would never again seek employment in the linen draping/fabrics/mercantile sector, and within another year he was employed as a clerk at the Board of Ordnance in the Tower of London.

The clerks at the Board of Ordnance worked constantly during office hours, but the office hours were from 10:00 a.m. to 4:00 p.m., Monday through Saturday, leaving an inordinate abundance of time both before and after normal hours.[173] And Granville, no goldbrick he, took full advantage of his excess time to study both contemporary and classical languages, including ancient Greek and Hebrew. With his natural aptitude for learning, he excelled to a remarkable degree in these endeavors and very soon was able to offer a professional level of discourse in debating the theology of both Old and New Testament in the original languages with Unitarian/Socinian and Jewish scholars. In scholastic circles in London, his reputation for theological exegesis grew. In 1764, he applied for and was accepted as a clerk in the Minuting Division of the Board of Ordnance, which rendered him more logically in alignment with his personal linguistic skills and personal philosophy of pacifism. And then, in 1765, he found himself in debate with the esteemed Benjamin Kennicott, Hebrew scholar and Bible publisher, regarding a syntax error that Sharp was quite convinced he had identified in all prior translations of the Old Testament. At the conclusion of the public dialogue, Kennicott was convinced that Sharp was…absolutely correct.[174]

The third eldest brother of Granville Sharp, William, had studied medicine, and by 1765 he was already engaged in medical practice in Mincing Lane, London.[175] As an observant Anglican, he opened his home every morning to the indigent ill, and on Sundays, with no office hours of his own, Granville would volunteer to assist. One day in 1765, Jonathan Strong, a Black African, appeared at their dispensary in Mincing Lane.[176] He was clearly badly injured and nearly comatose, having been beaten by his master, David Lisle, an attorney, using a pistol. Strong related that he had been beaten until the butt of the pistol broke off the lock, and then, nearly dead, thrown into the street to die (in that world, even defensive retaliation by a slave would guarantee an immediate one-way visit to the gibbet). Granville brought him in, cleansed his wounds, and called William.[177] William took one look at him and immediately arranged for him to be admitted to St. Barts Hospital, where Strong would remain and convalesce for four- and one-half months. At the end of that time, Granville was able to arrange an employment situation for Strong at Brown's Apothecary Shop in Fenchurch Street as a medical assistant/courier, with a room. Here Strong lived and recuperated and grew healthy once again over the next two years.

One eventful day in 1767, Strong was helping Mrs. Brown make deliveries when who should appear but David Lisle.[178] Lisle immediately recognized Strong as his former slave and followed the coach back to Fenchurch Street. Rather than raising an alarm, Lisle decided to hedge his losses in not laying claim immediately to Strong but instead surreptitiously advertising Strong for sale in the local publick houses. One David Kerr laid claim to him, but with the price of £30 to be paid *only* after Strong was safely loaded aboard a slaver captained by David Lair, bound for Jamaica. Lisle arranged for two thugs to accost him in a local publick house and take him to the Poultry Compter (a local holding cell).

Unbeknownst to his previous owner, Strong had been baptized sometime between 1765 and 1767 under the directive of two abolitionists, Stephen Nail and John London, who had served as his godfathers. So now, from the Poultry Compter, Strong sent out an appeal to both of them, as well as to John Brown, his employer. But when Brown came to enquire about Strong, Lisle accused him of "receiving stolen property" and threatened litigation. In response, Brown called...Granville Sharp. At first, Sharp didn't recognize the name, but when Strong was brought out of his holding cell, Sharp immediately made the connection. Sharp applied to the jailer to hold him until he heard from Sir Robert Kite, Lord Mayor of London.[179] Eleven days after Strong's abduction, he was delivered to Kite's courtroom for a hearing. Appearing for Lisle and Kerr were Captain David Lair and Kerr's attorney, William MacBean. Kite listened to the presentations from both Sharp and MacBean and then promptly responded that Strong had committed no crime, and therefore the City of London had no right to detain him further. He released him without fanfare.

Then an unusual response from Lair ensued. He immediately grabbed Strong by the arm and announced that he was "Mr. Kerr's rightful property" and that he was taking him to the ship. Chaos ensued as Thomas Beech, watching the proceedings, whispered to Sharp, "*Charge him!*" Sharp immediately called a "citizen's arrest" against Lair for battery of Strong, with Kite and Beech as witnesses. Lair cursed him, cursed Strong, released him, and stalked out of the courtroom. Strong returned to the apothecary shop and his situation. Sharp went home.

Two weeks later, Lisle appeared at Sharp's house, pounding on the door. When Sharp answered, Lisle launched into a rant and challenged him to a duel. Sharp remained calm and encouraged Lisle to pursue his concerns through the courts. The following week, Granville and his older brother James were sued by Kerr, rather than Lisle, for lost property (Strong being considered "property"). But the writs filed for this suit were a travesty, and the attorney retained by the Sharps was easily able to gain a continuance, but not for the reason that Granville had hoped. Their attorney wished to advise the brothers Sharp that this suit, regardless of the legal incompetence of the filing attorneys, was not winnable, at least not by contemporary standards.

There was at that time in British jurisprudence a non-decision decision known to all solicitors as the "Joint Opinion," which, while only a legal opinion delivered at a dinner conference in response to the issue of "Does the baptism of a slave in Great Britain automatically make him or her free?" had been rendered by Attorney General Yorke and Solicitor General Talbot in the negative. Therefore, since all paths to decision by the King's Court came through those two individuals, it had over time achieved the status of common law in the realm.[180] The Lord Chief Justice of the King's Bench, Lord Mansfield, was said to cite this opinion repeatedly and to always restore baptized slaves to their masters. Thus, Strong could not be declared free by any British court.

Sharp would not accept this conclusion. He sought other opinions from the various barristers in London, all of whom told him the same: settle this and release Strong to Kerr. Sharp then decided that there was no other alternative left to him: he would have to defend Strong himself, and in order to do this, he would have to apply himself to intensive study of British law. With absolutely no prior education in the law, Sharp devoted his free hours to perusal of the bookshops of London for legal textbooks, and in the course of his search, he came upon a volume titled *Short Account of that Part of Africa Inhabited by the Negroes,* by a writer he didn't recognize, Anthony Benezet. In reading this book, Sharp learned that Benezet had taken his concept of abolitionism one step further. At this point in time, the Anglican abolitionists like Sharp were outspoken in their condemnation of human slavery but at the same time espoused an opinion that the African Blacks were intellectually and morally inferior to whites. Along with Sharp, this opinion was held by Hume, Voltaire, Jefferson, and Edward Gibbon (*The Decline and Fall of the Roman Empire*). Benezet challenged this, finding that in his experience at his school in Philadelphia, Blacks were every bit as capable of learning and following moral codes as whites. In the margins of the book, Sharp commented on Benezet's "errors of Quakerism" but was otherwise impressed enough to 1) contact, and initiate an ongoing exchange of correspondence with Benezet, and 2) plagiarize and reprint a Benezet abolitionist pamphlet for distribution in London.[181]

After maneuverings and multiple continuances, Sharp was ready to take on the suit against Kerr and his brother, filing a brief of sorts called *A Representation of the Injustice and Dangerous Tendency of Tolerating Slavery, or Even of Admitting the Least Claim of Private Property in the Persons of Men, in England* (whew!).[182] The pleading itself was printed and circulated by Sharp among the various justices of the Court of King's Bench, where it received uneven reviews, some extremely critical ("Sharp presents the law as he would *like* it to be, rather than the law as it *is*"). Kerr, meanwhile, filed a second suit and then inexplicably dropped it. Lisle once again went directly to Sharp and demanded that he turn Strong over to him, and Sharp again informed him that he was not *holding* Strong, and that neither he, nor Lisle, nor anyone else in Great Britain had the right to claim Strong as property. Lisle departed and would not be heard from again.

Kerr's original suit still had to be defended, and to this end, Sharp employed two of the best legal minds of eighteenth century London, John Dunning, the solicitor general, and Sir William Blackstone, author of the famous *Commentaries on the Laws of England,* and puisne justice to Lord Mansfield on the Court of King's Bench. Blackstone's position in the suit was of the opinion that Strong's obligation to Kerr was a form of apprenticeship and that Strong would be legally forced to comply, an opinion with which Dunning concurred. Sharp, for his part, told his "dream team" attorneys that they were both quite wrong and asserted that, as per Montesquieu, an African slave in bondage could not legally enter into an apprenticeship contract, since such agreement constituted coercion because the two parties (owner and slave) were not of equal standing.

While the Kerr lawsuit was still being actively defended, a manumitted Black African named John Hylas came for help to Granville Sharp.[183] Already, Sharp was rapidly gaining a reputation as the "man to call" in London for slavery and abolition questions and problems. Hylas had been brought to London by his owner, Judith Alleyne, in 1754, while a Mr. and Mrs. Newton brought a slave named Mary (officially owned by Mrs. Newton) to London at about that same time. In 1758, John and Mary were wed in a Christian ceremony, with the approval of Ms. Alleyne and Mr. Newton. Ms. Alleyne immediately manumitted John to allow him to live with Mary. In 1766, with no warning to John Hylas, the Newtons had Mary "taken up" and shipped to the West Indies for resale. John was totally at a loss as to how he could recover his wife…until he heard about Granville Sharp.

Sharp found the Hylas case intriguing and thought this might be the opportunity he needed to manumit a British slave through the courts. He felt that her being transported out of Great Britain violated the *Habeas Corpus Act* of 1679 and that by common law which equated "husband and wife," the manumission of John *de facto* accomplished the manumission of his wife. But before Lord Chief Justice Wilmot in the Court of Common Pleas, Sharp's counsel feared the "Joint Opinion" and did not plea for manumission but merely for a cash settlement. Wilmot asked Hylas if he wanted cash or his wife, to which Hylas replied "my wife." Wilmot would find for Hylas, awarding him one shilling in damages (about fifty cents), and ordered the Newtons to return an enslaved Mary back to London.[184] This was *not* the outcome Sharp desired. It was time to have a private discussion with Lord Mansfield.

Legal experts and historians have long held that Mansfield and Sharp were working together throughout this time, trying to identify a case that would allow legal manumission of a single slave.[185] The motivation was not entirely clear. Mansfield for his part was always of the opinion that what held for one case would not hold for all cases. But at the same time, he recognized Sharp's acumen as an amateur attorney, but more importantly, his zeal for the abolition of slavery. And in the open Court of King's Bench, where anyone could readily attend, Sharp was making something of a nuisance of himself when Mansfield's court was in session. Sharp, for his part, seemed to hold the opinion that were a single slave on British soil set free, *all* slaves on British soil would have to be manumitted immediately. Neither party ever disclosed any other motivation for their congress. For Mansfield, he was of the opinion that Granville Sharp was incredibly well-read and wise but lacked the basic thought processes that comprised the professional aspect of the practice of law. Mansfield felt, as did the best justices, that every case devolved upon *one key question*, and that the duty of the justice was to 1) identify the single question of law being asked, and 2) render the correct legal answer to that key question. Therefore, he realized that Sharp always *wanted* to ask, "Can this slave be set free?" but the cases he provided simply were not asking that question. For example, the Hylas case was not really asking "Can Mary Hylas be set free?" but rather "Did the Newtons have a legal right to secretly send Mary Hylas out of Great Britain?" While the answer to the latter question was a definite "No," that did not change the status of her bondage to the Newtons. So Mansfield encouraged Sharp not to relent, but rather to identify a case where the answer to the question at hand would entail manumission of the plaintiff.[186]

As to the Kerr lawsuit and its conclusion in the dealings over Jonathan

Strong, civil cases in the British court system had to be decided within eight sessions of the court, or they were automatically dropped. There is nothing to suggest that Kerr or his attorneys were impressed or intimidated by the various opinions Granville Sharp provided to the court. More likely, Kerr had simply lost interest and didn't want to spend any more money on legal fees. For whatever reason, he ultimately failed to appear, and the case was closed, without any opinion. While Sharp was awarded twenty pounds in damages, he would not collect the award until 1774, by which time 1) Strong had died, and 2) Sharp's *A Representation* would make him the British champion of the abolitionist movement.

Interlude: Chapter 3

In the American colonies of about 1750, it is estimated that no less than one in every four persons, at any given time, was the property of another person. For the colonies south of Pennsylvania, that number might have been closer to one in *three*. From our viewpoint, this statistic seems almost implausible, but slavery was not the only status to be considered. There were two other components of society that involved persons as property: apprenticeships and indentured servitude. Both were extremely common in the eighteenth century. To put the issue in its appropriate perspective, it is essential to understand what the development of colonies in the New World meant to the lower classes living in Europe. In the four hundred years following the dreaded Black Plague of Europe, the nations had become progressively repopulated, and there was simply a finite amount of real estate available for the burgeoning population. As a result, outside of the nobility, few people held any expectation of *ever* owning property, including the property upon which their homes stood. In Great Britain, the instances of non-noble landowners were so rare that they had their own designation and subsequent surname: they were known as "franklins." With the discovery of North and South America and the progressive development of colonies, the possibility of land ownership became at least feasible, and as the safety, cost, and frequency of trans-oceanic travel improved, more and more "disenfranchised" peoples of the lower classes looked to America for a better future for themselves and/or their descendants.

Passage across the Atlantic was not inexpensive, however, and for many, if not most emigrants, the only reasonable way to relocate to America was to sign on as an "indentured servant.[187] This social contract simply stated that the signatory promised to work, for a finite and stated amount of time (typically between five and seven years), at a stated trade (and sometimes for *unstated tasks*!), for a specific person or family, in exchange for the cost of passage.[188] In this circumstance, the signatory was more or less at the mercy of the "master" during the period of servitude for housing, food, clothing, and health care. Some masters were empathetic, but many were not, looking upon indentured servants as nothing more than slaves with an "expiration date."[189] And indeed, that was precisely how they were defined by law: African slaves were considered "servants indentured for life." The other group was apprentices, young people (the vast, vast majority were male, by law) whose parents or guardians had signed over their rights, care, and basic needs to a "master" who was expected to teach them a trade for which the apprentice would hopefully, ultimately, become self-sufficient at the conclusion of the apprenticeship. Once again, once apprenticed, the young boy was at the mercy of the master for subsistence, and they were often badly mistreated. One example of an apprentice badly mistreated was Benjamin Franklin, whose own *older brother* James mistreated him to the point where Franklin fled Boston to get out of his apprentice obligation (v.s.).[190] But slaves, indentured servants, and apprentices who fled were considered outlaws from the perspective of the British legal system, and the "recovery system" was relatively brutal. In order to recover any of these *unfree* persons, the master would run an advertisement in the local press, or on broadsheets posted in the local businesses, or both. And there was some money to be made in the apprehension, confinement, and return of these unfree persons. As a result, the less educated, marginally employed, and brutish men of the community would often go out seeking runaways in order to be paid a reward as a supplemental or sometimes sole source of income.

In most of the American colonies, apprehending an escaped African slave was a relatively straightforward exercise, made even easier by 1750 by laws in the colonies that prohibited free Blacks from being on the streets after sunset or 7:00 p.m. So any Black persons seen after dark, or truly any unaccompanied Black persons at any time, were subject to apprehension by these wandering gangs. The gangs for their part were more likely to simply accost and confine a Black adult first and ask questions later. African slaves on an errand for their masters were expected to carry a writ (essentially a "permission slip") to allow them to be in public without their masters. Free Blacks had a problematic existence all their own in the American British colonies: they had to carry proof, at all times, that they were indeed "free" in order to prevent them from being "taken up." For children, the situation was, if possible, even worse. *Any* child of any ethnicity, Black, white, or "mulatto," was subject to being seized if unaccompanied by a parent or guardian and promptly sold as an indentured servant, apprentice, or slave. This too was considered a business venture on the streets of colonial America.

Apprenticeships were purchased and sold as commodities, by adults, based on the demand of the trade for which the apprenticeship was offered. Thus, for a goldsmith or silversmith apprenticeship, a master might *charge* the parents as much as fifty pounds, essentially the cost of the child on the open market. On the other hand, for a trade that already had surplus labor, such as a drover, or even worse, a "gold-digger" (necessary shoveling and emptying), the master might have to *pay* a parent ten pounds or more in order to secure help. In most jurisdictions, apprenticeships lasted seven years or until age twenty-one, whichever came last. For families of more than six or seven children, the dealing in child labor was considered an acceptable and appropriate method of financial support of the family. Sadly, nearly every metro area in the colonies also had a share of homeless children abandoned by family, orphaned by parental illness or unwanted pregnancy, or running away from a horrid home or apprentice situation, and these children, like runaways, were subject to being "taken up." The bounty-hunters would "take up" these children, runaways, unaccompanied Blacks, teens, etc., and sell them for profit, usually at the local docks, where ship captains were ever willing to whisk them away before they were missed. Franklin reported in his "Autobiography" that, after fleeing the cruelties of his older brother, and appearing in a disheveled condition in New York, he realized that he was in grave danger of being "taken up" and hid during the day and snuck off to Philadelphia by night.

In both Great Britain and the American British colonies, there were also roving "impressment gangs," either working freelance or for the Royal Navy, who would seize young men from about age twelve to about age twenty-five, beat them, and load them onto ships of the Royal Navy for a set fee. There was a chronic shortage of sailors in the Royal Navy due to the severity and hazards of the work. The impressment gangs had quotas to keep in order to be paid, and as a result they would congregate around the publick houses near the docks, take up young, intoxicated men, and spirit them onto ships. When these men recovered from their drinking sprees and/or beatings, they were already far out to sea.

For runaway slaves that had been recaptured, the response of the master was problematic and often based on the relative value of the slave. This was assessed by the talents of the slave, the age, and the underlying behavior. In most cases a slave would be taken back once, but an habitual runaway would not be redeemed by the master. Rather, the master would direct the slave to be taken to the docks and loaded aboard a "slaver" (a ship outfitted specifically for transport of slaves). The ship's captain would then be instructed to take the slave to the "West Indies" (usually, for the Brits, Barbados, Antigua, or Jamaica; for the French, St. Domingue, Guadeloupe, or Martinique) and sold for whatever the market would pay, the captain to keep the cost of the transport and return any profit. For the slave, this was for the most part capital punishment; the life expectancy of a slave in the West Indies was less than eighteen months in the harsh, hot, humid conditions of the sugar plantations. It was remarkably rare for a slave discharged by a master to the West Indies ever to be heard from again.

On July 3, 1770, Sarah Banks appeared at Granville Sharp's home, the Old Jewry, noticeably upset.[191] She told him about a young Black male, George August, also answering to "Thomas Lewis," who had been "taken up" the previous night by two rivermen and loaded aboard the *Captain Seward* bound for Jamaica, captained by a Captain Philip Sawyer. She described a relatively violent contest in a rowboat, with Lewis calling out, "Help me, Mrs. Banks!" several times. She recognized the voice. It seems that the status of this man was of some question, both during and after the case, as to whether he was a former slave or a free Black. But Sharp wasted no time taking the dowager Mrs. Banks in hasty tow to the Rotation Office in Litchfield Street (the "Rotation Office" was a magistrate's office where a judge could be procured without appointment), pressing for a warrant to return one Thomas Lewis, signed by Justice Saunders Welch, and delivered by one of the famous "Bow Street Runners" to Gravesend, where the ship lay in the estuary, ready to set sail. The warrant was ignored by Sawyer, and Lewis was not released. The next morning, Sharp went directly to the office of the esteemed Brass Crosby, Lord Mayor of London, and there filed for a writ of habeas corpus under the *Habeas Corpus Act* of 1679. This was secured and this time delivered by one of Mrs. Banks's own couriers to Spithead, at the Downs, where the *Captain Seward* was trying to move out into the North Sea but facing headwinds. Now, with the writ signed by Lord Mayor Crosby, Sawyer feared severe reprisals for failure to comply and released Lewis to the Lord Mayor of London. None of the rivermen, or their leader, filed a challenge to the writ. The case was likely to simply fade away at this point.

But Sharp was quite convinced that this was the case he was seeking and pressed for arraignment of the kidnappers. He first needed clarification of the status of Lewis: was he an escaped slave, or was he free? In this regard, Sharp hoped that he was still considered a slave. But therein lay the issue. He and Mrs. Banks were both interested in pursuing this case, and to that end, Lewis was able to name the two rivermen, as well as their ringleader, one Robert Stapylton, a career seafarer, now old and blind.[192] The two rivermen were Aaron Armstrong and John Maloney. An indictment was filed against these three for wrongful assault, imprisonment, and kidnapping. Mrs. Banks insisted, over the protests of Sharp, on covering the court fees to file the case. And then Stapylton, for uncertain reasons, decided to fight the charge. He first requested that the venue be changed from Crosby, to the Court of King's Bench, and therefore to, yes,

Lord Chief Justice Mansfield. This was granted. Now Sharp became concerned; as a private citizen, Mrs. Banks had assumed the cost of trial, and at King's Bench this would not be inexpensive. Sharp offered to assume the cost moving forward. Mrs. Banks declined and insisted that she would see this case to its conclusion. She had an attorney under retainer, a solicitor named Lucas. But as this case was to be heard at King's Bench, they would need a barrister. The two most likely candidates were Serjeant John Glynn and former Solicitor-General John Dunning. [The title "Serjeant" has nothing to do with the military but rather was a Crown title granted in the seventeenth and eighteenth centuries in Great Britain to those few attorneys considered the best, and most prestigious, in pleading cases before the courts of the Crown in London, v.i.]. In the end, they elected Dunning.

John Dunning was considered in late eighteenth century in London the quickest, cleverest legal mind in the realm, with never any testimony being offered without his careful assessment, and rapid-fire objections whenever appropriate, and always correctly applied.[193] At the same time, he and Lord Mansfield were almost invariably at odds, both in court and in Parliament. It is perhaps somewhat tragic, and even ironic, how often the Creator chooses to place a remarkable talent in so hideous a vessel, and so it was with Dunning. It was said at the time that any courier seeking Dunning in a publick house, and not knowing him on sight, could invariably request the house master to "send out the ugliest man in the room," and Dunning would appear every time. Poor complexion, pinched face, a voice raspy and broken with frequent coughing, and at times almost inaudible, Dunning was a legal mind with which to be reckoned but within a countenance never to be forgotten.

This case for Mansfield was to prove his own undoing in tortuous logic and legal contortionism to the point where he, by the conclusion of the sentencing, appeared hopelessly lost. It would prove for him the legal equivalent of the tragic "Dred Scott case" for Roger B. Taney in America eighty years later.

The *Lewis v. Stapylton* trial did not open until February 20, 1771. Dunning would have the opening statement. He averred that the status of Lewis was unclear and that Stapylton had no right under British law to claim ownership of Lewis, or of any other human being. "The laws of this country admit no such property. I know nothing where this idea exists, I apprehend it only exists in the minds of those who have lived in the countries where it is suffered."[194]

He then called Lewis. Lewis proceeded to tell a remarkably convoluted tale of his life to the present, being born in Sierra Leone, serving with his uncle in a servant class to the king there, and as per Dunning's encouragement, "always being free."[195]

At that point, Mansfield, hearing no objection from Stapylton's attorney, chose to interject on his own, "You don't prove his being free by himself." Dunning paused. Depending upon why Mansfield adopted that stance, he feared it could prove impossible to establish to a jury a positive statement of Lewis's freedom that could satisfy the court. At face value, Mansfield appeared to imply that, as a Black African, Lewis could not simply say, "I was never a slave," and accept this as proof. Sharp and Dunning were taken aback. It was time for Dunning to provide one of his masterful responses.

But it was not to be. "The boy has always understood himself to be free," was all Dunning could respond. This response was, in a word, lame.

But then, without a clear basis, Mansfield replied, "I shall presume him free, unless [defense] proves the contrary." Rather than calling Lewis out for the color of his skin, Mansfield had provided him the benefit of British personal liberty. The clouds parted.

Lewis continued. He had voluntarily, as a child and with his uncle's best wishes, boarded a ship for Santa Cruz, where he would, in turn, live with a ship's captain who died, then a nobleman who died, then to a cooper who died, then to the nobleman's clerk, who took him to a British merchant named Robert Smith. From there he boarded a ship, which was overcome by a Spanish privateer captained by Stapylton. He was then taken by Stapylton. Here Mansfield noted a point of British law: the taking of a slave as a war prize was considered one of the few legal methods for securing a slave in the British Empire. Then to Savannah, then to Havana, where he was employed ("and paid wages" Dunning quickly pointed out, to imply that he was *not* a slave at that point) in a publick house. Stapylton then reappeared in Havana, took Lewis aboard his ship, and went to New York, where Lewis worked for wages in a wine merchant's shop, then back to Santa Cruz and Robert Smith for eighteen months, until Smith died, and then, again under the control of Stapylton to Pensacola, where he was a house boy for a judge ("and was paid wages" Dunning interjected again and was greeted with a scowl by Mansfield), and then was taken by the judge's hairdresser to Boston. Mansfield was growing weary.

Lewis droned on: then to Charleston, then to Jamaica, then back to New York, and then finally to Great Britain with Stapylton, where they settled in Chelsea. Then Stapylton had him loaded on a ship—here Mansfield interjected, "Yes, we are aware of this."

But then Lewis countered, "No, that was the *second* time. The first time he tried to send me to Jamaica, the ship wrecked, and I came back to London."

Now even Dunning had grown weary. Mansfield pressed for details on the final kidnapping engineered by now *three* rivermen: Armstrong, Maloney, and Coleman. Here Lewis recounted the events of July 2, 1770, once again, from the assault, to the crying out for help, to Mrs. Banks, to the gagging, to the binding his leg, to Captain Seward asserting that he had "a bill of sale from Stapylton," to the writ that convinced Seward to release him. At this point, Stapylton's attorney, Walker, began his questioning. He asserted that there was indeed a bill of sale for Lewis and a title held by Stapylton. Mansfield had heard enough.

In eighteenth century British court proceedings, the justices were adept at deciding verdicts quickly and were known to clear a docket of one hundred cases in less than six hours. Sometimes the principals in the cases were unaware that a verdict had been rendered in their cases, so rapidly were cases opened and closed. To that end, the justices held a healthy distrust of rogue juries and cases that threatened to go "off the rails," and could, in situations where the facts in evidence blurred a point of law, request from the jury only a "special verdict."[196] This maneuver stripped the jury of the authority to pronounce a defendant guilty or not guilty and rather simply called upon the jury to stipulate whether a fact presented was credible or not. And so, in *Lewis v. Stapylton,*

Mansfield requested that the jury answer only a single question: Was Thomas Lewis the property of Robert Stapylton? That was it. Mansfield had found the key question in the case, and it was the answer to that question that he would leave to the jury. Their answer would provide Mansfield the ability to render, as a result, a verdict as to whether Lewis had been illegally assaulted, kidnapped, and confined. His part would be simple.

In eighteenth century British court proceedings, there was also an established practice both justices and a critical press referred to as "dithering."[197] In cases where a justice was reticent to establish a precedent of conceivably enormous consequence, he would seek minute errors in the filing of the case or obscure points of law that could avoid a direct response, or otherwise so obfuscate a decision as to leave all parties confused. And here, Mansfield, against his typical desire to "modernize" British jurisprudence, dropped back into a deliberate mode of "dithering" in order to avoid rendering a decision on the legality of human slavery in the British Empire. He felt quite strongly that this was simply not the correct case upon which to lay a precedent; there was too much confusion as to the legal status of Lewis (free or slave?), and he was willing to walk down that dithering path instead.

So now Walker was tasked with proving that Lewis was aware that he was the property of Stapylton. He produced the nearly illegible "bill of sale," but none of his witnesses could state unequivocally that they had witnessed the transference or when it might have occurred. Walker pressed on, calling two brothers of Stapylton, who each in turn testified that Lewis always referred to Robert Stapylton as "my master." Dunning stepped in and took the questioning one step further: did they ever hear Lewis refer to himself as "property of Robert Stapylton? To which Miles Stapylton answered "no" and Bryant Stapylton answered… "yes." Dunning called Bryant a liar, and at this point both sides rested. Dunning's summation was that Lewis could not possibly be Stapylton's property, simply because there was no legal mechanism in Great Britain that would allow that conveyance of one human being to another, except as a war prize, which clearly Lewis was not. It fell now to Mansfield to instruct the jury on answering the question of Lewis's legal status. "There is no bill of sale, there is no witness to the conveyance of Thomas Lewis to Robert Stapylton as property, so therefore it is manifest that they did not prove the contrary." It was almost as if Mansfield were handing them the answer he wanted. It took the jury less than five minutes to render a verdict: Lewis was "no property."[198]

On the heels of the special verdict, Mansfield's verdict was straightforward. Stapylton and the rivermen were found guilty of assault, confinement, and kidnapping. And once again, there was no manumission of a slave by the Court of King's Bench, simply because there was no slave involved in the trial of *Lewis v. Stapylton.* Mansfield and Dunning were satisfied; Sharp most assuredly was not. By British law, sentencing could not occur for another four days, and the defendants had to be present for sentencing. But none of the defendants appeared within the next three *months.* Finally, at Sharp's stern insistence, the barristers for the prosecution prayed for sentencing *in absentia* on June 17. Mansfield feigned amnesia for the case; Dunning's best friend and noted barrister in his own right, Sir Elijah Impey, recalled the specifics of the case and demanded the defaults of the absent defendants.

And here Mansfield lapsed into soliloquy regarding the points of law, and most importantly, whether a Black could establish his own status as free. And he seemed to think in the negative generally; he recalled that Walker was given ample opportunity to object to Dunning's assertion that Lewis was free simply because Lewis believed himself to be. And therein, Walker failed to take the initiative. But then Mansfield clearly and conveniently chose to ignore that he had rendered the stipulation that Lewis would be "presumed free unless the defendants prove the contrary." He then returned to that concern about the Spanish privateer taking Lewis a slave, which would satisfy the notion that British law recognized slaves if they were taken in wartime as prizes. But in that notion, only Lewis had provided a positive witness; therefore, Mansfield wondered aloud once again whether a slave could impeach his own defense, that is, whether the testimony of a Black could be used in a court of law to establish his status as *either* free or slave. It was all simply too confusing, and therefore Mansfield advised Dunning and Impey that he simply was not going to impose any sentence whatsoever on the defendants.

Sharp was furious. They had received a guilty verdict from this justice—the chief justice. But no sentence was forthcoming. The simple responsive question from Sharp was why?[199] And here Mansfield probed deeper: Stapylton had never proven Lewis to be property. But Lewis, having been taken as a war prize into slavery, never proved himself to be free. Therefore, his status before the court was, as yet, unknown, or at least, unproven. And therefore, no sentence against the defendants would be forthcoming. Sharp would not let go so easily and asked Dunning to press for a sentence. But upon return to court that evening, Dunning found neither the defendants nor Mansfield and went home. One last time, on November 28, 1771, at the close of the Michaelmas term, Dunning tried again. Mansfield was absolutely sick of hearing about Lewis, or Sharp, or Banks, or Staplyton, or any of it and bluntly advised Dunning that Mrs. Banks had achieved the return of Lewis and for her own good should drop the matter. Then, turning to the paperwork at his desk, he signed that aforementioned writ of habeas corpus for one James Somersett, among his other tasks. And he closed the session, leaving Dunning standing alone in the gathering darkness of King's Bench as the lamps were being extinguished.

William Murray was born to Scottish nobility in 1705 to a family with definite tendencies to supporting the former Roman Catholic King James II (known in Great Britain as "Jacobites," "Jacob" being the Hebrew equivalent of "James").[200] Murray was a fourth son and therefore had no claim to his family title, but all the same, he demonstrated from an early age a remarkable aptitude for reading and learning and was academically successful throughout his early education, right up to his matriculation at Oxford. He entered in 1723 and earned his bachelor's degree from Christ Church College in 1727. He then went to London to read for the bar and successfully entered the bar in 1730. Continuing his proficiency for legal studies and for understanding both Scottish and British law, Murray proved invaluable in interpreting both in the House of Lords. In 1742 he entered Parliament and was appointed solicitor general. With adept appointments and timely decisions, he rose to the rank of attorney general by 1754 and from there to Lord Chief Justice in 1757, at which point he was, by tradition, requiring a title for the chief justice to be designated a "Lord" and elevated to the peerage. He was therefore designated First Earl Mansfield. He has been acclaimed universally as among the most perceptive and brilliant jurists in Great Britain during the eighteenth century, clear in his interpretation of the law and in his fair judgment in his many cases. So esteemed were his decisions that his protégé, Sir William Blackstone, used Mansfield citations throughout his *Commentaries* that are still read today. And so it was to this esteemed and experienced justice that Somersett entered his plea. And it was this same Lord Mansfield who, fifteen years before the Somersett case was tried, advised Franklin in the Cockpit at Whitehall to apply moderation to the taxation of the Penn estates. His profound influence pushed the bill through Parliament, achieving approval as the *Supply Act of 1759*.

Interlude: Chapter 4

When Somersett appeared at the door of Granville Sharp seeking guidance on that cold afternoon in January 1772, Sharp calmed him and advised him of a safe house in which to reside pending his upcoming appearance at King's Bench before Lord Mansfield on January 24. Insofar as Somersett was under a surety bond, which was one of the highest, to that point, ever assigned by the British court in a matter so apparently trivial, Sharp realized that this placed the finances of Elizabeth Cade, and the safety of Somersett, under dire threat of Somersett's impressment and transfer to Jamaica. Once Somersett departed, Sharp began a flurry of activity at the Court of King's Bench. His first order of business was to find Dunning. While the "Lewis matter" had not ended to Sharp's satisfaction, he felt no malice toward Dunning; indeed, he felt that Dunning had acquitted himself well and had shown atypical passion in pleading for the freedom of Lewis while condemning the inherent evil of the British slave laws. Here was the perfect barrister to plead for Somersett. Upon arriving at Westminster Hall, he spotted Dunning and approached him.

S: "Mr. Dunning, I believe we have finally identified a case of significance that may force a decision from the King's Bench on the legality of slavery in the empire. I would like to tell you about it, in order to secure your services on our behalf."

D: "Pray tell, Mr. Sharp, would this matter concern an African negro who goes by name 'Somersett'?"

S was somewhat taken aback and now on his guard: "Why, yes, it does. And so you apparently have heard?"

D: "Indeed, sir, I have, and have been retained by George Steuart to serve as his primary defense counsel."

Now Sharp turned crimson and lashed out at Dunning. "How can you, of all barristers, *support* the defense of a slave owner in such a matter? You, who condemned the institution of slavery before the bench not two sessions previously! You?"

At this point, Dunning assumed the coign of vantage as a professional and cautioned Sharp, "Sir, at this point it would be better for both of us, and for your supplicant Somersett, if we terminated further discourse in this matter. Mr. Steuart approached me two weeks ago seeking my services, and in the spirit of equity and fair representation before the law, I had to agree that he was entitled to due process to the best of my abilities to provide. This is my first duty as a barrister, and I will do no other." He turned and walked away, leaving Sharp to his frustration.[201]

Sharp needed time to regather his thoughts in the matter, and in so doing he realized that here was a worthy cause, and a worthy case, and that there were other capable barristers in Westminster who should be willing, in the same spirit as Dunning, to take up the cause of abolition to "the best of their abilities." To that end, he began to formulate a list in his mind of the capable attorneys he had heard in his various visits to Westminster, to the Inns of Court, and to Lord Justice Mansfield's Court of King's Bench. From these he decided to have his solicitor approach Serjeant William Davy and Serjeant John Glynn.[202] Both attorneys had extensive experience with pleas before the bench of Mansfield and knew the justice well, both personally and in his professional opinions and conduct in court. Davy for his part was the outspoken gregarious rascal, unafraid to stand toe-to-toe in verbal jousting with any man, and unintimidated by the prestige of the Lord Chief Justice. Glynn, on the other hand, was more thoughtful and mature. At aged fifty he was, by the standards of the day, one of the older learned counsels in Westminster, and while it was said that Dunning was the master of the law that he knew, Glynn was the master of *all* British law. It was simply a matter of Glynn having acquired so much experience because he had lived so long in the Courts of Westminster.

On January 24, 1772, James Somersett reappeared before Lord Mansfield to answer the subpoena. The return of Captain Knowles was read before the court (a *return* being a sworn legal document explaining a legal relationship of a defendant to the plaintiff, in response to a summons to appear), and then Serjeant Davy addressed Mansfield.[203] He opined that the circumstances of this case being of a grave and serious matter, there was insufficient time remaining in Hilary term to adequately address them and therefore prayed for adjournment to Easter term. Mansfield briefly considered and then acquiesced to a point, declaring a continuance but only to February 7 of Hilary term. But then Mansfield added that, considering the gravity of the issues, he might well ultimately consider deferring a decision to the "opinion of all the judges on it." The uniqueness of the statement, in this setting, was received by both Davy and Dunning as a warning. During the recess, Dunning would confer with Mansfield, who strongly encouraged him to seek settlement in the case. Dunning was advised that if he pressed this to a decision, his client might be disappointed, but far more importantly, it could disrupt the entire economy of the empire. Dunning promised to discuss the situation again with Steuart.

Meanwhile, Providence appeared to Sharp in the guise of one Francis Hargrave.[204] On January 27, Sharp received correspondence from Hargrave. He was familiar with Granville Sharp, as they had exchanged letters, and ideas during the Hylas trial three years previously. Now Hargrave presented to Sharp that he had had time to reflect on his ideas regarding the evils of human bondage, and regarding the *Representation* authored by Sharp, and in the interim had been called to the bar of Westminster. In that role, he had applied his legal education and training to the issue and had now heard about a *Somersett* case before Mansfield. Hargrave suspected that Sharp was aware of the case and that he might even be involved. Further, Hargrave had been advised of the curious statement at the close of the hearing from Mansfield regarding the potential gravity of the issues of that case. He closed by advising Sharp that if he were interested, *I am very ready to communicate any arguments that occur to me on the subject, with as much pleasure as if I had been retained as one of the Counsel in the Cause.* The following day, Sharp responded to Hargrave and assured him of his welcome in participation of the prosecution of Steuart on behalf of Somersett *and that you do a great act of private charity, as well as public good.*

On January 29, Sharp went to the office of his solicitor, Mr. Priddle, where he enquired as to the success of retaining both Davy and Glynn as counsel, proceeding forward.[205] And when Mr. Priddle's clerk, Mr. Hughes answered in the affirmative, Sharp gladly handed him six guineas, which was about the full amount of his available resources. And Mr. Hughes equally gladly poured them right back into Sharp's hand. "They won't accept them. They have already spoken with your Mr. Hargrave." Sharp privately brushed away tears and headed home.

Now the clock was ticking for Sharp, and he set to work outlining the case of Somersett as he understood it, from his birth in Sierra Leone to his sale into slavery and his service as the clear and uncontested *property* of George Steuart (Sharp was determined not to let Mansfield dither this case away!), their travels together in front of literally hundreds of witnesses who could be invoked as needed, and the events of their time in London, right up to Somersett being apprehended by a bounty gang for export to Jamaica.[206] He prepared three copies for his now *three* counselors and brought them to Hughes for distribution to allow his learned counsel time to prepare their prosecution. Regrettably for Sharp, these briefs would not be delivered by Hughes until the day before the case opened. Such are the human errors on which history often turns.

No sooner had Sharp returned home from Priddle's office delivering the briefs to Hughes, but there was correspondence waiting for him.[207] It was a curious parcel from another acquaintance and abolitionist, John Fothergill. And the packet was bulky! Inside was a letter and a copy of Sharp's *Representation*, but in an unusual format, from an unknown printer. He leafed through it and found a foreword written by the famous Philadelphia abolitionist, Anthony Benezet, who acknowledged the authorship of Granville Sharp of London, and an apology for the editing of the length of the original. He smiled. Anthony Benezet! Editorial efforts duly accredited were commonplace among the abolitionists, who recognized that their various pamphlets and tracts often had to be modified for the appropriate audience. There was no sense of outrage here; this was considered the highest of compliments. Smiling, Sharp now turned to Fothergill's letter. He and Sharp had been in intermittent correspondence over the past two and a half years on the issues of charity and manumission of slaves.[208] Fothergill congratulated him on the American publication of his *Representation* and advised him *that an anonymous benefactor with whom I am acquainted, of international renown, has taken an interest in your Somersett case, and has pledged his financial support for your efforts in this regard. He is prepared to come forward at the conclusion of the case and wishes you every success.*

Sharp rapidly penned a response to Fothergill, requesting any other copies of Benezet's redaction that he might spare, adding that Benezet, despite his abridgment of the work, *had very judiciously extracted the very marrow of my book.* He then commented in his letter to Fothergill that the bearer of the letter was none other than Somersett. It seemed that Sharp had realized that Somersett for his part could best aid in his own prosecution of Steuart as a courier among the various principals concerned. Off Somersett went toward Harpur Street, Bloomsbury. As Somersett departed the Old Jewry, Sharp followed him out onto the front stoop. The winter sun was shining brightly that day!

George Steuart was not quiescent in the days leading up to February 7.[209] He too had heeded the warning issued by Mansfield and was now publicizing his concerns in different spheres and soliciting support. Realizing that were Mansfield to find for the plaintiff in this case, it could possibly culminate in the legal manumission of an African slave purchased in the American colony of Virginia, he went to the agents of the southern colonies of Great Britain, including Virginia, the Carolinas, Georgia, West Florida, and the West Indies, offering two possible responses. They could either pursue settlement, with reparation of Steuart's personal losses of legal fees, and, of course, his investment in one James Somersett, *or* mounting a legal defense that would resolve the question of slavery in the British Empire, with the power of the chief justice to create precedent throughout Great Britain and its colonies. Steuart advanced, at that point, that he was prepared for either response. The mainland southern colonies from Maryland to the Gulf of Mexico were not impressed with the gravity of the situation and declined to respond. But the sugar plantation lobby of the British West Indies listened carefully to Steuart's arguments and decided that it was indeed time to take a stand. They compensated Steuart for the costs incurred already for Dunning and pledged to cover his expenses moving forward. From there, they proceeded to retain Mr. James Wallace to assist in the defense. It was an astute choice. Wallace was considered yet another legal superstar in the firmament of the British bar of the late eighteenth century, and this would raise the stakes to a level seldom seen at King's Bench.

When the trial opened on February 7, 1772, *everyone present* took notice. Two serjeants-at-law stood for the prosecution with two associate barristers (Hargrave and James Mansfield), and Dunning and Wallace stood for the defense. Lord Chief Justice Mansfield, flanked by three puisne-justices, Sir Richard Aston, Edward Willes, and Sir William Henry Ashurst, entered at the bench. This was clearly not to be some settlement hearing; this was historical.

The serjeants-at-law in the British legal system were one of the oldest bodies of attorneys in the empire.[210] Created by King Henry II, the author of the British court system, the serjeants-at-law were a select group of barristers entrusted with providing legal counsel to the monarch. It was, for an attorney, the highest post to which he could aspire. And it remained such for nearly four hundred years, until the reign of Elizabeth I, at the close of the sixteenth century. In that time, she created a separate, private group of counselors, the "Queen's Counsel," due to concerns of privacy and loyalty at the height of Protestant/Roman Catholic disputes in the history of England. Henceforth, the monarch would maintain an independent legal "Counsel," and the prestige of the serjeants-at-law suffered. But throughout the eighteenth century, they remained an influential collection of barristers who provided much of the day-to-day legal counsel at Westminster, having exclusive jurisdiction in the Court of Common Pleas and precedence at the Court of King's Bench and the Exchequer of Pleas. These exclusivity rights were withdrawn in a reform act in 1873, and no serjeants-at-law were named after 1875, allowing those extant to maintain their status. The final British serjeant-at-law died in 1921.

As the trial opened, the "return" (the response to the writ of habeas corpus, explaining the relationship of the "corpus" to the defendant) of George Steuart was read into the record.[211] It related in brief the life of Somersett, especially related to the time of his purchase by Steuart and the subsequent years. And it contained one glaring error, which was never challenged by either party, nor by the bench, through the remainder of the trial: it stipulated that Steuart and Somersett had come to Great Britain in 1769 *from Virginia* and totally skipped the time they had lived in Massachusetts. This return was clearly the work of Steuart himself, and while he could have corrected it at any time during the trial, it is likely that he thought it advantageous to his case to have himself and Somersett living under the slave laws of Virginia until their emigration to Great Britain. Massachusetts had *never* recognized slavery as a legal entity within the colony and only through the theory of legal comity with the other colonies had chosen to "look the other way" when slaveholders and slaves entered the colony.

From the standpoint of the prosecution, it is highly likely that Sharp and probably Hargrave, at least, had noted it. And they had made the deliberate decision to let it go unless a question of its veracity derived from the bench. From Sharp's standpoint, this case was simply too close to his ideal, and to that apparently of Lord Mansfield as well, to give it up on this technicality. Sharp may well have even advised Somersett to "keep it under his hat," as it were, until Sharp told him otherwise. Somersett was no Jonathan Strong, or John Hylas, or Thomas Lewis. While he lacked formal education, in his years as an office servant for Steuart he almost certainly had acquired at least some literacy and was better-spoken than any of Sharp's previous plaintiffs. He was, in short, intelligent and fully aware of the stakes this case would determine for his life. If

Sharp told him to keep quiet about Massachusetts, then "mum was the word." And so, moving forward in the irony of the British-American legal system, the prosecution had to do everything possible to present Somersett as a slave, while the defense had to do everything possible to minimize his slave status.

And so Serjeant Davy began.[212] As previously noted, he was not intimidated by Lord Mansfield and had "knocked it about with him" in court in the past. At the outset of a previous trial, "Bull" Davy had presented an opening argument before Mansfield, during which Mansfield interrupted him, saying "If this be your concept of the law, Mr. Davy, I should have to burn all my law books." To which, without missing a beat, Davy responded, "I could only wish, your lordship, that you read a few of them first."

In his opening, Davy attacked any notion of comity with Virginia slave laws by any court in Great Britain. Just because a man brings another man, recognized in Virginia as his property, this does not allow him to assert him as his property *here*. Were a British citizen to return from the Orient with six wives, they would not be allowed to continue as such within this land. He then attacked all the former notions of slavery once recognized in Great Britain. The best known and most widely asserted of these was the theory of *villeinage* that existed in England before the Norman conquest of 1066. Before that time, peasants living on a specific manor in a specific locale were deemed by law to belong to that manor and had no right to depart from the site or from the occupation they were expected to pursue; or alternatively they belonged to their lord or master, from whom they likewise had no right to depart. This concept died out rapidly after the time of the Conquest, and by the sixteenth century there were no remaining *villeins* in England. From this he launched into the old *Rex v. Cartright* decision, a legal legend dating back to at least 1569 or earlier and quite likely what we would term an "urban myth" about a Brit named Cartright who purchased a Russian slave in Russia, returned to England, and promptly found his Russian slave confiscated. He filed suit for the return of his property under the old Norman English legal theory of "trover." Trover stated that a man had the right to any property that he could legally prove was his own and typically was applied to tools, livestock, produce, and the like. As the precedent went, the justice, whose name was lost to antiquity but whose decision was not, had declared that "England possessed an air too pure for slaves to breathe" and therefore would accept no man being kept a slave once brought to this land.

Davy next sketched for the court an England where slaves could be legally imported by British citizens: farms filled with Black slaves, blacksmiths forging chains and instruments of torture to subjugate Blacks, estates and manors staffed by dozens of enslaved Africans. And what of the offspring of these slaves? What would be their status? At that point, Serjeant Davy would have served well to have taken his seat. But no, he droned on, having already spoken for nearly two hours. And became enmeshed and befuddled in the "Holt cases." In the case of *Smith v. Brown & Cooper*, Lord Chief Justice Holt voided the sale of a slave transmitted from Smith to the firm of Brown & Cooper in London, stating in his opinion that Smith would have better served himself had he assigned a legal fiction of selling the slave from Virginia rather than from London. Davy, citing this opinion, stated that the slave had never left Virginia. Here both Lord Mansfield and Justice Willes tried to straighten out his confusion on the citation, and ultimately Davy simply said, "nothing further" and finally sat down, fifteen minutes too late.[213]

Now Serjeant Glynn arose and stated from the first that he had received the briefs regarding Somersett only two hours previously, leaving him little time to prepare.[214] Ruse or not, he then immediately stated that no matter, the case was so clear and of such great province that further time would be unnecessary. He then tore into the thought of Steuart prevailing in the case: were Steuart to somehow abridge the liberty of Somersett, British law would have to chisel out a position to accommodate this, and the only feasible location for this would be villeinage. Therefore, let Steuart attempt to resurrect the legal theory of villeinage for a person who was, without dispute, not born in England. He then defended the cases of Chief Justice Holt with clarity, likely as damage control over the muddled mess that had ended Davy's presentation. Glynn offered that there was no law to support the plea of Steuart, and "a man cannot be a slave in England upon any authority whatsoever." He closed with the statement that Holt's "determination has been adhered to ever since and there has been no contradictory determination." Glynn had very slyly set a trap and would simply wait for another counselor or justice to stumble into it. He sat, having spoken for over an hour. There yet awaited two more attorneys for Somersett, James Mansfield (no relation to Lord Mansfield, whose surname was Murray) and the newly minted barrister, Francis Hargrave.

Lord Mansfield now addressed Somersett's barristers. "Is there any traces there ever existed such a case as that of the Russian slave?"

Davy spoke for the group. "We know nothing more than what we have presented."

Now Mansfield looked at all the barristers still in line to testify. "This thing seems by the argument probable to go to a great length, and as it is at end of term, so it will be hardly possible to go through to the end without recess." He raised his gavel. "We stand adjourned until next term."[215]

This pause in the proceedings was enormous by the standards of that time: nearly three months. The case would not resume until May 9, 1772 in Easter term. In that seeming abundance of time, Sharp felt he had not a moment to lose. Fothergill had provided him five copies of the Benezet edition of Sharp's *Representation,* and Sharp promptly provided these to Somersett to distribute to the justices and to Lord North, British Prime Minister.[216] Meanwhile, the press was filled with opinions of anonymous abolitionists, likely including both Sharp and the Quaker friends of Franklin. There was a gathering "buzz" resonating throughout London and on into the surrounding districts. Something "big" was happening at the Court of King's Bench, something historic. In the midst of all the gathering hoopla, Sharp, now no longer spending his own shilling, was directed by Dr. Fothergill to add yet one more barrister to his team, John Alleyne, who had been invited to the bar of London only since the previous court session![217] Sharp was assured by Fothergill that this young barrister was not only brilliant but would also bring a fresh, colonial "angle" to the proceedings. And lacking the funds for the wig and robe and various accoutrements of the proper barrister, young Alleyne had had to solicit a fifty-pound loan from his American friend and patron, Benjamin

Franklin, who despite the remonstrances to the contrary by the inner circle, now insisted upon his addition to the plaintiff's counsel.[218] Between Hargrave and Alleyne, the Court of King's Bench was about to hear from the future of British jurisprudence. And in an unusual and perhaps unseemly display, the Lords Justice were about to hear something different at the Court of King's Bench: *passion! Somersett* was quickly developing into a "case of the century," and Franklin was willing to betray his personal interest in the success of this case.

Upon resuming the case of *Somersett v Steuart* on May 9 in Easter term, twelve year George III, James Mansfield rose for the plaintiff.[219] Not plowing much new ground, Mansfield offered that for Steuart to prevail, Britain would have to devise a new species of slavery, a change in English law so vast as to require an Act of Parliament. "I hope that such a kind of slavery will never find its way into England, and I apprehend that, by your Lordship's decision, this man will receive his liberty."[220]

Hargrave was next to speak, but he was ill with acute influenza.[221] Lord Mansfield recessed *again*, for five days, to allow the convalescence of Hargrave, and in the interim proceeded to clear the burgeoning docket of King's Bench. By May 14, the courtroom was packed with bystanders, tourists, curiosity seekers, cutpurses, suitors, and a variety of idle solicitors and barristers who simply wanted to be able to say they had witnessed the spectacle.[222] And a spectacle it was. Two young barristers were about to usher British jurisprudence into the modern era.

Francis Hargrave rose first, aged thirty-one and with his baby face, looking perhaps ten years younger, and began his statement. He opened with, oddly, an apology to the justices and to the two serjeants on his own team, for his very appearance before them, disclaiming that his presence was worthy of their attention. And then looked across the crowded gallery, and...there was Granville Sharp, smiling, nodding, encouraging. He looked back to the bench and in a trembling voice stated the question is "not whether slavery is lawful in our colonies, but whether in England? And not whether it has previously existed in England, but whether it is not now time to be abolished? George Steuart's return clearly asserts that the basis of his action is slavery, and therefore this brings the question of the lawfulness of slavery in England, directly before this English court."[223] He then clearly alluded to the deliberate erroneous statement that Somersett was transferred directly from Virginia to London, claiming that by avoiding "this artifice" of rightfully citing a conveyance from Massachusetts, Steuart deliberately begged the question of the status of Somersett. In that moment, he had not only called Steuart out on his lie, but at the same time he had artfully precluded both the bench, and Steuart's attorneys, from "walking back" this assertion. Hargrave had locked the question before the court as to whether Somersett was a slave in London, in the eyes of the law, and there would be no escape from it. He had, in effect, ended any possibility of "dithering" this decision away.

He went on, his voice now gathering strength, reviewing briefly the history of British slavery, but unlike his teammates, he asserted that villeinage had never been abolished, that it was still an accepted legal theory and never abridged by act of Parliament or common law.[224] But villeinage would not lie for *Somersett* insofar as Somersett was not born in England. He then discussed whether the "air of England was too pure for a slave to breathe," having heard the question of Mansfield clearly. "*If* the account of the case is true, the plain inference is that the slave was become free by his very arrival in our land." Now he went on about a case from France regarding an escaped criminal from Spain apprehended in France, and the lack of comity recognized by the French court for Spanish law, and therefore the pardon of the Spanish criminal. Here Lord Mansfield interjected, "And rightly, for the laws of one nation cannot condemn offenses supposedly to be committed against those of another."

To which Hargrave rousingly concurred, "Quite right, m'lord. The lack of morality in the laws of one land cannot expect comity from the laws of another." There was spontaneous applause from the gallery.

He continued, turning the arguments for Steuart inside out. Steuart, Hargrave asserted, was *trying to introduce slavery into Great Britain*. This was the only logical conclusion from his return in the case. He wanted a new form of slavery recognized throughout Great Britain itself. Steuart was asserting that Parliament had already accepted slavery in the American colonies, through its tolerance of this peculiar institution. And now Steuart needed only this decision to press his case before Parliament to extend slavery throughout the empire. And was it not true, Hargrave pressed on, that the natural step following a court decision in support of slavery would be commencement of slavery in our land? Hargrave was winding up to his thundering conclusion with further punctuations of applause from the gallery. "How opposite to natural justice Mr. Steuart's claim is, in firm persuasion of its inconsistency with the laws of England, and how much we can pray this court to as much honour to your Lordships from the exclusion of this *new* slavery, as your ancestors obtained by the abolition of the old."[225] The gallery exploded in applause, shouting, and drowning out the gaveling of Mansfield.[226] The demonstration went on for minutes. Sharp was shamelessly weeping. Lord Mansfield looked about the roaring gallery, smiled momentarily, and quietly set his gavel down.

Out of all the annals of British jurisprudence, John Alleyne had to be thinking at this moment, "How do I follow this?" But as the gallery was gradually brought back to order, Alleyne acquitted himself well. He wanted to simply revisit the concept of comity. Comity is an ancient legal theory that generally states the moral rules of a nation are to be respected when the citizens of that nation travel to other countries. The question to be weighed in this case was where comity ends, according to Alleyne. For Alleyne, there existed two distinct bases of parliamentary law: municipal acts unique to a jurisdiction and general/national laws based on the inherent human sense of justice, of recognition of "right from wrong." And comity would lie for the latter, but most assuredly not for the former, nor could it. Who could vote, who paid taxes, who served in the military, who stood for public office in Japan or Egypt, could not be enforced in Great Britain. But at the same time, an institution like slavery, approved by municipal law in Virginia or South Carolina, clearly violated the concept of British morality and was therefore not entitled to comity. No, the national morality controlled the national law and forbade that the principles of humanity in this land ever be corrupted by the admixture of slavery customs.[227] With that, Alleyne took his seat, and the plaintiff's attorneys rested their case.

Interlude: Chapter 5

A ttention shifted to the defense counsel. Dunning was in big trouble here, and he knew it. Wallace was ready to soldier on, and both barristers had already prepared to base their defense upon the impregnable "Joint Opinion" of 1729.

Any student of American slavery, or the American Revolution, must absolutely be familiar with the Joint Opinion of 1729, since it controlled the lives of twenty thousand slaves in Great Britain, and another estimated hundred thousand slaves in the British colonies north of Maryland, and had tethered the slavery laws of the British colonies in America to Great Britain for forty-three years.[228] It came about at a dinner party in London, hosted by plantation owners from the West Indies (essentially Barbados, Antigua, and Jamaica) and their attorneys. The featured guests were British Attorney General Philip Yorke and British Solicitor General Charles Talbot. In a mood seasoned by steaks, cigars, and fine wines, the planters wished to pose a question of the two jurists. The planters were aware that essentially *all* cases brought to the Crown courts had to funnel through their two offices, and therefore, a consensus from the two of them would appear to preclude any legal challenges to their assertion in answer to the question. The issue stemmed from a pair of deep-seated apparent misconceptions about the status of slavery in the British empire. For centuries it had been asserted that 1) any slave who could emigrate to England and free himself from the direct control of his master was instantly, automatically, and perpetually free, and 2) any slave who was baptized was then considered Christian and thereby was instantly, automatically, and perpetually free, because only infidels could be enslaved.

For the prosperity of the colonies, and secondarily the prosperity of Great Britain, the planters needed to know, were either or both of these assertions true? The first premise appeared to have arisen from that mythological case of *Rex v Cartright* that had been adjudicated sometime before 1569; there is no known record of such a case in the vast annals of the British courts dating to the Domesday book and earlier, but it was a "decision" cited frequently enough over the previous hundred years as to make it nearly common law. In brief, it related that a Brit named Cartright traveled to Russia, acquiring a Russian slave and returned to England. The slave was promptly confiscated, and Cartright sued for his return. An unknown justice in a court of significance enough to render the decision as common law ordered the release of the slave, famously declaiming that "the air of Britain is too pure for a slave to breathe." It was odd that the court and the justice could not be cited, but the phrase took on a life all its own. The second premise was perhaps far older and may have been established by Moses himself, writing in Leviticus 25: 39-54, where "brothers in your midst" were not liable to be "bondsmen" (slaves); rather only "infidels" could serve as "bondsmen." This was extrapolated over decades of urban myth to the point where many slaves, and some whites, believed that slaves in Great Britain could force their own manumission by the simple act of baptism (which *de facto* would render the slave "Christian" and therefore a "brother in your midst" rather than an infidel, and would, based upon this supposition, inspire generations of abolitionists to surreptitiously "baptize" hundreds of African slaves).

The planters wanted an answer so that they could direct their own assemblies at home, and their agents in Great Britain, as to strategies to preserve the peculiar institution of slavery in their home colonies. Yorke and Talbot conferred discreetly, and briefly, and then rendered their joint opinion:

neither escape from a legal owner in Great Britain, nor Christian baptism in any jurisdiction, would render a slave legally acquired in his homeland to be free. And thus spoken, a scribe immediately copied the opinion for their signature, and it was duly recorded. For the next forty years, it would be held over the heads of the abolitionists as powerfully as an Act of Parliament or a decision from a King's Court, to the point that it had acquired its own name in the legal vernacular: the "Joint Opinion."

Into this setting arose James Wallace. Here, Lord Mansfield interrupted the proceedings before Wallace commenced, curious as to his financial sponsor.[229] And here Wallace confirmed that he was present through the request and retainer of the West Indies plantation owners. Mansfield simply nodded and begged Wallace continue. Wallace approached the question from a fresh point of view: tradition. He pointed out that fully three-fourths of the entire world currently practiced slavery: all of Asia, Africa, the Americas, as well as Russia and Poland in Europe. And that contrary to *Cartright*, in the age of English villeinage, the peasants apparently functioned without respiratory difficulties for many centuries. He paused and noted that Mansfield was somewhat bemused. He went on: Parliament had been complicit with American slavery for over a hundred years, and by their trade laws and duties, they were fully aware of the practice in the Americas and had never challenged its legality. Further, by the colonial law of Virginia, Somersett was indeed the property of Steuart, and British law did not call for stripping Steuart of his property upon his arrival in Great Britain.

Aware of Mansfield's judicial support of mercantilism in the empire, Wallace averred that the contracts of Virginia were honored in London and throughout the empire.[230] That strategy instantly failed; Mansfield halted the proceedings again and asserted to Wallace that the relationship between master and slave could *never* be interpreted as a contract, due to Montesquieu's legal theory that coercion by definition invalidates any contract, and prayed Wallace move on. Wallace then touched on the unresolved decisions of Holt, and then delivered his *coup de grace,* the dreaded "Joint Opinion of 1729." Here Justice Aston added that the Bishop of London had agreed with this statement that baptism does not change the legal status of a Black African slave. That Yorke and Talbot, the authors of the opinion, had both been personal mentors of Lord Mansfield and had aided him early in his legal career was common knowledge in the Inns of Court in London. So *none* of the attorneys, on either side of the dock, or beside him on the bench, were prepared for what Mansfield was now about to say.

Lord Mansfield drew a breath and started, "This case [the Joint Opinion] alluded to was upon a petition in Lincoln's Inn Hall, after dinner; probably, therefore, might not, as he believes the contrary is not unusual at that hour, be taken with much accuracy." He continued, "The principal matter was then, on the earnest solicitation of many merchants, to know whether a slave was freed by being made a Christian. And it was resolved...not."[231] There was an audible stirring in the gallery, and not a comment from the attorneys gathered. In a stroke, the vaunted "Joint Opinion," because it was *never* rendered as the answer to a case of law in any British Crown court by any seated justice, had simply ceased to exist.

After a prolonged pause, Wallace swallowed hard and soldiered on. There was much commerce to be disrupted if this decision outlawed slavery in Great Britain. Thousands of pounds would be lost, and slaves in Virginia could win their manumission simply by fleeing to a country that did not recognize slavery. Wallace was unwittingly laying the first tracks of the Underground Railroad. At this point, Wallace dropped to his chair. Dunning started to rise, and Mansfield asked him to be seated. Mansfield wished to adjourn once again for another week, but prior to adjournment, he wanted to raise the issues of Alleyne once again, that of comity, or from a legal standpoint, "choice of law."[232] He pointed out to Steuart's attorneys that Franklin's protégé Alleyne was well-taken here, and that the slave laws of Poland or Russia would not lie in Great Britain. He then gave them perhaps the most direct order he ever rendered from the bench: "If the merchants think the question of great consequence to trade and commerce, and the public should think so too, they had better think of an application to those that will make a law [i.e., Parliament]. We [i.e. the Court of King's Bench] must find the law; we cannot make it."[233]

Mansfield had clearly made his decision. It was up to Steuart, Dunning, Wallace, and the West Indies plantation owners whether to make it the law of the empire.[234] And for reasons of their own, they decided in that final week that Mansfield had mercifully afforded them not to take the easy way out, the settlement and non-judiciary manumission of Somersett. They were willing to stake the decision on the abilities of Dunning.

Resuming for the defense one week later, Dunning clearly wished he were seated in the opposite dock. He opened almost apologetically for his position in paid support of a slave-owner. He then encouraged the justices to decide the case based on law and not sentiment. But then Dunning offered only sentiment.[235] Without the Joint Opinion, a rock for forty-three years in the courts of Westminster now reduced to little more than a pile of sand, Dunning launched into a further recitation of the economic impact of complete manumission. The cost to the empire would be over twenty million pounds sterling. The loss of labor would throw production of basic and manufactured goods into chaos and seriously disrupt British defense. Millions of Black Africans would pour out of the colonies and into Great Britain to be manumitted. Then Dunning launched into the tired myth of the "happy Negro" and how slavery wasn't "all that bad." Somersett enjoyed a better life than he could have hoped for in Sierra Leone. The free servant class of Great Britain enjoyed no greater freedom than Somersett now, due to their poverty.

Dunning finally tried a different approach based on Holt that said Steuart was *not* pursuing trover, but rather the loss of Somersett's *labor* and not the loss of Somersett's *person*. Here he might have achieved some traction with the justices, but…as noted, Hargrave in his statement had sealed the question of Somersett's return to be based on Virginia slavery law, which clearly asserted ownership. Dunning had been cut off in that theory of defense by the baby-faced young barrister in his first appearance at Westminster. And now Dunning was reduced to foolishness: how do we know how Somersett became a slave in Africa? Maybe he was a war prize, which would render him a legal slave by British law. Maybe he was a debtor and had been imprisoned by the African equivalent of the London sheriff. No one here had controverted these possibilities. He was exhausted of all possibilities and clearly could not bring himself to answer Serjeant Davy's opening question: "Upon what principle is it that a man can become a dog for another man?"[236] The correct answer, that Dunning could not, or would not, bring himself to utter, was "Under the laws of the Colony of Virginia."

The only remaining portion of this eighteenth century trial at the Court of King's Bench was rebuttal by the plaintiff, which was handled by Serjeant Davy, simply and succinctly praying to the bench to uphold the moral high ground that all Brits aspire to, for "the air of England has been purifying since Elizabeth and is now too pure for a slave to breathe in."[237] Davy closed. The case now went to the judges. Normally this might have required no more than five minutes, with a unanimous verdict. But here Lord Mansfield deferred.[238] The issues at stake were simply too grave, and too complex, to allow for an emotional decision. He chose rather at that point to launch into a lecture to both sides. Wallace and Dunning were there, but Steuart had been noticeably absent. Mansfield dismantled the Steuart defense, point by point, and finally, twice, practically *implored* Steuart and his benefactors to settle this suit prior to judgment. He then, yet again, gave both sides another month to make this case go away. And he finally stated that failing that, *fiat justitia ruat coelom* ("let justice be done, though the heavens may fall").[239]

In that final month, neither side would ever discuss settlement with the opponent. It was never offered, and no conference was ever called. Sharp never directed Somersett to refuse a settlement. Steuart was not ordered by his benefactors to settle. He never demanded of them the right to settle. Quite frankly, Steuart had absented himself from the process after the day of Hargrave and Alleyne. He was certain that he had heard the sound of his losing his case that afternoon. On the morning of June 22, 1772, seven attorneys sat in the dock, two on one side, and five gathered around a very dark African on the other. There was no Charles Steuart. There was no Granville Sharp. Steuart felt this was a formality. Sharp feared he would risk impacting the decision or even jinxing it.

Mansfield appeared and began to speak. He provided legal background for the case, brought up once more the Joint Opinion, more or less called it nonsense, along with his mentor Philip Yorke's decision in 1749 of *Pearne v. Lisle*, in which Yorke had incredibly attempted to assert that trover would lie for a case of slavery, and that a man in the eighteenth century could be considered a villein. He then went directly to the Steuart return and focused on the issue of Somersett's elopement, the overarching critical refusal by Steuart to have Somersett returned to his custody, and Steuart's effort to have Somersett shipped out of London to the West Indies. Clearly to Mansfield, the non-return and deportation for subsequent resale was a much more serious issue than simple return of lost property. Had Steuart accepted the custody of Somersett and *then* attempted to have him taken up and sold at auction in the West Indies, the court might well have simply directed Somersett's return to the custody of Steuart. But that status of custody and thus that possible resolution no longer existed; Steuart had willfully rejected it. And in this current state of affairs, Lord Mansfield asserted that no man had a right, in British law, to behave toward another man in this way, and that barring the establishment of positive law (i.e., to permit an owner to direct the sale of a slave taken out of Great Britain), and regardless of the consequences of the decision, he could not say that the case was allowed or approved by any law of England, "and therefore, the Black must be discharged."[240] There was a stunned silence. And then pandemonium while Hargrave patiently explained to Somersett over the roar all around them that yes, he was free. And Hargrave asked Somersett, as his first task as a free man, to go to the Old Jewry and tell Mr. Sharp.

End of Interlude

Chapter 14

I n the spring of 1767, Franklin had received a packet mailed from The Hague, Netherlands, from Charles Guillaume Frédéric Dumas. Perplexed, Franklin anxiously opened the packet and found a letter and a book on electricity and the experiments of Pieter van Musschenbroek from Leyden, with the development of the Leyden jar. Franklin smiled; he had met van Musschenbroek in 1761, when he and William were travelling in Europe. The other book in the packet was *An Historical Account of the Expedition against the Ohio Indians,* authored by Dumas, and this edition printed in London. Franklin's printing shop had first published this little tract in 1765, listing the source as "published by a lover of his country." But the London edition was refined and bore a personal inscription from Dumas on the frontispiece. Dumas had been made aware of Franklin's interest in the late Professeur Koenig and wished to replace him as a surrogate to continue a correspondence. Never one to overlook a potentially valuable acquaintance in Europe, Franklin was happy to oblige.[241]

Charles Guillaume (sometimes "William," the English equivalent) Frédéric Dumas was born to a French family in 1721 in Brandenburg-Ansbach in Germany. He was educated in Geneva at the Academy of Charles Frederick Necker after Dumas's family moved there about 1726 and was from an early age quite precocious, particularly in languages. He would also become personally acquainted with the Necker family during that time, which would provide a valuable lifelong contact in the French court. While he studied mathematics and philosophy under Louis Necker, he also learned classical Greek along with his Latin and as an adult would learn Spanish in addition to his native German and French. He could read Russian and was fluent in Frisian due to his relocation to the university at Utrecht to take on the chairmanship of the linguistics department. And in the exigency of life close to Great Britain, he would become fluent in English as well, albeit with a significant Alsatian accent. From his mathematical background, he had taken up a personal hobby in cryptography.

He had one further request for Franklin: he wanted to know about his prospects in relocating to the British colony of West Florida and especially Pensacola and valued Franklin's opinion as an American native. Pensacola had a more temperate climate than his native area of Switzerland and the Palatine, and Dumas apprehended, from a distance of 3,500 miles, that it looked like a paradise in comparison with his current locale in the United Provinces. In fact, Franklin discouraged him from relocation to Florida, insofar as the Pensacola of 1767 was a hotbed of yellow fever and malaria, among other serious illnesses.[242] Here Franklin was reminding Dumas of the fresh memory of their personal military hero, Henri Bouquet, and Bouquet's abrupt, tragic fate in West Florida. By the standards of that day, the climate of the Caribbean was considered extremely unhealthy and was to be avoided by the inexperienced, "unseasoned" European émigré. At the same time, this exchange marked the beginning of a valuable friendship by mail, which would pay rich dividends for Franklin and for America. And in the end, this correspondence would prove one of the most individually prolific series of letters in Franklin's life.

In March of 1772, Franklin grew frustrated and angry. At age sixty-six, he was already exhausted by the mundane tasks of his daily routines and feared his opportunities to achieve his goal of freedom for Pennsylvania were slipping away. The Crown was clearly not going to wrench his province from the hands of the hated Penn family, and Parliament was simply disinterested in the matter.

Any consideration of manumission of American slaves appeared exhausted; the Crown enjoyed the fruits of slave labor to bolster its global economy and was not going to move to upset that delicate balance of relative immorality for relative wealth. And once again, Parliament was not inclined to make any movement to end slavery in Great Britain and was not empowered to press toward manumission in the colonies. It truly appeared that Franklin's efforts had reached an impasse. He was staring at a blind alley, and there were no doors in which to turn.

One night, at a dinner meeting of the inner circle in late March, his anger overflowed and he lashed out, "Just one! Just one slave, and perhaps we could still build this."[243]

Pownall was supportive but equally disappointed. "Dr. Franklin, this simply cannot happen. We have tried everything. We have made a noble effort toward your goal. And we simply have exhausted our remedies. I have nothing further to suggest." And they both sipped their ale. Clearly, they had already identified a potential motivation for the plantation owners in the southern British colonies to join the cause of Massachusetts in separation from the Crown. The letters were waiting in Benezet's school in Philadelphia. The ensuing silence was pervasive, and almost everyone present fell victim to their despair. But then a voice, from the other side of the table.

"Dr. Franklin, thou hast said, 'One,' is that correct?" It was the naturally tremulous, timid but eloquent voice of John Fothergill.

"Pray, go on, doctor," responded Franklin.

"Well, there is a man here in London that may be able to deliver thee but one, manumitted."[244]

"What? How?"

Fothergill now sighed, audibly. "There is a man named Granville Sharp, a mirror of thine own Anthony Benezet in Philadelphia, but more legally inclined, an Anglican, working steadfastly, but so far unsuccessfully, at legal manumission through the courts."[245]

Now Franklin sat upright, intrigued. "Yes, I've heard of this Sharp but have yet to meet him. All the same, I am aware of dear Benezet and his efforts for unfree persons and native Americans in Philadelphia. He works to support them and to educate them but certainly has neither the inclination, nor the resources, nor the background, to pursue legal remedy in the colonial courts. It would be difficult to conceive of a like-minded individual here in London who would have a better chance of it."

Fothergill gently contradicted him. "Oh, but it seems that Sharp is something of a self-taught solicitor and an exceedingly bright and talented man. He has appropriated for himself an extensive knowledge of English common law and now has the ear of a key jurist on the King's Bench. They are said to be working together quietly to identify the case that will reveal to all Great Britain the immorality and failed social contract of human slavery."[246]

And now Franklin slumped down again, demonstrably skeptical. "There is no such jurist on King's Bench. They are all sworn to adjudicate their cases in support of the Crown, serving as agents of the king, as they understand their role on the bench."

"Ah, yes, Dr. Franklin, that is true, but there is one."

"And, pray tell, who is this 'enlightened jurist' of yours, Dr. Fothergill?"

"None other than the chief justice, Lord Mansfield." And the room fell silent at the audible exhalation of Franklin. Fothergill continued, "But I must implore thee humbly, Dr. Franklin: do *not* attempt to contact, far less intervene with Sharp at this point. He works in the shadows of Mansfield, much as we Honest Whigs work with thee, and at the first signs of disturbance, is forsworn to abandon his mission. And will, as he is a quite moral and upright individual. In thy zeal, thou couldst readily accomplish quite the opposite of thy stated goal. Pray, let him work in secrecy."

"I trust you will be able to keep us apprised of his progress in this mission, Fothergill?"

"Only as much as I am able, only as much as I am able. He is a very quiet and thoughtful man."

Franklin looked straight at Fothergill now and sighed with a grimace. Once again he had to trust, and he so dreaded this dependency. But this was all that was left, and he simply had to press on, entrusting to a stranger and an obscure young barrister the entire success of his revolutionary plan.

Now Pownall looked up, suddenly reanimated. "Shall we press on, Dr. Franklin?"

Franklin blankly responded, "We have no other option, Pownall. Where do we stand in the colonies?"

Pownall replied, "There is currently a likelihood that Parliament, having rescinded the Townshend levy, will initiate a new taxation on the surplus British tea burgeoning daily in our warehouses and ports, in so doing to leave a symbolic levy to assert Parliament's ability to further assess levies on the colonies. And at the same time to unload the excess tea upon the reliable American market. My gawd, how your people drink the stuff! The behavior in the colonies in response to the Stamp tax and the Townshend levies have not been soon forgotten, nor forgiven, by many of my colleagues."

"And what, pray tell, will retention of a 'symbolic levy' accomplish in Boston and Philadelphia?" Franklin wondered.

"Parliament desires to remind the colonials of their position, and their subservience, to their monarch. And will hear of no other stance in this regard. I anticipate that this will indeed be the outcome of the pending legislation now in Commons."

Franklin eased back, thoughtful, and then smiled. "Samuel Adams will have his day on this one."

Franklin was not a born revolutionary. That indisputable designation fell to two men in Massachusetts, both named Adams and both living in Boston, but no more closely related than second cousins. The older, Samuel Adams, was born in Boston in 1722 and was one of only three children of Samuel Adams, Sr., of twelve born, to survive to adulthood.[247] He attended, like Franklin before him, the Boston Latin School for his elementary education, but unlike Franklin, he went on to matriculate at Harvard in 1736, graduating with a bachelor's degree in 1740. While his family always assumed he would enter the ministry, Samuel had by that time embarked upon political science studies and went on at Harvard to earn his master's degree in 1743. After a failed effort at opening a mercantile establishment, Samuel entered the family business as a "maltster," preparing and cooking malt for the local brewers of Boston.[248] In 1748, he gathered a group of friends in launching a weekly newspaper, *The Independent Adviser,* which featured political commentaries by...Samuel Adams. In 1747, with the support of the Boston Caucus, Samuel was elected to his first political office as a clerk at the Boston Market. In 1756, he was elected local tax collector through the Boston Town Meeting, a post that would end disastrously. He had no heart for the role and knew that his constituents in arrears were often among the indigent, and thus he would not sue for payment.[249] As a result, he was chronically deficient in his duties, a situation for which he was held personally fiscally responsible. Ultimately, he would be fined £1,463 in 1768, for which friends would pay the majority, and the Town Meeting would negotiate cancellation of the remainder. Yet through it all, Samuel Adams remained a champion of the common man in Boston.

On the heels of the British victory in the French and Indian War in North America, Parliament sought reparation of war debt on the part of the colonies it had paid to defend and passed the *Sugar Tax.* The Boston Town Meeting rebelled and asked their tax collector, Samuel Adams, to draft the response to Parliament. Adams borrowed from his Boston colleague James Otis the term "taxation without representation" in the text, while at the same time referring to Bostonians as "tributary slaves." The gauntlet had been thrown down, and a cause was born through the pen of Samuel Adams. In the wake of the *Sugar Act,* Parliament passed the *Stamp Act,* which would galvanize the colonies' response against Parliament.[250] From Virginia came a protest that clearly was drawn from Adams's response to the *Sugar Act,* while in Boston, Adams went a step further and called for a boycott of *all* British imports and not only sugar. The "Boston rabble" would seize the moment, and on August 14, the home of Andrew Oliver, a stamp tax collector and future lieutenant governor of Massachusetts, was destroyed by an angry mob. Two weeks later, the home of Thomas Hutchinson received like treatment. Blame for the mob violence was laid at the feet of Adams. But ultimately, the stamp tax collectors were all but forced out from the various colonies; during that time the relocation of the receiver general, Charles Steuart, to Boston would occur. Steuart found that collecting the tax was nearly impossible with threats of personal violence directed toward him and his valet, James Somersett.

Ultimately, Parliament stepped in, and the collection was suspended. Parliament held hearings about the impact of the tax and heard from various British international traders and from none other than Benjamin Franklin himself, and ultimately rescinded the tax. In Boston, Adams was hailed a hero. But by 1767, Parliament was back again with the *Townshend Act*. This act included a modest tax levy from Parliament, asserting the right to tax colonists in the British colonies, and after much "back and forth" between Boston and the Crown, the colonists would threaten the safety of Governor Bernard and the local tax collectors, culminating in the British response of sending troops to Boston to restore order. It was at that point that, citing exhaustion, Steuart requested and was granted a personal leave to return for rest and recovery to London and departed Boston with Somersett in tow.[251]

The younger of the two Adams second cousins, John, was born in 1735 in Braintree (now Quincy), and partly home-schooled and partly attended Braintree Latin school.[252] In 1751, he entered Harvard and graduated in 1755 with an A.B. degree. He started teaching elementary school but found it wearisome and began reading law under James Putnam in Worcester. He earned an A.M. degree from Harvard in 1758 and embarked upon a career in law. Early in his career, he began writing opinion editorials about the elite Bostonians who pandered to the British government seeking plum opportunities in service to the Crown.[253] While not citing Thomas Hutchinson by name, the implication was obvious. By the time of the *Stamp Act* of 1765, he was openly critical of both taxation without representation and restriction to due process by a jury of one's peers, two immoral restrictions that he felt were being pressed by the British government against loyal British colonists in America. The following year, the Town Meeting of Braintree would elect him a selectman, launching his political career. In 1767, with the introduction of the *Townshend Act*, violence ensued as noted. By March 1770, with British soldiers posted in Boston around the Old State House, a sentry was confronted by a local mob, and eight other soldiers came to his aid. A young tough hurled an ice-ball, and in response the British sentries aimed their rifles. Someone in the crowd shouted, "Fire and be damned." The later testimonies would differ as to whether the shout came from a British officer or a colonist, but the British sentries indeed fired. Five Boston locals were killed, and the British soldiers were arraigned for murder.

Samuel Adams was accused of instigating this crowd violence, while John Adams volunteered to defend the British soldiers, asserting that "they are entitled to fair trial and the right to counsel."[254] And John Adams succeeded in achieving acquittal of six, and a reduced sentence for involuntary manslaughter for two. Such was the prevailing reputation of the Adams men regarding revolution. For a fleeting moment, Franklin, receiving this news in London, even believed that this might be the beginning of the "revolution" he so desperately sought for Pennsylvania. Yet in the wake of the "Boston Massacre," the outrage from the Adams cousins would cool significantly.[255] Thomas Paine envisioned them in his second *Crisis*, seven years later, with his reference to "Sunshine Patriots": zealous in fair weather but realizing in the flurry of a violent repression that their lives could be at stake, and stopping far short of actually taking up arms against injustice. In the aftermath of the Boston massacre Samuel Adams would focus upon his personal political career, while John Adams would withdraw from politics to focus on his legal practice.

Chapter 15

In the evening of June 22, 1772, John Fothergill appeared at the doorstep of Mrs. Stevenson, in Craven Street, seeking Dr. Franklin. He was in his study, reading. Mrs. Stevenson allowed him in, and knowing that Fothergill could find Dr. Franklin, she stepped aside. Fothergill entered the study and said quietly, "A word with thee, Dr. Franklin."

Franklin removed his glasses, set them on his desk, and closed his book. "What could possibly bring you here at this hour? Is someone ill?"

Fothergill carefully closed and latched the door to the study. "Dr. Franklin, I beg to inform thee that today Lord Mansfield manumitted a Black African slave, James Somersett, at the Court of King's Bench."[256]

And then he fell silent. There was an eerie quiet for a minute. Then a few tears fell on Franklin's book. Franklin collected himself. "Dr. Fothergill, would you be so kind as to gather Mr. Pownall and Mr. Barclay and return to this room in precisely one week?"

Fothergill said nothing but nodded and backed out of the study. Then he was gone.

Now Franklin went into action regarding this stunning notice. He had composed an editorial and submitted it to William Strahan for publication in the *London Chronicle*, which was previously filed and now authorized to be published anonymously, in the June 18–20 edition (note the dating compared to the decision from King's Bench) of *The London Chronicle*:

It is said that some generous humane persons subscribed to the expence of obtaining liberty by law for Somersett the Negro. It is to be wished that the same humanity may extend itself among numbers; if not to the procuring liberty for those that remain in our Colonies, at least to obtain a law abolishing the African commerce in Slaves, and declaring the children of Slaves free when they become of age.

"By a late computation made in America, it appears that there are now eight hundred and fifty thousand Negroes in the English Islands and Colonies; and that the yearly importation is about one hundred thousand, of which number about one third perish from the gaol distemper on the passage, and in the sickness called the seasoning before they are set to labour. The remnant makes up the deficiencies continually occurring among the main body of those unhappy people, through the distempers occasioned by excessive labour, bad nourishment, uncomfortable accommodation and broken spirits. Can sweetening our tea & with sugar, be a circumstance of such absolute necessity? Can the petty pleasure thence arising to the taste, compensate for so much misery produced among our fellow creatures, and such a constant butchery of the human species by this pestilential detestable traffic in the bodies and souls of men? Pharisaical Britain! To pride thyself in setting free a single slave that happens to land on thy coasts, while thy Merchants in all thy ports are encouraged by thy laws to continue a commerce whereby so many hundreds of thousands are dragged into a slavery that can scarce be said to end with their lives, since it is entailed on their posterity![257]

The author would be readily identified in the press as Franklin, and the ensuing fallout from his editorial would be varied in the various areas of its circulation. In Great Britain, much would be made of attempting to parse out precisely what this decision truly meant; while thousands of Black African slaves would be manumitted, Mansfield would constantly "walk the decision back" for the next ten years, pointing out for any that would listen that it was *not* a generalized manumission at all.[258] In fact, the fine point of the case was that Steuart had inadvertently *de facto* manumitted Somersett himself, when he refused to accept his returned property! And in so doing, he had rendered himself an agent powerless to direct any part of the disposition of Somersett moving forward. In other words, once Steuart had refused custody of Somersett on British soil, *he* had made Somersett a free person. And once he had made Somersett a free person, he was most assuredly not permitted to order him deported for sale, or for auction, or for any other dictate on Somersett's life. *That fact*, and that alone, was why Somersett was ordered free at the Court of King's Bench, or so Mansfield would assert for the remainder of his career.

So as the clamor died down in London, the warmth over the Franklin editorial did as well. Some were confused about his use of the "Quaker pronouns." Was this some sort of parody of his close circle of friends, such as Fothergill and Barclay? He had never made use of these before and never would again. Was this because of the letter from Benezet in May? Sharp, a devout Anglican, had decided for unspoken reasons to side with Franklin on the issue of slavery and agreed that the source was Great Britain, who provided the slaves and reaped the profits. And the Quakers would again take the stance that the corruption was universal and that the "peculiar institution" provoked as much existential harm for the slave trader and for the slave owner as for the slave.

In America, the decision and Franklin's editorial would create an almost immediate geographical dichotomy.[259] While the message of Somersett would not arrive until late summer, once it did, it triggered visceral reactions throughout America. In one home and school in Philadelphia, the reaction from Benezet had been to find that unusual little package that had been sent by Fothergill months earlier and to mail it in care of John Hancock to New York. North of Pennsylvania, the colonists agreed with Franklin that the sin was slavery, but Satan's agent in the sin was British. In the South, the plantation owners and slave traders reacted with grave concern over the threat of loss of livelihood, loss of land, loss of, well, everything they held dear, including the real possibility of loss of life. Agents in Great Britain had become concerned about the economic fallout from *Somersett* and began watching the mails for any correspondence emanating from Franklin or his Whig friends in the summer of 1772, but would identify nothing, for those letters had been sent from London *six months* previously, in a package posted by Dr. Fothergill. And in the American colonies in the fall, Tories watched the post for letters from abolitionists like Benezet and his colleagues, directed to the slave owners, but again, they noted nothing more than letters from Hancock. But by the winter of 1772–73, the plantation owners of Virginia had become extremely anxious over the issue of the slave trade. In early 1773, Virginia would select its first "Committee of Correspondence" to address the concerns of their slave owners; Virginia was "in"! Hancock and New York were "in"!

On June 29, 1772, Fothergill, Barclay, and Pownall were ushered in by Dr. Franklin at Mrs. Stevenson's home in Craven Street. He had been waiting for them. They entered the study, and Franklin closed the door and then latched it, an unusual demonstration of extra security.

Fr: "I truly never dreamed this day would arrive. Not within my lifetime."

Fo: "I almost regret to say that it is here. By now, many have read of the case of 'Somersett v. Steuart.' And already many others are raising the issue of what this decision means for Great Britain. And of course, for her colonies."

Fr: "For the African slaves of Great Britain, it can only point toward manumission. I'm told, however, that this will not be obtained in the colonies. At least not yet, based upon this decision."

Fo: "True enough, but at the same time, the clock now begins to toll for thee and thy fellow colonists."

P: "For our part, a decision is to be made, and 'if it were done when 'tis done, then 'twere well it were done quickly.'"[260]

Fr: "Ah, yes, your beloved Bard. Pownall, I have addressed that nasty business of the slave trade through the London press. My greater concern now is that from Massachusetts we hear little. That untidy business in March of '70 has chilled the ardor of Adams for liberty.[261] How do we proceed?"

P: "We must rekindle his zeal for zeal. Your thoughts?"

Fr: "Hume and I resolved that a cause would be necessary to foment and to sustain revolution. And of course that cause, in the northern colonies, cannot be African slavery. What news of Parliament? New taxes to be levied against our beloved Massachusetts? That could reignite the Adamses."

P: "Nothing at this point. Parliament is quiet on the issue of taxes.[262] Burke is having his day there."

Fr: "We must identify a cause to keep Massachusetts and New York in the fray. Something to kindle the wrath of Samuel Adams and of the people of Boston, once again."

At this point, Pownall rose quietly from his seat and walked to the study door. And then to the windows, one by one, checking the latches, looking for strangers outside. Finally, reaching into his coat, he withdrew a packet wrapped with a silk ribbon. "Dr. Franklin, your tinderbox."[263] He tossed it onto Franklin's desk. Franklin looked first at Pownall, then at the parcel. He reached toward it, held it for a minute, and then slit the ribbon with his penknife. He opened the flap and withdrew a packet of papers. Unfolding the top leaf, he read for a few moments, and his eyes opened wide. "Oh, my. Oh, my."

Fothergill looked over. "What is it? What does it say?"

Franklin looked first at Pownall. "Are these real?"

"Quite real," responded Pownall, "and quite authentic."

Fothergill tried again. "What are they?"

Franklin passed the first leaf over to Fothergill. Fothergill put his glasses on, read for a few lines, and likewise repeated, "Oh, my."

In turn, he passed one of the letters to Barclay, who read in silence.

✑

Chapter 16

The "Hutchinson letters" were an exchange in correspondence from both Thomas Hutchinson and his brother-in-law Andrew Oliver, addressed to Thomas Whately, the private secretary of George Grenville.[264] At the time of the *Stamp Act* in 1765, Grenville was prime minister and Hutchinson lieutenant governor of Massachusetts (under Sir Francis Bernard, governor). Andrew Oliver was serving as Hutchinson's private secretary and had received the appointment to administer the Stamp Tax in Boston. In the wake of the mob violence against the homes of both Hutchinson and Oliver in protest of the tax, they sent letters to Grenville via the posting of Thomas Whately as his secretary, advising Grenville, and through him Parliament, that the only way to control colonial violence was through "abridgment of what are called English liberties," thereby advancing the concept that 1) colonists were not entitled to the same rights as their English counterparts, and 2) that military force would be necessary to produce this "abridgment."[265] By requesting the presence of military force, it was at least implied, if not clearly stated, that quartering of British soldiers in the homes of random civilians throughout Boston would be necessary. Connecting the dots, it appeared that now-Governor Thomas Hutchinson, once a friend of Franklin but now a perpetual Loyalist, and now-Lieutenant Governor Andrew Oliver, were already calling for the quartering of British soldiers in Boston as early as 1767! And maintaining that presence for the sole purpose of suppressing the rights of the people of Boston, rather than for defense of the colony. It was clear that Hutchinson wanted and needed a military presence in the late 1760s to deal severely with those colonial Patriot partisans who would react in violence to any Parliamentary effort of taxation. So Hutchinson insisted upon continued quartering of British soldiers in private homes in Boston, drilling the soldiers in public view and suppressing any opinions orally, or in the press, that criticized edicts from the governor, Parliament, or the Crown. In so doing, Hutchinson and Oliver, with the complicity of Grenville, had brought about the Boston Massacre. Or so the revolutionaries in Boston would interpret (v.i.).

Having achieved the provocation of the southern plantation owners over the *Somersett* letters, and subsequently confirming their appropriately animated response in late 1772,[266] Franklin now proceeded to "leak" the Hutchinson letters to Massachusetts in December.[267] Thomas Cushing received the letters from Franklin in March 1773 and immediately enquired as to whether they could be shared or published. Franklin's response of June 1773 was that sharing was acceptable, but the letters should not be published verbatim. Cushing decided then to share them with Samuel Adams, who promptly published them in the *Boston Gazette* in July.[268] Within days, the publick houses throughout Massachusetts colony were abuzz.

Meanwhile, Parliament was asserting its right to attach duties to colonial imports, and as promised in the wake of the *Townshend Act* revocation, focused its eyes on tea. The British East India Company had accumulated a spectacular surplus of tea due to smuggling of Dutch tea into Great Britain, and as a result a depressed market there for British tea. Therefore, crates of British tea from Sri Lanka ("Ceylon") began to overflow in the warehouses of Southwark on the Thames, right across the river from Parliament in plain view, and generally throughout the English ports. In response, Parliament authorized the East India Company to export its surplus to the colonies at a dramatically cut rate, but with an import tax to be applied when the tea arrived in the colonies.[269] This would have the double impact of undercutting the cost of Dutch tea imported through independent merchants and smugglers, while at the same time allowing British government agents to collect a tax for Parliament and unload their tea directly to the public. The impact on the colonies, of course, was to drive up the cost of *all* tea imported into the colonies. In an oddly timed but absolutely providential turn of events for the inner circle, Parliament approved this tax on tea, the *Tea Act* on May 10, 1773. And with the publication of the Hutchinson letters, it appeared to the people of Boston that once again British troops were returning to suppress any resistance. News of this *Tea Act* would reach Boston by August 1773. And once again, the Adamses were outraged!

Into this bubbling cauldron of political unrest, and with Thomas Hutchinson still ensconced in the governor's mansion in Boston, the first three ships loaded with British tea and stamped with the new tax arrived unwittingly at Boston harbor in the second week of December, 1773.[270] On the night of December 16, 1773, Samuel Adams was addressing a packed Old South Meeting House about his outrage over the horrors of the Hutchinson papers and the impact upon the homes and safety of the people of Boston. He was bluntly implicating the authors of the Hutchinson letters, Governor Thomas Hutchinson and Lieutenant Governor Andrew Oliver, in calling for this suppression of the civil rights of the citizens. While he was yet speaking, shouts of anger and frustration erupted from the audience, and with Adams imploring the mob to desist, *and to curb their outrage,* they tore from the confines of Old South Meeting House at Milk and [Washington] Streets and headed directly toward the harbor.[271] Boston rebels boarded *Dartmouth, Eleanor,* and *Beaver,* dumping a total of 342 chests of tea into Boston Harbor, a total equivalent loss of about £10,000. The fire was thus reignited and was burning brightly in Boston in the dawn of 1774. The short recess from 1770–73 was officially at an end. The Adams cousins were back.

Franklin did not have to long await the news of the response to the Hutchinson letters. The news of the "Boston Tea Party" arrived in London on January 20, 1774, and the response from the Privy Council and from Commons was immediate and furious.[272] John Pownall quickly responded to the news with an offer, as first secretary of the Board of Trade, to draft a response of appropriate severity, by Acts of Parliament, to this audacious act of treason against the Crown. To his surprise and confusion, his brother Thomas volunteered *further sanctions* while John read his draft to him. Thomas seemed acquiescent and almost…supportive. It was "most odd." Thus reassured of the rightness of his cause, and with his brother Thomas's support, John pressed his draft before the Privy Council. They approved all points unanimously and sent it to Parliament. And for the first time in British history, Parliament, and not the Crown, was going to set policy over an American colony.

Known forevermore as the "Intolerable Acts," the first was delivered by February and closed Boston Harbor completely, pending payment of reparations for the destroyed tea.[273] The second was considered the worst of the lot, revoking the Massachusetts charter and establishing Parliament as the controlling source of all future political appointments in the colony. Never had Parliament assumed this degree of control and usurpation of Crown authority. The third allowed a change of venue for native Brits arraigned for crimes in Massachusetts to London, thus effectively assuring that colonial witnesses for the prosecution of cases against British military personnel would be hard-pressed to appear. The fourth allowed Great Britain to "quarter" or house British soldiers in any building they so desired. And the final act, although technically not a response to the Boston Tea Party, would be seen that way by New York, Pennsylvania, and Virginia, as it awarded the Northwest Territories to Quebec, thwarting any subsequent initiative from the colonies to expand their borders and their influence through land patents and stock companies. The "Quebec Act" thus effectively ended all the land speculation by affluent colonials and their British friends, including Franklin, his Junto in Philadelphia, and the Club of Honest Whigs in London. The Patriot fires in Boston would now rage on, extending right into 1775.

While the significance to the American Revolution of the release of the "Hutchinson letters" to the Boston press can be debated, they would have a direct impact upon Franklin and his life in London. George Grenville had died in London in 1770, and Thomas Whately gathered up his correspondence, likely neatly sorted and filed, through Whately's role as secretary.[274] Upon Whately's unexpected demise on May 26, 1772, this correspondence was delivered for safekeeping to his brother, William Whately. Seeing little further use for this correspondence, William Whately advertised its availability for anyone who had originated correspondence addressed to Grenville to reclaim as archives or destroy. John Temple appeared, due to his previous role as provincial governor of New Hampshire, and reclaimed some letters. Later that morning, Thomas Pownall appeared, due to his role as previous governor of Massachusetts, and reclaimed the file listed as "correspondence from Governors of Massachusetts." He subsequently returned the letters of his immediate successor, Sir Francis Bernard, but Whately failed to realize that the Hutchinson letters had been retained by Pownall. Franklin, upon receiving the packet of letters from Pownall, proceeded to "leak" them to Boston in late 1772, sending them to Thomas Cushing, speaker of the house in the Massachusetts Assembly, and a revolutionary in his own right.[275] In the attached letter, Franklin warned Cushing not to allow the letters to be leaked further, and especially not to Samuel Adams. Which was clearly yet another subterfuge (as Franklin had written so many years previously, in *Poor Richard's Almanac,* "three may keep a secret, if two of them are dead"), insofar as the letters appeared in the Boston press in July 1773. This action stoked the flames in both Boston and London all that much more, especially as suspicion arose regarding *how* this private correspondence between Hutchinson and the now-deceased Grenville was leaked to, of all places, the Boston press of Samuel Adams. Suspicion immediately fell on William Whately as the custodian of the correspondence. And Whately, for his part, pled innocence, and at the same time wondered how they could possibly have left his safe keeping. And then he remembered, "Temple!"[276] The only one he remembered seeking correspondence from the files of his deceased brother Thomas was John Temple, the former governor of New Hampshire, and the only person who was a colonial, not a Brit. It simply had to be.

Here the entire issue of Franklin's inner circle, and their deliberations, turned frightening. Both Franklin and Pownall had to be watching this inquiry with pounding hearts: would Whately remember the visit from Pownall? So they watched and waited. And watched even as in early December 1773, Temple, absolutely livid now over the accusation of theft from Whately, and *knowing* that he himself was innocent of the crime, demanded a duel against Whately to address the false derogation on his character.[277] Whately, certain of *his* innocence and the guilt of Temple, agreed. In the duel, Whately was dealt a saber wound to the arm, which was not fatal but rendered Whately incapable of lifting a sword then or during his recuperation. Both men agreed that once Whately was recuperated, they would repeat the exercise. At this point, the inner circle met again at Fothergill's house.

Fo: "We cannot be a party to two innocent men repeating this horrid act."

P: "For my part I am willing to come forward and will in the interim devise a story that will attach my behavior to the correspondence with Cushing."

"No, no, no!" Franklin slammed both palms on the table and arose heatedly. "Gentlemen, it is I who sent the letters and the associated correspondence. And Cushing will, if asked, yield my correspondence to the authorities here. At that point the jig will be quite up, for all of us. No, I am going to the press before the month is out, confessing my *sole* involvement in the affair. Neither of you will be named, and perhaps with my reputation in London, the matter will be laid to rest and subside. It is, in the end, our only hope."

And at that, Fothergill, Barclay, and Pownall could offer nothing further than muted agreement. Franklin was correct; either the authorities would accept his story, or the entire matter of fomenting revolution was once again at an end.

So, on Christmas Day, 1773, in Franklin's chosen organ of propaganda, Strahan's *The London Chronicle*, appeared the letter of Benjamin Franklin acknowledging that *he* had acquired and sent the Hutchinson letters to Cushing in Boston, praying that they be not revealed to any other persons, and that both Whately and Temple were innocent of any malfeasance. And four prominent public figures in London awaited the ensuing firestorm.[278]

Chapter 17

T hey needn't have waited long. The official response of the Massachusetts assembly (as opposed to the *unofficial* response, which was the Boston Tea Party) was a formal petition to the Crown to recall both Governor Hutchinson and Lieutenant Governor Oliver, as "based on correspondence now in our possession, we find these two officials no longer disposed toward the better interests of the colony of Massachusetts."[279] Receipt of that petition was acknowledged by the Privy Council on January 11, 1774. On January 20, reports of the unofficial response in Boston Harbor first appeared in London. By January 29, the Privy Council had decided it was time to address this "Petition" from Massachusetts and requested that the official agent of Massachusetts, one Benjamin Franklin, appear to provide an explanation of the petition in anticipation of the council vote.[280]

Here, Franklin was to make the gravest political error of his career, which came desperately close to a culmination at the gibbet.[281] He first offered to Arthur Lee, the associate agent for Massachusetts in London, that he saw no need for personal counsel, but he wished Mr. Lee to accompany him to the "meeting." Lee, as a trained attorney and thereby thinking much better of it, encouraged Franklin not to wade into the "Cockpit at Whitehall" without his own counsel. Franklin reluctantly agreed, and at the recommendation of his new disciple Granville Sharp selected none other than John Dunning to come along for what Franklin believed would be a quick disposition of the petition and the "Hutchinson matter." He then enlisted a tight circle of friends: Dr. Joseph Priestley, Edmund Burke, and his editorialist acolyte Edward Bancroft, to join him at Whitehall for moral support.

Israel Mauduit, as a loyalist agent for the Massachusetts governor, but on that day serving as proxy for Hutchinson, had been invited to this little meeting as well, which should have given Franklin some pause.[282] But as Mauduit had demonstrated himself to be little more than a sycophant for his employer, Franklin grossly underestimated the extent of opposition awaiting him. Upon arrival, he found the Cockpit absolutely packed with members of the House of Lords, including the most influential colonial overseers of the day, among them Lords North, Dartmouth, and Hillsborough. Now discomfited, Franklin was thankful Dunning was at his side. The event was opened by Mauduit, who answered perfunctory questions regarding his status as proxy for Hutchinson and his role in the Massachusetts government. And then Mauduit was dismissed, and the chair, Earl Gower, Lord President of the Privy Council, recognized Alexander Wedderburn.

Alexander Wedderburn was born in East Lothian, Scotland, in 1733, eldest son of a well-respected Scottish barrister, Peter Wedderburn, and thus born to the role of attorney.[283] He received the best education of its day in Scotland and was accepted to the Scottish bar in 1754. As one of the earliest editors of the *Law Review of Edinburgh,* he was verbally accosted by Lord Covington, a lord of sessions in Scotland and well-known as one of the most verbally adept barristers of the bench, regarding a review taking issue at a decision previously rendered by Lord Covington. When Wedderburn retorted with like (or greater?) eloquence and verbal assault, he was subsequently ordered by the bar to stand down. So he promptly resigned from the Scottish bar.

Resurfacing in London, Wedderburn employed two British attorneys of his day to aid his conversation skills and to forswear his deep Scottish brogue. Coincidentally, he approached Franklin's long-time London friend, William Strahan, the printer from Scotland, to introduce him to the society of the day in London. Lord Bute arranged for Wedderburn to gain a seat in Parliament in 1761, and by 1764, he was accepted to the British bar. Marrying well in 1767 left him independently wealthy, and he focused on the legal and political intrigues of the British court. By 1774 he was known by all, including Lord Mansfield, as a most intimidating and verbally gifted barrister, and while perhaps not further gifted in legal intellect, he was theatrically every bit the consummate prosecutor.

So up to address Dr. Franklin, the most esteemed and best-known colonial personality throughout Europe at that time, strode Mr. Wedderburn, the most feared prosecutor of his day. In this role Wedderburn did not disappoint. He began with a brief review of the petition from the Massachusetts assembly, dismissing it out of hand as the grievances of uneducated colonials who simply did not understand how the authority of the governor of their colony emanated *not* from the colonials, but rather from the Crown. And how the Crown was well-pleased with the performance of both Hutchinson and Oliver, who were, after all, simply colonials like the petitioners, but who had elevated themselves to their current office by being loyal subjects of the Crown. The "dig" at the Massachusetts Assembly here was obvious. But Wedderburn was merely warming up for the main course: the frying of Franklin.

Now Wedderburn addressed directly the "esteemed" Dr. Franklin and proceeded to hurl invectives for a solid hour or more, the likes of which most of the Privy Council had never before heard in their collective careers. Wedderburn was unrelenting: he pointed out clearly and accurately that it was Franklin, by his own admission, that had acquired by some unknown artifice, the private correspondence of the brothers-in-law Hutchinson and Oliver, clearly addressed to Grenville, and clearly, according to several letters in the collection, for Grenville's eyes only. And that Franklin, for his part, had deliberately provided this personal correspondence to the Massachusetts assembly and to a "six-man junto, whom I will not here name, unless requested," and then copies of the letters had been allowed, at Franklin's permission, to be created and disseminated, asserting (by Franklin) that this was not the same thing as distribution of the originals. Mauduit, Mansfield, Burke, and Lee, among others in the gallery, reported that many statements of Wedderburn were greeted with "laughter and applause" by the lords, but at the same time, the severity of the verbal assault had to ultimately be producing some discomfort on the part of the audience. Several times Wedderburn referred to the "unknown basis" for the acquisition of the letters, but this did not appear to be a source of curiosity beyond the casual statement that Franklin had, heretofore, not been forthcoming on providing details of the acquisition. On and on the assault continued, until it was clear beyond any doubt to anyone present that Franklin had indeed allowed publication of personal and private letters between private parties. It was further affirmed that Franklin's explanation, which said correspondence was nothing different than "public statements from public men," could not lie for his defense.

But then a strange thing happened that would make Franklin's grave error here no greater than that of Wedderburn. For Wedderburn concluded the inquisition by asserting that "therefore, the response to the petition from the Massachusetts Assembly" for the recall of Hutchinson and Oliver "should be in the negative." And that was it. There was no further pressing of Franklin for details about acquiring the letters, no further invective hurled his way. Franklin had stood resolute through that hour with that perpetual smirk on his face that would beguile and bewilder everyone he met throughout his long life as to his thought processes and had spoken not a single word.[284] At this time, as the murmuring died down in the Cockpit, Earl Gower asked Franklin, "Do you wish to be examined at this time?" to which Dunning interjected immediately, "He does not, m'lord." With that, the inquisition, disguised as a review of the petition to recall Governor Hutchinson and Lieutenant Governor Oliver, came to an end. Anticlimactically, the petition was, of course, unanimously rejected by the Privy Council.

For Franklin, however, the matter was not quite yet concluded. The following day, he was advised by his London friend and ostensible superior, Lord Le Despencer, that his position as deputy postmaster for the American colonies had been vacated as a result of the "Hutchinson affair."[285] While this most assuredly did not leave Franklin destitute, it was a political face-slap that left Franklin all the more determined to see his secret plan to its successful conclusion. His contempt for the House of Lords was permanently established on that day.

Meanwhile, Thomas Pownall had taken up the olive branch in Parliament, at least at face value, speaking of attempting reconciliation with Boston.[286] In so doing, he was unwittingly focusing the wrath of Samuel Adams upon his own head. Adams likewise would go to his grave never knowing the identity of the person who had provided Franklin the "Hutchinson Letters," thereby ensuring the onset of the American Revolution by the now unified American colonies. Pownall responded with warnings to the Committee of Correspondence in Boston generally, and to the Adams cousins in particular, "judge not of the tree by the color of the blossoms, but wait for the bearing time and judge by the fruits." Adams, ever impatient and ever outraged, was not interested in waiting for anything from a Parliamentary partisan. Pownall would spend the summer of 1774 speaking as much as he was allowed in Parliament in favor of reconciliation with the colonies, but to little avail.

Franklin began planning the possibility of a hasty departure to America. On the heels of the debacle in the Cockpit, and fear of impending arrest and imprisonment in the Tower, he had taken the expedient of temporarily removing himself from Craven Street to Chelsea, outside London, following the adage of "out of sight, out of mind." But he had certain unfinished business pending, of which only his inner circle was aware. As the revolution now appeared to be a foregone conclusion, with Massachusetts seeking congress with the other British colonies in North America, Franklin turned toward the next phase. It had already been made clear by Barclay and Pownall that a national purse would be essential to outfitting a revolutionary American military, and the most obvious sources were France, the Netherlands, and Spain, likely in that order. To that end, Franklin would be travelling in Europe in the coming months to years. He would need an acolyte essayist in America to maintain the spirit of revolution through the uncertain length of time needed for success. This would be a difficult position to fill, and to maintain. They had already rejected Bancroft in this role, as his loyalty to their cause was suspect. The writer would have to appreciate the sincerity of the inner circle but at the same time agree completely with the need for strict confidence and apprehend the frightening personal danger of the task. And currently, neither Fothergill, nor Barclay, nor Pownall, nor even Franklin himself, could proffer a name. Providence, or incredibly good luck, was about to come calling on the inner circle once more.

❦

Chapter 18

Thomas Pain was born in Thetford, England, January 29, 1737, the son of a "staymaker," this vernacular description most likely implying a cable-maker supplying the "sheets" [rope rigging] for the many ships between Clacton-on-Sea and King's Lynn (as opposed to a "corset-maker" as most biographers list him).[287] His father had spelled the surname "Pain," as did his ancestors, but Thomas would add the "e" at about the time he relocated to the American colonies in 1774 [so we leave it as he wished, henceforth in our story]. He attended grammar school in Thetford until aged fourteen, at which time he was apprenticed by his father into the family business. At age seventeen, he attempted to join the crew of the privateer *Terrible,* but his father discovered the scheme and bore him back home.[288] At age twenty, he was more successful at fleeing from his father and his apprenticeship, joining the *King of Prussia* for about a year, during the Seven Years' War, in 1757. For the next three years, he wandered from London to Dover to Sandwich, finding work in the brisk trade of "staymaking" at a time in the "Age of Sails" when the most common conveyance in Europe was a ship. By 1760, he was a master staymaker in his own shop in Sandwich. At that time he married Mary Lambert, daughter of an exciseman. His staymaking shop promptly failed, a trend which would follow Paine through much of his life: a demonstrable and frequently repeated total inability to manage finances. He and his young wife moved then to Margate, and by the following year, she had died of unknown cause.

Based upon his brief acquaintance with the Lamberts, Paine decided to have a go as an exciseman, a notoriously difficult career, grossly underpaid and with few prospects of advantage.[289] To that end, he returned to Thetford and took preparatory studies for the Excise. In a nation that was considered in the eighteenth century to be the major sea-trader of the entire world, the Excise was of critical importance in collecting import duties and preventing smuggling at the literally hundreds of ports that lined her shores. This duty fell to the excisemen, who labored nonstop for less than £50 net wages per year, barely enough to support themselves, let alone any consideration of families. On December 1, 1762, Paine received his first appointment to the Excise, capping a frenetic six years of his life. In August 1764 he received his first independent assignment in Lincolnshire and was discharged from the Excise in August 1765 for "stamping." The excisemen were expected to inspect all imported goods unloaded from every ship in their port, opening the crates, looking for contraband, marking the crates (with their personal "stamp"), and confirming that the contents of the crates were indeed what the bills of lading said they were. It was a near-impossible task in less than eighteen hours per day, and because of this, the excisemen would develop a sense of the trustworthiness of their regular shipping companies, and unless something appeared clearly awry, they would simply stamp their crates without inspection. The practice of "stamping" was apparently commonplace but also quite illegal. And in any case of smuggling identified after the fact, the "stamp" of the exciseman on the crate bearing the contraband was clear evidence of the offense. So it was for Paine.

In July 1766, starving and broken, Paine groveled for reinstatement with the Excise, and his petition was accepted. One is left to wonder how anyone would pursue such employment except for the simple fact that the salary was regular. But the demands of the position were beyond the pale. And the excisemen worked in relative isolation in the smaller ports, unaware that their general condition was being shared throughout the empire. Now, by this time, Paine had demonstrated an unexpected gift for turning a phrase, earning modest supplementation of his modest salary by writing slogans, songs, and poetry. So when no positions at the Excise came available during 1767, he took on preaching jobs for local churches as a lay deacon, as well as a tutoring position for boys in Kensington. In 1768, he finally received an excise position at Lewes, Sussex, taking him far from home.[290] He moved into a spare room in the home of Samuel Ollive. There, perhaps with the maturity of his thirty years, he finally made a modest success for himself, providing inspections not only in Lewes, but also in Brighton. It was at Brighton that he would garner the attention of other excisemen as a clever writer and speaker. It was also there that he would remarry; his new wife was ten years his junior, a pretty girl, the daughter of his landlord.[291] In this time, Samuel Ollive died, leaving his widow, Paine's mother-in-law, in some financial straits. The wedding took place in 1771; by 1772 Paine found himself enlisted by his fellow excisemen in authoring a petition to Parliament for better working conditions, shorter hours, and higher salaries. Suddenly, Paine was finding himself overwhelmed: his mother-in-law and new bride asked him to take on his late father-in-law's grocery and tobacco mill, in addition to his excise and excisemen-lobbying responsibilities. So he produced his first essay of significance, *The Case for the Officers of Excise,* and through the winter of 1772–73, Paine traveled back and forth from Brighton to London, lobbying Parliament on behalf of his brethren in the Excise. Ultimately, his efforts proved fruitless; Parliament was impressed by his writing but had no intention of providing any form of relief for these lowest-rung bureaucrats who clearly needed the positions more than their government needed them.

Now, his efforts at lobbying failed, his grocery and tobacco mill neglected, his excise work being covered in likely haphazard fashion by fellow inspectors, Paine was summoned to the Office of the Excise in Lewes on April 8, 1774, where he was summarily discharged for absenteeism (due to his travelling to London and Parliament!) and advised that as a second discharge, he was permanently ineligible for reinstatement. With debts rising, Paine found himself in real danger of being arrested and convicted of indebtedness, or "taken up" by the impressment gangs. On April 14, he sold all his possessions to successfully discharge his debts; on June 4, his young wife moved out, his marriage unconsummated after more than two years.[292] His world was crashing in around him. At that point, Thomas Paine took stock of his life.

He had, while travelling to lobby Parliament in London, made the acquaintance in the "Publick Houses" of London of Oliver Goldsmith, the playwright, and through him, Dr. Benjamin Franklin, a less regular frequenter of these establishments but quite taken by clever songs and poetry and thus naturally drawn to both Goldsmith and Paine.[293] And now Paine, having heard of Franklin's undoing in the Cockpit, wondered if one discharged bureaucrat would commiserate with another.[294] In that hope, Paine, with his career, his finances, and his personal life rapidly disintegrating, turned his sights and his hopes back to London.

One Saturday in April of 1774, Dr. Franklin went out from Craven Street to Covent Garden, seeking out the company of Oliver Goldsmith for amusement. At a publick house outside Covent Garden, he spotted Goldsmith with a raucous group of revelers singing loudly and poorly and begged that he be allowed to join them.[295] Goldsmith laughingly bade him welcome and proceeded to introduce some of his choristers, "...and this is Thomas, Thomas something or another..."

"*Thomas Paine*," the man said, clearly more sober than Goldsmith.

Franklin offered, "Yes, we've met, but tell me, Oliver. What does your Thomas Paine do?"

Goldsmith said, "He is a writer of songs, ribald songs. And poetry. And is really quite good. And gets even better as the evening wears on."

And he broke into raucous laughter with his besotted entourage once again. (Tragically, Goldsmith would be dead within two weeks, the victim of a kidney infection.) Paine, for his part, was fascinated to find himself the subject of interest of Dr. Benjamin Franklin and moved closer for a private conversation.

Franklin addressed him, "So, do you write in the fashion of Mr. Goldsmith?"

P: "I am no playwright, but I do write lyric."

Fr: "Is this your livelihood?"

P: "Oh, no. It has provided me with only a modest supplemental income source."

Fr: "And so how do you support yourself?"

P: "Not well."

Franklin was amused.

"I was an exciseman, but I have of late been discharged from my situation. I was in Brighton and noted that the excisemen were, to a man, overworked and grossly underpaid. To the point where they fell natural victims to stamping, smuggling, and bribery. My fellows sought me out to petition Parliament for a redress of grievances. And this, I regret to say, went poorly. They were most unreceptive, and upon my return to Brighton, I was advised that my frequent absences had accomplished my being turned out."

Franklin could certainly identify with the recalcitrance of Parliament. "And now?"

P: "On account of my discharge, I will be forced to sell my assets to avoid debtors' prison. My wife is moving out from our home to her mother's, with her remaining possessions."

Fr: "And so now, what is your opinion of Parliament, in regard to their willingness to redress grievances for British citizens?" Now Franklin was fishing.

P: "They are but knaves and scoundrels, without a worthy in their lot that I ever found. Are we not all men? Do we not have rights? I was treated as unworthy, and as a beggar or a thief."

Fr: "I might be able to use a writer and would be willing to pay you for your service. Would you be willing to accompany me and provide a sketch of your talent?"

P: "I would be much obliged, Dr. Franklin, but I fear my skills in that regard are meager at best, and that I have a Parliament to prove it."

Fr: "We will see about that. After all, I too have just been turned out from my situation in the colonies." Smiling, Franklin rose and bade Mr. Paine accompany him to Craven Street.

Upon arriving, Paine was relieved, and then greatly heartened, by his reception at Franklin's quarters in Craven Street. Franklin appeared truly delighted to have him, ushered him inside, provided him a meal with fresh, hot tea, and later took him to the haberdasher for a new suit of clothes. Franklin then advised Mrs. Stevenson that she would have another boarder living in his quarters for the next few weeks. Then, curtains drawn, Franklin and Paine began to chat. Within the hour, Franklin produced quill and ink, and paper, and asked Paine to write an impromptu essay on the ills of the excisemen.

It became quite clear to Franklin after only this initial dialogue and essay study with Paine that 1) he was a gifted writer and speaker, 2) he was a zealot for liberty and the rights of the common man, and 3) he was absolutely, hopelessly strapped. In that circumstance, Franklin took Paine into his confidence, and by the end of June 1774 had hatched his next plan. It was time to introduce Thomas Paine to the inner circle, and Franklin now invited him to join them at Harpur Street. Paine was fascinated and eager to assist Franklin, his benefactor and newfound idol.[296]

The following week, Paine and Franklin ventured out together to Harpur Street, Bloomsbury, and Paine was immediately smitten by the beauty of the home of Fothergill.

Franklin advised him, "Dr. Fothergill is my personal physician and perhaps the single most successful physician of this town."

Looking all about him at the decor, Paine could only breathe, "Yes, he must be."

Ushered into Fothergill's private study, the two were greeted by Thomas Pownall and David Barclay, already in congress. They rose and welcomed Paine, smiling at him and nodding to Franklin. Franklin would speak first. "Gentlemen, Mr. Paine has been advised of the purpose of our regular meetings here, and is in sworn agreement with all our expectations and designs."

Fothergill said, "So, pray tell us, Mr. Paine, of thy intentions here and thine understanding of thy tasks in service to Dr. Franklin."

Paine started slowly, but as he spoke, his comfort level rose and he noticeably relaxed. "M'lord, I hope to aid Dr. Franklin's cause by conveying his thoughts, and mine, to the colonists in America seeking redress of grievances with Parliament. We are together of a mind that the only recourse for the colonials is separation from the Empire, in order to gain their respect. Anything less, at this point, would appear to Parliament as capitulation rather than reconciliation and would be greeted with retribution of a most severe nature. I will not betray his kindness, nor his trust. And will provide service faithfully for your cause, until its successful conclusion. I am most grateful to all of you for providing me this unique opportunity in the cause of freedom."

Barclay smiled broadly and nodded. Paine was everything that Franklin had promised. Pownall exhaled deeply; this could just work out, and there simply were no other candidates. The ensuing ninety minutes were consumed in a vigorous discussion of the political theories of Hobbes and Locke, as well as those of Montesquieu and Franklin's dear friend, David Hume. Paine then produced a folio containing perhaps a half-dozen essays on the basis of government and the rights of citizens, written in concert with Franklin over the previous four weeks. His three confederates passed them around and looked through them with growing admiration and wonder; how had Franklin managed to find this diamond in the rough? Afterward, Paine again addressed his benefactor.

"I should be indebted to all of you for the opportunity to meet Dr. Hume."

"All in good time, Thomas," said Franklin. "For now, we yet have much work to do."

[As fate would have it, Paine would never have the opportunity to meet David Hume. Paine was already being prepared to move to Philadelphia in the fall, and Dr. Hume would not survive the American Revolution.] After two hours, Franklin rose. "We have abused your hospitality, Dr. Fothergill, and the hour is late. But we shall be seeing you regularly this summer. For now, you need your rest." And without further discussion, Franklin and Paine departed Harpur Street.

Awaiting Franklin's return to Craven Street were correspondence and books from Charles Dumas.[297] In the letter, Dumas thanked Franklin for some previous books he had forwarded, and after the greetings, expressed his amusement: *What has just happened in America in relation to tea gives me infinite pleasure.* He continued to pledge his support, moving forward, for the American colonies in their effort at independence, and their future development as *a system of nations as brilliant as ancient Greece or modern Europe.* Franklin was both amused and intrigued. He needed this emotional boost following the debacle in the Cockpit, and at the same time he recognized the value of the author. He carefully folded the correspondence and placed it in his active file. Then, packing some personal effects into his valise, he returned to Chelsea with Paine to avoid any curiosity about the comings and goings of a destitute exciseman in his company.[298]

Over the long summer of 1774, Franklin was remarkably absent from many of his more frequented homes and businesses in London, leading King George III to ask Lord Dartmouth of his whereabouts. "I believe, sir, he is in town. He was going to America, but I fancy he is not gone," Dartmouth offered.

"I heard," the king countered, "he was going to Switzerland."[299]

But Franklin would return from time to time to Craven Street and meet quietly but regularly with both the Honest Whigs, and with the inner circle, now including Pownall, Fothergill, Barclay, and Paine, but no others. Since no one in Franklin's circle of friends was asked directly about him, none offered any information. Franklin's absence during this time, however, was working a certain magic regarding the opinions of the members of the Privy Council toward his character. The overarching tone was one of genuine regret for having behaved in so insulting and personally degrading a fashion toward him in the Cockpit.[300] At the same time, there arose a deterioration in the overall perception of the behavior of Alexander Wedderburn. "We should not have disgraced him so," became the nearly unanimous theme. For those few, like the fourth Earl Sandwich, who held alternative viewpoints about Franklin and his loyalties to the Crown, Dr. Franklin's absence did little more than fuel further suspicion; Sandwich was clearly developing a paranoid fear of Franklin's influence both inside and outside of Westminster. And so, without offering any defense whatsoever, and without speaking or publishing a word, Franklin was rebuilding his status in the ranks of the House of Lords. This would serve him well in the coming year.

What Franklin *was* doing was engaging Paine in ongoing dialogue regarding political theories about the concepts of good government, correct construction of a centralized administration, division of powers, hereditary v. elected legislators and administrators, and where Great Britain had succeeded and failed. Pownall renewed his interest in his published *The Administration of the Colonies* and visited at length with Paine until Paine felt that he knew the southern colonies better than Franklin did. Barclay lectured on finances and banking and the fiscal essentials of the military, in terms of both arms and materiel in the field. It was, in summary, a massive course for Paine in political and military science of the eighteenth century, at the conclusion of which this pauper lyricist found himself the premier political writer of the age. The turn of events and the outcome was beyond remarkable. And no one was more amazed with the progress and the outcome than Thomas Paine. His proclivities both for drink and for the company of famous and influential men were strategically overlooked, and the topics were avoided. By September 1774, all four of the inner circle were in unanimity: not only was Thomas Paine ready for the colonies, but the colonies were, most assuredly, quite ready for Thomas Paine.

The only trail of Paine's transformation remaining to posterity today is the record of payment of passage and letter of introduction to Richard Bache, both by Dr. Franklin (while of course the proof lies in the literary output of this most eminent pamphleteer beginning from his arrival in America).[301] In the letter of introduction to Mr. Bache, Franklin's son-in-law, Franklin bade him find work for Mr. Paine of a teaching or writing nature to free him for at least the semblance of time to write. In reality, the first two major essays produced by Paine were already in his possession upon his arrival in Philadelphia. By consensus, the inner circle had agreed that his very first publication must be an essay condemning African slavery in the colonies, in order to draw the attention of every northern colony, from Pennsylvania to Massachusetts, and reassure them that Paine was a staunch abolitionist.[302] Then Paine was to await the reception of this essay, to ensure that 1) it was greeted favorably by the general public, without evoking any retaliatory responses from the South, and 2) it drew extensive interest from the northern colonies. Only with those two responses in evidence was Paine to drop the final bombshell into the fray. Franklin privately advised Paine to reserve the second essay until he, Franklin, had returned to the colonies; Paine agreed.

Paine and Franklin had spent a great part of the summer of 1774 in coauthoring that bombshell treatise that would forever change the colonies and political science. Franklin had drawn up the initial outline for this essay, which would ultimately comprise forty-seven pages. But Paine proved more than competent to the task, and in time, he would write and rewrite the drafts until the document became his own, in language, and more importantly, in passion. Paine initially labeled his treatise "Plain Truth." At which Franklin burst out in spontaneous laughter. Paine was noticeably perplexed, whereupon Franklin went to his desk and withdrew a yellowed broadsheet he had written many years ago in Philadelphia during King George's War, excoriating Thomas Penn and the proprietors of Pennsylvania for their cheeseparing and cowardice, entitled…"Plain Truth."[303] Now it was Paine's turn to laugh and to clap his hands together. Providential, most assuredly. Franklin then said, "Something else." And Paine and Franklin thought, and then Paine smiled again, carefully placed the draft upon his writing desk, dipped quill into ink, and scrawled in large letters across the top of Page One, "*Common Sense.*" Franklin responded, in a word, "Perfect!" Ultimately, this essay would be the opening of a series entitled *The American Crisis*, which would eventually run to sixteen treatises released between 1776 and 1783.

But Franklin was quite adamant that the first essay for Paine would be that statement in opposition to African slavery, in order to garner the attention and respect of both New York and the "Boston rabble." True to the plan, on March 8, 1775, "African Slavery in America" appeared in *The Pennsylvania Gazette*, a severe critique on the slave trade and those whose purchases supported it and published anonymously. Surprisingly, the only criticism leveled at Paine on behalf of the First Continental Congress emanated from a Massachusetts source, rather than any southern delegate. That source of outrage was, of course, John Adams, who felt that the essay was unnecessarily inflammatory toward his southern colleagues. Through 1775, numerous small essays would also appear in the Philadelphia press from the pen of Thomas Paine. But *Common Sense* would remain in Paine's private folio, awaiting the correct moment to strike.

Chapter 19

Meanwhile, the inner circle was now moving rapidly forward with plans for the revolution. Barclay had realized that attempts to finance an army by a national purse were fraught, at least at the outset of the revolution. There were simply too many political obstacles in the way of any single European nation to provide financial support for a revolution of British colonies against its monarch. Such a move was certain to bring war upon that nation against the British Empire, and with the possible exception of France, no other European nation, less than fifteen years after the Seven Years' War, was ready to consider this again. Especially not in support of rebellious British subjects. No, the finances would initially have to be arranged secretly from private sources. There was at that time only one person in the inner circle who had friends and colleagues with the capital, and the interest, to provide this.

David Barclay was born in 1728 to the Quaker family of a successful linen-draper in Cheapside, London.[304] His mother was a daughter of the Freame banking family. As a young man, he was involved in mercantile trading to the American colonies, and it was there, during the French and Indian War, that David Barclay dealt in firearms and other materiel with the Pennsylvania militia, and thereby made the acquaintance of Benjamin Franklin. He married in 1749; the union produced two daughters, one of whom died in childhood. His first wife died in 1763. Barclay married again in 1767. His surviving daughter married in 1773 and had two children. Sadly, his daughter died in 1776.

David inherited bank stock through his mother and joined the Freame Bank in the 1750s. At that time in London, the banking industry was still in its infancy and was finding its way to success for its owners by trial and error; some trial, and quite a bit of error. In the seventeenth century in London, more banks would fail than succeed by a factor of perhaps ten to one. As a result, banks developed a bad name among the public and were not used by the affluent generally. But by the 1730s, banking started to take on a different atmosphere altogether. It seems that an extended family of Quakers surnamed Freame, Barclay, Gould, and Bevans, among others, was developing a true knack for handling relatively large sums without losing them, and sometimes with returns of over thirty percent per annum for their investors![305] The difference for the Quaker bankers was multifaceted: they generally tended to be much wealthier people, they did not abide risk, they did not abide bankruptcy, they were well-connected throughout Great Britain, the British colonies in America, and Europe, through the Society of Friends, and they approached banking as an adjunct to business rather than an enterprise unto itself. Initially, much of their business was based on the "real bills doctrine," where the bank would buy the debt due to a supplier at a modest discount and then pursue timely collection of the debt by the original buyer. Due to the Quaker wealth, they were in a unique position in London to purchase debt, known as "bills," with ready cash.[306] And due to their extensive connections in the empire, they had a remarkably good idea about whose debts were "good" and likely to be repaid promptly. In this way, the Quaker bankers acquired vast revenues relatively quickly (by twenty-first century standards, their personal holdings were all in the millions of pounds). Over time, more and more urban builders and merchants would approach the Quaker bankers for loans, knowing that they could get credit for three to six percent and that they seemed to have an endless flow of ready cash for good credit risks. These Quaker bankers simply seemed to have an uncanny knowledge of good credit risks.

By 1776, David Barclay's bank was known as Barclay, Bevan, and Co.[307] Over the next twenty years, David and John Barclay would acquire, through mergers and purchases, consolidation of the bank known today as the Barclays Bank, one of the largest banking establishments in the world. During the 1770s, David would establish contacts with some of the largest banking families and firms in Europe, including the Necker family in Switzerland and France, as well as the Grand family in France and the Netherlands. With these contacts, and with his personal influence in London, David Barclay encouraged Dr. Franklin to initiate a secret correspondence with these other banking families. To that end, he felt that encryption of correspondence through an intermediary would be the safer approach. Franklin thought on this and then broke into a smile. He knew just the person to assist with this multinational encryption.

But while the preparations were being laid out for this endeavor, the discussion in the inner circle turned to Dr. Franklin and his role in revolution moving forward. It was quite clear that after the Cockpit incident, Franklin could no longer live safely in England. Already there were rumors that as relations between Great Britain and her colonies had deteriorated there were many in Parliament that wanted to bring charges against him for treason. For those convicted of treason in the London of that era, the punishment was summary execution. Furthermore, it did not make sense, from the standpoint of both Pownall and Barclay, for Franklin to return to any location within the colonies, and most assuredly not Philadelphia.[308] His mere presence there would render Philadelphia perhaps the single most plum target during the revolution, and it would certainly bring turmoil, if not bloodshed, to the streets of Philadelphia.

No, they wanted Franklin directly involved in the securing of funds and the procurement of supplies for the revolution. The two most likely places for Franklin to relocate were Paris or The Hague.[309] They felt that he would be safest in either of those cities. Franklin was more comfortable with his French and spoke no Dutch or Frisian. Furthermore, Franklin secretly relished the idea of living within three days' messaging to Parliament and the Crown. The three of them decided that Robert Morris was their best bet for making this happen and asked him to intervene on Franklin's behalf to have him appointed to the Continental Congress and subsequently to the Ministry to France.[310] Morris, the wealthiest and most influential man in Philadelphia, assured the inner circle that this was quite feasible and welcomed Franklin's input both with the Continental Congress and the *Ancien régime*.

The inner circle met several times during the closing days of summer in 1774, sometimes at Albemarle Street and sometimes at Harpur Street. It was becoming more and more clear with every passing day that the revolution stone had been nudged from its perch on the hilltop and was now more rapidly gathering energy and speed. It was time for the three leaders to map out their course in the coming conflict. Pownall advanced to the group that he was quite capable of continuing to foment insecurity within the ranks of Commons, and confident in his ability to weigh the sense of Commons, and to alert the others of any changes of significance in Parliament's point of view toward the American colonies. He had begun correspondence with Washington, which would continue throughout the revolution. He would provide the best topographical maps of the colonies to the colonial military, and he would continue his ongoing surveys and pamphlets in support of his beloved American colonies. His theories of employing dragoon regiments for rapid deployment where needed on short notice, and his development of topographical maps to aid troop movement were, in 1774, well, revolutionary.

Franklin, now preparing for departure to Philadelphia but already mapping an outline of his ultimate destination in France, produced a letter he had recently received for the other three to examine.[311] Written from Charles G.F. Dumas at The Hague, United Provinces [now The Netherlands], the author spoke highly of the colonies and their goal of independence and freedom for the common man. This man, Franklin advised the others, was fluent in five languages and had already made several key contacts in the United Provinces. Further, living in The Hague, he had working knowledge of the labyrinths of European diplomacy, and how it worked, and what did *not* work, in the cities of London, Paris, Berlin, Vienna, Rome, and Madrid. Finally, he had already worked out a system of encryption of correspondence that made similar concepts appear, frankly, primitive. He had sent Franklin a key and a test: Franklin had failed the "test," but his grandson, William "Temple" Franklin, found it quite legible, and more importantly, quite usable.

Barclay was immediately intrigued. Already moving toward the financing of a revolution on a massive scale, he knew several things: 1) the revolution would require at least 6 million pounds sterling to keep a military in the field for at least five years; 2) that degree of finance would require a national, rather than private purse; 3) no European country would publicly contribute financial support to any colonies in revolt against a legitimate monarchy in Europe for fear of entering into war against that monarchy; 4) the American colonies could not supply their military with weapons or ammunition without the assistance of European firearm sources due to lack of American foundries and factories; 5) Great Britain was currently the largest empire and possessed the most feared and respected military in the world; 6) the British navy would almost certainly blockade the American Atlantic seaboard, severely restricting the ship traffic in and out of American ports; and 7) the British would be attempting to undermine every effort at American success from the outset of hostilities. And he threw open the table for discussion. Pownall recommended that they take Barclay's list point by point, for the whole made the prospects almost insurmountably impossible.

Franklin frowned and sighed. "When it was a plan, a nebulous dream, it could be imagined. But laid before us in this fashion, it seems beyond formidable."

Barclay rejoined, "But if this be thy goal, and if this is the point of our meetings, these issues must be faced, and they must be faced before we can move forward. Otherwise, we are lost."

Pownall spoke. "Well, let us then take David's list from the first. How did you arrive at that figure?"

Barclay offered, "Thomas, thine own Parliament gives us this as the rough cost of the French and Indian War, an effort of seven years. The figures at this point are of course immature by half. But this provides a general goal of finance and need for loans or grants from Europe."

Franklin said, "But that takes us into your second point. Where do we look for this amount of loans?"

"We look to the countries who are most likely to have the funds, and quite frankly, who don't like Great Britain very much." And Barclay smiled.

Pownall put in, "That list is long. France, Spain, the United Provinces, Italy, Russia come immediately to mind. Less likely are Prussia and Austria, who have shared alliances with the Brits of late and have more modest treasuries."

"But with your third point, the plan fails," said Franklin. "What can we do with this? Do you think we can achieve a European alliance against the Brits simply to support our revolution?"

Pownall for his part, was simply baffled. He couldn't come up with any plausible answer to this dilemma. Barclay smiled. "Thou art thinking like revolutionaries rather than bankers. The challenge is to disguise the source of the loans and grants, to evade audit. This, I regret to admit, is *not* a grave challenge in this world of complex European financial transactions. We simply need to employ a common depository inaccessible to audit."

Pownall frowned. "There is no such place."

That brought a laugh from Barclay, "Oh, Thomas, but there is. And thou canst find it in every city in Europe and the Americas."

Now both Pownall and Franklin were baffled and intrigued. Barclay continued, "The Roman Curia! It has gone unaudited now for over 1,200 years. The finances of the Roman Curia are so arcane as to defy all the accountants of Europe."

With this Franklin became skeptical and responded flatly, "The papists are not going to finance an American revolution!"

"Ah, but Dr. Franklin, they will never know. The Roman church in France, Spain, the United Provinces, and Italy can serve as depositories, take their five percent, and then deliver the finances to the Continental Congress. It will be extremely clean and clear of audit. His Holiness will likely be unaware." Now Franklin was brightening. What seemed to him, and to Pownall, insurmountable proved to be little challenge to the financial genius of Barclay. "The court of

Louis XVI can provide access to the finances of the Roman curia through their commendatory abbots.[312] And at The Hague, your colleague Charles Dumas certainly must be familiar with the Abbé Desnoyers. The abbé is quite used to controlling finances for Vergennes, from the protective environs of the United Provinces, without raising suspicions. He can serve his Crown, his Prince of the Church, and the Americans quite well."

Franklin moved on. "Our colonial military is going to need assistance with materiel, and most assuredly we cannot look to Great Britain."

Now Pownall stepped in. "The financial instruments collected in the various countries need never leave Europe. They can be delivered to the weapons and munitions factories of Spain, France, Italy, and the Palatine. No one will challenge the transaction, and the colonies will receive not negotiable currencies and bonds, but rather the materiel they truly need."

"Precisely! Negotiable instruments during a revolution might prove too often less than worthless. We will provide thy colonies with what they can use." And now it was Barclay's turn to ask of Pownall and Franklin, "What of point number five?"

Franklin said, "We are maneuvering as we speak to assure that Washington is designated the leader of the colonial military. His leadership is essential to our success. He is an integral part of the 'motivation' for the entry of the southern colonies, and his war experience on American terrain is unsurpassed. And..." here Franklin recalled the experience of the Braddock debacle, "he has learned how to lose a battle without losing an army or a cause."

Pownall added, "We have spoken with him in the past regarding the strategies learned in the late French and Indian War, about ambuscade tactics, deployment of dragoon forces, and the importance of topographical awareness in siege and fortification. His leadership skills are unequalled."

Barclay said, "It is absolutely critical that he understands that he is never, never to undertake entry into a pitched battle against British regulars. This would be the aim of the British leaders and could cost thee the entire revolution in a single day." Both Franklin and Pownall nodded in agreement. They would regularly remind Washington of this concept, but Washington was already well-versed in the techniques of the "Fabian defense" and would continually execute this defense in expert fashion throughout the ensuing nine years.[313] Barclay continued, "And what of point number six? How are we to get the materiel to our colonial military? Blockade running would seem to be a risk not worth taking."

Franklin suddenly brightened. A different idea struck him suddenly. Once again he was thinking about the French and Indian War and the Forks of the Ohio. "Fort Pitt! We must take immediate possession of Fort Pitt. That's the key."

Barclay was puzzled, but Pownall's knowledge of Pennsylvania geography kicked in.

"Of course! The Ohio!" The Atlantic ports would be difficult to enter and depart, but New Orleans was Spanish territory, as was the Mississippi, and the Ohio was, if anything, French territory. (In practicality it was truly no one's, or anyone's, but definitely not controlled by the British Empire.) "We could sail ships up from New Orleans all the way to Fort Pitt. And from there we could distribute arms to the military in all the colonies."

Now Barclay interjected, "This seems like a fantasy. Can this be done? Can a ship's captain bring ships that deep into American territory?"

Franklin sat, looking up to the ceiling. Who was it? Who was it? Name? Name? Then, suddenly, "Oliver Pollock! Oliver Pollock! Of course!" Now Pownall and Barclay looked at Franklin as if he were some sort of wizard.

Pownall asked, "Who, pray tell, is Oliver Pollock?"

Oliver Pollock was born in Bready, a town in what is now Northern Ireland, in 1737. In 1760 he sailed with his father to Philadelphia and settled in Cumberland County to attempt farming. It was during that time that he made the acquaintance of Benjamin Franklin and visited him several times in Philadelphia. But the sea was in his blood, and by 1765 he was sailing trading vessels throughout the Caribbean and New Orleans, where he struck up a friendship with Alejandro O'Reilly, a colorful character who introduced Pollock to the Spanish ruling class of the city. He was well-received by the Spanish and would become a favorite son of New Orleans, providing staples from the various Caribbean islands to the city in times of poor harvest and food shortages. By 1772 he was one of the wealthier residents of the Crescent City. He owned property throughout the city and had a plantation outside Baton Rouge. At the outset of 1775, he was the obvious candidate to accomplish the "blockade running" via New Orleans and Fort Pitt, for the colonies.

Pownall knew the area of the Forks of the Ohio and knew that it was, in theory, navigable. "Yes, it is possible."[314]

"We would need to seize Fort Pitt in order to achieve this goal."

Pownall said, "My dear Dr. Franklin, are you aware that Fort Pitt is currently under the ownership of the colony of Virginia?"

"What's that? Are you quite sure?"

"Two years ago, the British military decided to abandon the fort, as the French were no longer operative in the area. It seems two speculators, William Thompson and Alexander Ross, filed a request with the Board of Trade to purchase the fort from its commander, Major Charles Edmonstone. The sale was certified, by a very good friend of mine, John Pownall."[315] Here Pownall smiled broadly.

"We would be entering through New Orleans under the noses of Great Britain. This system would require maximum secrecy if we are to use it more than once. It could be the sole uncontested shipping pathway for all the colonies. But," and here Franklin grinned broadly, "we also know that the First Lord of the Admiralty has a peculiar affliction, dysfranklinalgia, that keeps him fondly attached to the vast majority of His Majesty's ships." Fothergill now also smiled at the 'inside' medical humor. "And he will be very reluctant to allow them out of his personal oversight in the Channel and the North Sea. Any feint in the direction of Southampton, Dover, Land's End, or Plymouth, will send his navy scurrying for home in abandonment of the blockade of North America." That concept would prove embarrassingly easy for Franklin to accomplish throughout the American Revolution. And from the vantage point of Passy, it would prove easy to "send an alert" to the British admiralty at less than one week's notice.

Barclay concluded, "This entire enterprise will require a system of encryption in all our correspondence. The postal systems throughout Europe have become totally corrupted, and couriers are the safer method of delivery. But couriers will most assuredly be far too expensive for trans-Atlantic communication. The only answer to this issue is a system of encryption that would be impossible to decipher. This will require serious thought and serious practice."

Franklin was beginning to think that with careful planning, this could still all be brought to fruition. And further, Franklin and Pownall were well aware that the inability of any European nation to respond to a problem in America in less than six months would tilt the balance of military and political power dramatically toward the colonies, which could intercommunicate within days.

Chapter 20

P aine departed Great Britain around September 30 with a letter of introduction from Franklin to Franklin's son-in-law and Philadelphia printer Richard Bache.[316] He would arrive in Philadelphia November 30, 1774, deathly ill, likely from scurvy and/or infectious dysentery, which would require both quarantine and careful nursing. By the end of the year, he had recovered sufficiently to seek out the local taverns of Philadelphia. There he would make the acquaintance of Robert Aitken (sometimes "Aitkin"), a rival printer of Bache and a bookseller. It seems Bache had shown only passing interest in his father-in-law's protégé and had secured a modest tutoring position for him. Aitken advised Paine of his new *Pennsylvania Magazine*, just at that time being readied for the press, and invited Paine to write an introductory essay for the first number. Paine promptly responded with his first published essay independent of Franklin, a brief passage about the superiority of current culture to that of the ancients, and of the colonies to that of Europe. Amused and impressed, Aitken promptly named Paine editor. Providential, indeed!

During the remainder of 1775, Paine would keep busy with pen and press, providing ongoing essays for his *Magazine* under the *nom de plume* of "Atlanticus" or "Amicus," the previously promised separate essay against slavery on March 8 (*Justice and Humanity*), announcements with plates, of inventions introduced in Great Britain and as yet unknown in the colonies, multiple lyric odes (recalling his previous vocation in the taverns of London), including "On the Death of General Wolfe," a ballad with music commemorating the loss of Wolfe on the Plains of Abraham, and "A New Anecdote of Alexander the Great."[317] He was only starting and already had augmented the circulation of this publication by two hundred and fifty percent. Aitken had acquired his service for a salary of £50. It would be an investment over the ensuing eighteen months that would pay Aitken tremendous dividends. Paine would continue with essays in criticism of duels, criticism of cruelty toward animals, feminism, abolition of slavery (again!), abolition of the monarchy, federation of the colonies, revision of copyright laws, and binding arbitration in international trade. Paine was drawing incredible attention during his first year in Philadelphia; Franklin and the inner circle were quietly delighted. Paine's input in the American Revolution, initially a source of profound concern within the inner circle, would prove the bulwark of the entire process.

Franklin's 1774 would end in personal tragedy: his common-law wife, Deborah, would die from complications of a stroke just before Christmas.[318] His son William, himself now a self-professed loyalist, and privy to Tory commentary and gossip in a world that his father would never experience, perceived an ongoing undercurrent of animosity toward his father and implored him to get out of London and return home prior to Deborah's demise, but to no avail. Franklin had unsettled business of his own, and once again, his family, such as it was, took a back seat to his personal issues and concerns. He had pledged to Fothergill, and to Barclay, that he would indeed "take the high road" whenever offered in order to avoid the bloodshed of revolutionary warfare between Great Britain and her colonies. And in December 1774, this would be arranged by Fothergill personally in a series of personal discussions with the Howe family.[319]

The Howe family, at the dawn of the American Revolution, was one of the most formidable and influential gatherings of peers in a single family group.[320] The oldest brother, who carried the family title Lord Howe, was Richard, who had inherited the title from his oldest brother, who had died in the battle for Ticonderoga during the Seven Years' War. Richard would assume the command of the entire British fleet in America in 1776. Richard's younger brother, William, would be named commander-in-chief of the British army in North America upon the recall of General Gage in September 1775. And their reasonably outspoken older sister, Caroline, the thirty-eight-year-old widow of distant cousin Richard Howe (and therefore also "Lady Howe"), would be employed to entertain Dr. Benjamin Franklin at the family estate in the Christmas season of December 1774. This pretense would be used to allow discourse between Dr. Franklin and Lady Howe's two well-connected brothers. All three siblings were grandchildren of King George I and therefore second cousins to the Crown. On the second Tuesday of that month, Franklin accepted a personal invitation from Lady Caroline Howe to engage in a polite but competitive game of chess. Mrs. Howe was, by shades, demure but forthright in her chess and in her running commentary on the political relationship between London and the colonies.

H: "What is to be done about this dispute between Great Britain and her colonies?"

Fr: "They should kiss and be friends."

H: "I have often said that I wish the government would employ *you* to settle the dispute. I am sure that nobody could do it so well. Don't you think such a thing is practicable?"

Franklin, good-natured but not serious, responded that yes, it could still be solved, but not by him. Recalling the Cockpit yet again, he advised Mrs. Howe that he would never be an agent acceptable to the British government in such an endeavor. After accepting an invitation to return on Christmas afternoon for "another round of chess," Franklin went to Fothergill's in Harpur Street for a meeting with the inner circle.

Barclay this time took the lead. "I am quite convinced that thou couldst achieve successful mediation with Richard Howe. I would ask that thou make a plan for colonial reconciliation before thy next visit to their home."

Franklin remained skeptical but agreed and started writing "Hints for a Conversation," seventeen points of concession and conciliation that he felt could still achieve resolution without revolution.

And then a packet arrived from Philadelphia. It contained some of the minutes of the "First Continental Congress" as well as resolutions that seemed more threatening than conciliatory. It offered that the colonies felt that Parliament had far overstepped its bounds in the "coercive acts" against Massachusetts, but that the colonies remained loyal to the Crown. To that end, it proposed repeal of these acts by December 1, 1774; failing that, the colonies would have no choice but to boycott British imports to the colonies. Franklin, as agent for the colonies, dutifully presented the resolutions to Lord Dartmouth, along with his "Hints for a Conversation." In his turn, Dartmouth promised to present them to the Crown.

So Franklin returned to the Howe residence in Mayfair on Christmas afternoon, where Lady Caroline politely introduced him to her elder brother, Lord Richard Howe.[321] And Lord Howe, for his part, welcomed Franklin with exuberance and invited him to produce a statement of reconciliation suitable for review in the Board of Trade and the Privy Council. Franklin responded that Dartmouth was in receipt of such a document, adding that he personally had nothing further to append to the petition; it was quite satisfactory of itself. Lord Howe promised to confer with Dartmouth, and Franklin retired to the parlor for another series of chess matches with Lord Howe's older sister. Before his departure on that festive afternoon, Franklin secured yet another invitation for New Year's Day.

The new year of 1775 arrived on a Sunday, and Franklin hastened to Mayfair yet again. This time, Lord Howe appeared in the foyer, and the two men retired to Howe's study. Howe was more curt this time. "Do you think there might be value in sending an emissary from London to address your 'Continental Congress'?" Obviously, Dartmouth had shared the correspondence from Franklin's packet with Howe.

Franklin answered, "I think that it could be an excellent gesture, provided that the emissary is of rank and dignity."

Caroline now entered the study and the conversation. "Do you not think my brother, the Lord Howe, would be an excellent emissary for the Crown in this capacity?" She then looked to her brother. "I would think that you were a better emissary in that service than our brother William to be sent as a general of the army."

"I would think, Mrs. Howe, that Great Britain could provide William a more honorable employment."

Lord Howe breezed past the potential insult of Franklin's statement and produced a copy of the Dartmouth document, "Hints for a Conversation."

"Is this in your hand?" Franklin swallowed hard, but then answered in the affirmative. Howe replied that that was most unfortunate; the document as written was completely unacceptable to the Board of Trade, and he urged Dr. Franklin to make a better attempt. In so doing, Howe advised Franklin that a stance of contrition and reconciliation would be better received by the Privy Council and would ensure Franklin full pardon and "any reward in the power of the government to bestow."

Franklin snatched the document from Howe's hand, apologized for its content and for not staying for Mrs. Howe's entertainment, and departed. He was still smarting from the thought that Howe had offered a bribe and that Howe had actually thought that Franklin might well accept it. He felt Fothergill's and Barclay's enthusiasm for reconciliation rapidly fading away. But then William Pitt, Lord Chatham, attempted an eleventh-hour resolution and offered to present a plan to the House of Lords that would recognize the right of the Continental Congress to approve taxes and provide representation in Parliament.[322] The Crown would retain the privilege of sending troops for colonial defense and would allow Parliament to regulate British trade in North America, but nothing else. He begged Franklin to be in attendance at the House of Lords on February 1 for the presentation of the plan. Franklin reluctantly agreed.

In the meantime, Franklin contacted Dumas at The Hague.[323] Dumas was already dealing with fellow Huguenot refugees from Paris seeking asylum in Pennsylvania and had requested assistance from Franklin in helping these learned outcasts establish employment in Philadelphia. For his part, Franklin thought this could be a valuable method of aiding Dumas, thereby investing political capital in the career of this well-positioned diplomat. Franklin agreed to support their relocation to Philadelphia and to provide letters of introduction to Robert Morris. He was again quite conciliatory to Dumas in the overall tone of his correspondence. He felt a plan starting to grow.

On February 1, Franklin took a seat in the front row of the gallery of Lords, a place of prominence in line of sight and in status before the House.[324] Chatham made a powerful presentation outlining the plan of reconciliation toward the colonies, and then Dartmouth rose in well-rehearsed support. Now Franklin leaned forward; maybe there *was* yet a hope of recognition of colonial independence without bloodshed. But the next speaker was the Fourth Earl Sandwich (the initial namesake of the Hawaiian Islands and the perennial luncheon entrée), who almost took up Wedderburn's vilification of Franklin from the Cockpit! He averred that this "plan" could not possibly have been written by Chatham but rather had to come from one of the "bitterest and most mischievous enemies this country has ever known." He pointed directly at Dr. Franklin.

Chatham then attempted some damage control, but the plan was already shattered. Franklin stood fast in the gallery, refusing once again to respond to the political vituperation hurled into his face. But the sun was setting on Fothergill's last hope of peace. Franklin was privately pleased with the performance of Sandwich. The clear conclusion from his open invective directed at Franklin was a confirmation that he was, at that point, hopelessly paranoid over this American colonist with the worldly reputation and feared that Franklin was uniquely positioned to crush the entire British Empire. Sandwich had been warned that Franklin appeared to be conspiring in Westminster with some unnamed political figures in government against the Crown, and Sandwich was thereby spiraling into personal paranoia over Franklin's general influence in London. And insofar as Sandwich was Lord Admiral of the British Navy, that fear would serve Franklin quite well while embarrassing the largest naval power in the world.

True to his promise to the inner-circle Quakers, Franklin contacted a few remaining friends in the House of Lords, trying to find some common ground.[325] There was none. Now angered, he penned a petition to Lord Dartmouth demanding that Parliament provide reparations of no less than £100,000 for the blockade of Boston. Showing the petition to Thomas Walpole for his input, Walpole looked at it, read it, looked at Franklin, read it again, and looked at Franklin again, without comment. Franklin later commented, "He looked at me and the petition several times alternately, as if he apprehended me out of my senses."

Franklin dropped it. And then Chatham came to Franklin in early March, advising him to leave the country. "I can no longer guarantee your safety or well-being in London. There are many peers here that would have you taken to the Tower of London under an arrest warrant." That afternoon, Franklin booked passage on a packet ship for Philadelphia.

On March 14, at what would prove the final meeting of the inner circle prior to the outbreak of open warfare between Great Britain and the American colonies and their penultimate meeting ever, Barclay, having conveniently maneuvered by virtue of his financial status in London to assume a role as estate-holder for the Penn family, came with a message of the imminent demise of Thomas Penn in Stoke Poges, west of London.[326] Gathered at Harpur Street there was silence for a few moments; all eyes were on Franklin. His old nemesis, the man who was the maker of this thirty-year feast, was about to depart this mortal coil. How would Franklin respond? Was the game over?

Fr: "I suppose you, my dearest friends, are wondering whether this will resolve my heartfelt anger toward the Penn family. His son John remains the designated governor at this time, and independence of Pennsylvania is not currently assured. I have learned so much in these past ten years about myself, my adopted home city of Philadelphia, the government of Westminster, and the philosophy of the rights of man. And what I have apprehended in all this education is that Thomas Penn was never the problem,[327] but rather a symptom of the problem. The problem, for all of us, is the inherent corruption of a government that affords its power base to the few who, by accident of birth, have laid claim to the right to govern. None of this is currently changed, and until it is changed, we can never truly be free from bondage to Westminster.

In short, my dear friends, the death of Thomas Penn will change...*nothing*."[328]

P: "And so we continue?"

Fr: "As we have, and I believe we now understand our roles here. Thomas?"

P: "Yes, and I will continue to confer with Burke and Barre, and will keep you advised regularly and consistently on the mind and heart of Parliament.[329] Do not think for one moment that I lack the ability and wherewithal to sway Parliament, one way or another, to our cause. I will see to it. And at the same time, I will continue to monitor all the activities of the Privy Council through solid, intimate conversation with my most long-standing friend in Great Britain." And he gave the group a knowing wink.

Fr: "Barclay?"

B: "I have been in contact with Necker and with Grand, and they have responded favorably to our endeavor. I shall continue to work with Necker and his ministers and to communicate with Dumas through St. Eustatius and Amsterdam. I truly believe that both France and Spain are interested and willing to provide financial support for thy design. And never doth a thousand pounds sterling move, anywhere in Europe, without my foreknowledge."

Fr: "Doctor Fothergill?"

Fothergill sighed and set his eyeglasses on the table. "I must, at this time, express to thee my deep frustration and regret in my failing to secure a peaceful independence for thy colony, and thy friends in America, while preserving a reconciliation with my beloved nation.[330] In this I have failed thee, and this thine inner circle of friends. I apprehend that I have little left to offer in thy service beyond my communications to thee and thy friends, and my ongoing prayers on thy behalf."

Franklin reached out and squeezed Fothergill's forearm. "You have been nothing less than the most loyal of my friends, and the most sincere. Your efforts to secure peaceful independence for the colonies cannot be minimized and were well worth the attempt.[331] I will make no further demands upon your time but will always accept your correspondence eagerly and with great consideration. Your medical care for my many afflictions and complaints has brought me great solace in times of pain and has preserved a future vision for all men. Your prayers can be nothing but a great blessing for our colonies, and I can only hope that they continue through to our success."

"Thou art most kind, and most gracious. I shall not forget and shall also eagerly look for thy correspondence in the coming months. Be safe in thy travels and greet dear Benezet on my behalf."

There was, in that moment, little more to say. In a world where men rarely lived beyond age sixty, two members of the circle were already clearly well past their prime years, and their future was most uncertain. Fothergill would not live to see the successful end of the American Revolution. Franklin, for his part, would despair his own survival during the ensuing ten years but would always make it through. And while Franklin was at this point almost assured of the success of the plan, he could not foresee another eight years of constant exertion before realization of his dream. But always on his mind were the portentous words from Hume: "The path to success is wholly dependent upon the survival of the architect. Without him, the endeavor will die a natural death." The three men departed from Harpur Street while Fothergill's gentleman tidied the study and began extinguishing lamps.

On March 21, 1775, Thomas Penn drew his final breath and passed away. Dr. Franklin was two days out to sea, on his way home to Philadelphia for the first time since 1765. Before he would arrive in Philadelphia, indeed while still in the middle of the Atlantic, on April 19, British soldiers would move on the armory at Concord, Massachusetts and be met by militia from the Massachusetts colony. At Lexington, the British would fire upon the militia, killing eight. These same British soldiers would not be so fortunate, after finding the Concord Armory emptied. The style of guerrilla warfare that had so devastated Edward Braddock twenty years previously would cost over two hundred British regulars their lives or limbs as the Brits attempted the return march to Boston.[332]

එ

Chapter 21

T he Second Continental Congress, with Benjamin Franklin arriving on May 5, would read like a "Who's Who of Founding Fathers" two hundred fifty years thereafter: Washington, Jefferson, Madison, Adams, and Hancock were all arriving in Philadelphia at that time.[333] Franklin would remain almost eerily silent during many of the subsequent sessions, to that familiar point of outrage for John Adams: "I cannot fathom the esteem shown to this man, sitting in silence, a great part of the time fast asleep in his chair." It wasn't that Franklin was disinterested; he was simply on page three hundred of the inner circle's imaginary *Biography of an Independent United States* while everyone else was still reading the prologue. And as he sat in Philadelphia in meeting after meeting of committee after committee that summer, he knew two things that only five men on the planet knew at that point in time: 1) the colonies were going to war against Great Britain, and 2) Great Britain, the most powerful empire in the world at that time, didn't have a prayer.[334]

Thomas Paine notably brightened with the return of Franklin to Philadelphia in May 1775. Paine was already drawing attention with his ongoing editorials in the *Pennsylvania Gazette*. He and Franklin would discuss the timing of the publication of the document that both men knew would seal the fate of independence throughout the colonies. Not yet, too early. Not quite yet.

Franklin would sojourn in the American colonies for only sixteen months and then head back to Europe. But in that relatively tight timeframe, he would embark upon a literal tarantella of activity, serving on multiple committees of the Second Continental Congress, ostensibly helping lay out the groundwork in ramping up to revolution, while quietly carrying out his personal plan of resolution, having, within the inner circle, already laid out an entire design that was more straightforward than the American patriots could have imagined. Early in the session of the congress, William Bradford, now operating his father's print shop in Philadelphia, advised James Madison that many of the delegates had begun "to entertain a great suspicion that Dr. Franklin came rather as a spy than as a friend, and that he means to discover our weak side and make his peace with the ministers [of Westminster]."[335] John Adams was even more frustrated with the presence of Franklin in their midst and would never miss an opportunity to disparage Franklin behind his back. In retrospect, they had nothing to fear; Franklin's zeal exceeded that of the lot, and his plan was already playing out perfectly.

In that same month of May 1775, Franklin traveled with his grandson, Temple, back to New Jersey to meet with the governor of New Jersey, William Franklin, son of Benjamin and father of Temple.[336] While Benjamin spoke pointedly of William moving New Jersey toward revolution, William told his father that he felt this to be an impolitical move at that point in time and encouraged him to hedge his bets. There was, at that point, still much talk throughout the colonies of looking toward reconciliation with Great Britain; Benjamin did not tip his hand at that moment but instead focused on his need for Temple to be available to him. They agreed to let Temple stay with his father that summer, but only with the understanding that he would return to Philadelphia in the fall to attend college there. Their parting was polite, but little more. Their paths were rapidly diverging.

One major outgrowth of this conciliatory sentiment in Philadelphia that summer was the "Olive Branch Petition," which was approved by the Congress to send directly to His Majesty, George III.[337] It was, in short, an expression of contrition to a point, with a direct appeal to the Crown to mediate peace with Parliament in terms agreeable to both sides. Franklin, for the sake of unity in the colonies, agreed to sign his name to this, along with the other delegates. But at the same time, he knew full well that 1) he was then adamantly opposed to such an effort, and 2) so was the Crown.[338] By this point in the Congressional session, he was already serving on the Committee of Safety, requiring him to be in session at 6:00 a.m. daily, and it was here that he would begin to show his true colors, drawing up a declaration for General Washington that expressed colonial sentiment about the incoherency of the British stance on taxation: the Americans had to repay the British government for the cost of defense in the colonies.[339] Here Franklin and Washington called out the lie, stating that the "defenses" were already being borne, in both manpower and capital, by the colonists themselves.

Bradford would, after the Washington/Franklin declaration was approved in Congress, now assure Madison that the suspicions about Franklin had fallen away. He was clearly moving toward revolution. Toward the end of July, Franklin revealed the old plan he and Thomas Pownall had drawn up for the Albany congress of 1754.[340] The inner circle had made some modifications during 1774, which provided for independence from the mother country, while not totally excluding reconciliation. But the form of government was clearly geared more toward an executive based in Philadelphia than London. Without mention of Pownall, Fothergill, or Barclay, Franklin read the plan into the minutes of the Second Continental Congress but did not move for a vote. This was radical by half, and at that point there were not more than five or six people on the planet in agreement with it. Franklin could wait.

He had no time to spend "politicking" on this issue.[341] A committee was formed to separate the postal service from the Crown; Franklin was appointed chair. A committee was formed to pursue the establishment of a colonial currency system; Franklin was appointed to that committee. A committee was formed to address the issue of Indigenous persons, and trade within their nations, as well as those of Europe; Franklin was appointed to that committee. A committee was formed to pursue acquisition of lead for shot, and gunpowder;

Franklin slyly *volunteered* for that committee, having already formulated some plans with Barclay and Dumas. And then Pennsylvania's delegation asked him to assist with a plan of defense specifically for that colony, as he had provided similarly during King George's War as well as during the French and Indian War. Then Congress turned around and formed a Committee of Colonial Defense of its own, appointing Franklin Chair and directing him to meet with Washington in Cambridge, Massachusetts in October.

Now many of the delegates began to see Franklin in a new light: not only was he revolutionary, but it almost appeared as if he had previously orchestrated this entire enterprise somehow...

Franklin and two other committee members travelled to Cambridge in October 1775 to meet with Washington and the preliminary "Continental Army."[342] Now it was Franklin's turn to get out the notes provided from Pownall. He urged Washington to always consider a "Fabian strategy," both offensively and defensively, to preserve his army for a potential long haul. He proposed rules and strategies to maintain discipline in the ranks, straight from Lord Loudoun's directives to Pownall. And then from Pownall's own theories on dragoons and the "flying military," he discussed provisioning the army with portable rations, and the vigilance toward a favorable time for a decisive victory, when the opportunity presented itself to the faster army.

At this point, Washington took the opportunity of expanding upon the topic of rations and provisions for his army and advised Franklin of the importance of keeping his volunteer force well-compensated and well-fed. Here Franklin immediately went to the counsel from Barclay, assuring Washington that friends in Europe were at the ready to assist in that regard, and at the same time laying out money from his own pocket, thus also carrying out Barclay's recommendation of portraying "Franklin the spendthrift." Washington was pleasantly surprised as Franklin counted out £100 Crown sterling and pressed the sack into his hand.[343] The men exchanged smiles; it was the high point of the military summit.

It was during Franklin's visit that he had a quiet conversation one afternoon with Washington as they took a restful walk along the pasture fence where the officers' horses were grazing. Standing at the rail, they watched the horses swishing their tails and occasionally biting at their shoulders over the ubiquitous stable flies. Franklin offered, "The horses look miserable."

W: "Yes, and until we have a hard freeze, the flies will continue to pester them."

Franklin watched a bit longer as the horses twitched their ears repeatedly and swatted at the flies with their tails. "So who is winning?"

W: "I beg your pardon, Dr. Franklin?"

F: "Who is winning?"

W: "Between the stable flies and the horses? The horses, being much larger, I suppose have the upper hand here."

F: "And yet the flies persist and keep up their barrage. What do you suppose the horses will do?"

W: "They will finally have their fill of it and head to water. The flies will not follow them there."

F: "And so the flies end up with the pasture, and the horses return to the water."

Franklin now turned and looked directly at Washington. "Never forget the stable flies and the horses." Washington first looked puzzled but then grinned and nodded.

On November 29, 1775, the Second Continental Congress approved a Committee of Secret Correspondence.[344] The "Secret" part is somewhat misleading; as a federation of colonies, rather than an officially recognized nation in the eyes of any European state, America had no status to pursue assistance or alliance with other nations. But this did not deter the delegates from pursuing "friends of the colonies" in Europe who 1) had large purses and 2) did not like Great Britain very much. It was this committee, as much or more so than any other committee, including defense, that Franklin *had* to direct, insofar as much of this work in Europe had also already been prepared by Barclay and his sphere of financial colleagues.[345] Franklin had been advised by Barclay back in July that an emissary would be arriving in Philadelphia before the end of the year, sent from a high-ranking government official in

France. Having no official standing at that time to receive such a dignitary, Franklin feared that this somewhat brash move threatened to expose the efforts of the inner circle regarding solicitation of foreign aid. He hoped that by being a member of the Secret Correspondence Committee, he would have the basis to proceed with these negotiations without raising suspicion as to how the visit had come about. Furthermore, Franklin would need his "man in the colonies," Robert Morris, to be a part of this committee as well. Between them, they would direct the flow of both materiel and capital into the colonies throughout the revolution, and they would not brook any efforts to expose the tight network of men and influence that this effort would require. In this regard he prevailed, and ultimately the committee would include *three* delegates from Pennsylvania, adding John Dickinson, a relatively reluctant revolutionary in the early months. Once again, Franklin went into action with a whirlwind of activity.

In less than a month, he was advised of the arrival of an emissary from France, Julien Alexandre Achard de Bonvouloir, who helped cover Franklin's project by claiming to have arrived from Quebec. In actuality, he was serving as a confidential agent of Charles Gravier, Comte de Vergennes, the foreign minister under Louis XVI.[346] To greet him, Franklin brought a second agent, François Daymons, who worked as a bilingual librarian in Philadelphia, and John Jay, the delegate on the Secret Correspondence Committee from New York. Franklin advised that committee that in order to avoid drawing undue attention to this meeting, he did not want the entire committee to be present. Fortuitously, almost incredibly, they all accepted that line of argument, and the meeting (actually *two* meetings, several days apart) proceeded without incident or suspicion.

Achard advised Franklin and Jay that while the Court of Louis XVI was indeed sympathetic to the cause of the American colonies and would enjoy nothing more than vengeance for the previous defeat by the British in the French and Indian Wars, he could make no public declaration thereby, but rather would "enable" the gift of ₶1,000,000 to the cause of the American colonies by clandestine sources. He would further encourage support from

Spain and the Netherlands as well. At the conclusion of the second meeting on December 27, Franklin immediately sent word to Thomas Paine and advised him that the time had come; the French were in.[347] Paine headed to the printer's, carrying a fifty-page manuscript. Franklin then dashed off a letter to Dumas in The Hague, advising him (prematurely) that he, Dumas, had been retained by the Continental Congress as agent in the United Provinces in order to seek out nations amenable to commercial treaties with the colonies, as well as to secure the services of two military engineers, one for fortifications and one for field work.[348] In the letter he enclosed £100 sterling. Dumas would receive this correspondence ecstatically: he was now working for Dr. Franklin and America!

Jay thought that Achard's message was excellent news and was ready to convey this to the committee as a whole. Franklin, feigning circumspection, urged Jay to keep the content of the meeting in confidence until they were able to solicit and receive some sort of confirmation of this message from Paris. In reality, Franklin needed time to get a response to Barclay, through Dumas, via St. Eustatius and the Hague, which would take some two to three months. Feverishly, Franklin wrote Dumas to recommend that Barclay contact Vergennes immediately and funnel the funds through the Abbé Desnoyers and the Roman Catholic "Peter's Pence" to the church in Baltimore under the name of Robert Morris of Philadelphia.[349] By the end of February, Franklin deemed that there was ample lead time for Barclay, Dumas, and Desnoyers to conduct their surreptitious business in the Netherlands. At that time, a meeting of the Secret Committee was finally held to allow Jay to announce the support of France. Immediately, the committee named Silas Deane to serve as special (secret) agent for the colonies to France, and Deane began making his departure plans. Franklin was initially less than pleased with this choice but ultimately acquiesced so as not to draw further undesired attention to his clearly odd behavior of the past year.

Chapter 22

Meanwhile, the treatise that would be known to posterity as *Common Sense* by an anonymous (at the time) author was having an impact far beyond that which anyone other than Franklin and Paine ever could have predicted.[350] From Charleston, South Carolina to Boston, it became a topic of conversation in every coffee house and publick house. In terms of percentage readership in the colonies, it remains the single best-selling publication in American history. In essence, the author had clearly asserted that the colonies should pursue independence as a *nation*. By February 1776, Franklin was openly acknowledging the authorship by Paine, and by the time of the Declaration that summer, over 200,000 copies of the pamphlet were in circulation. The overwhelming sentiment of the politicians was, by that point, in the direction of independence. Paine was leading the way.

At this point in February 1776, Franklin was dispatched by the Second Continental Congress as envoy to, of all places, Canada, and specifically Quebec, to attempt to enlist those colonies in rebellion against the Crown.[351] Without belaboring the gruesome specifics of this diplomatic disaster, suffice it to say that Franklin physically barely survived this three-month debacle, the Canadians swore allegiance to the Crown and ordered the Americans to leave immediately, and Franklin returned to Philadelphia in late May in marginal health; he truly believed he might not survive the month. Deane was already finishing his preparations to depart to Paris.

But friends in Philadelphia reassured Franklin that he was returning to good news, as Richard Henry Lee of Virginia had already moved to resolutions of independence, with six colonies in agreement.[352] As he recovered his health, Franklin now learned that he had been appointed to the committee to draft a "Declaration of Independency" for all the British colonies from the St. Lawrence River to the Okefenokee Swamp. The full committee included Thomas Jefferson of Virginia, John Adams of Massachusetts, Roger Sherman of Connecticut, and Robert Livingston of New York. While all were formidably bright gentlemen of letters, they agreed, with Franklin in full support, that Jefferson should provide the framework for what would become the single most august document of the Revolution. And Jefferson rose mightily to the task. With minimal editing, the final document was produced in time for the vote, on July 2, 1776. While Jefferson felt that the truths therein espoused were "sacred and undeniable," it was Franklin who would overwrite, *We hold these truths to be* self-evident, *that all men are created equal.*[353] The Davids, Hume and Barclay, would have been proud.

The vote for Richard Henry Lee's motion to ratify the Declaration was debated on July 2, and Franklin's colleague and erstwhile friend John Dickinson made it quite clear to the entire Congress that Pennsylvania was not authorized to take this degree of liberty in voting for liberty. And in that moment, Franklin seized control of his delegation specifically and of the Congress generally and spontaneously and uncharacteristically blurted out, "Pennsylvania votes 'aye'!"

Dickinson immediately interjected, "With my abstention." The remainder of the Pennsylvania delegation remained silent, and the vote was therefore duly noted.[354] The next step for the inner circle had just taken place.

Stratford Hall was the legendary plantation home of Thomas and Hannah Lee, the parents of sons Philip Ludwell Lee, Richard Henry Lee, Thomas Ludwell Lee, Francis Lightfoot Lee, William Lee, and Arthur Lee, and two daughters, Hannah Ludwell Lee and Alice Lee.[355] After the death of the elder Hannah in 1749 and the elder Thomas the following year, the sons pretty much assumed ownership of the plantation and proceeded to lives of public service in varying roles. To this end, they remained one of the most prominent political families in the entire British colonies in the lead-in to the revolution. With cousin Henry Lee III playing a leadership role in Washington's army, the family would remain in the public eye for the ensuing generation. The seventh and eighth children of the family, William and Arthur, would seek roles of prominence as well, but were less successful, as we shall see.

Oddly, at the end of the month, Lord Richard Howe, now commander of the British military in North America, and Admiral of the Navy, reached out to Franklin yet again, and clearly under the insistence of the Crown, offering reconciliation with the promise for pardons for all the colonists (secretly, John Adams had been excluded from this offer of pardons, with the plan for his trial and execution in London).[356] The wording of this final offer was clumsy by half; Franklin responded in exasperation after reading the document to Congress on July 30. *[Your offer of pardons] can have no other effect than that of increasing our resentments.*

Pardons?? Pardons?? The Crown and Parliament had treated the American colonists as second-class citizens for the past ten years and ignored their pleas for mediation and fairness. And now the Crown came with pardons? But Franklin then shifted his stance and advised Howe that were Great Britain to offer independence for the colonies, peace negotiations would be worthwhile. Howe's response to Franklin's letter was subdued, and he declined to send a written version. They would initiate a personal meeting in Staten Island in August that would prove futile. Franklin wanted full independence from the Crown; Howe wanted a recognized America still within the empire. There would be no further "common ground."

In October, Franklin would be named to the one position he actively sought and absolutely had to have: minister to France on behalf of the colonies.[357] But this would be a delegation, including Silas Deane, already dispatched, as well as Thomas Jefferson. Franklin felt that Jefferson would be a welcome addition whom Franklin could control effectively. Silas Deane would prove more problematic, as it would remain unclear how sincere a patriot he truly was. But the worst was yet to come for Franklin and the inner circle. Jefferson declined this appointment, with its indefinite term of duty, "until the close of hostilities between the Colonies and the Crown," due to the chronic illness of his wife (she would not survive to see the Treaty of Paris of 1783), and Congress, in his place, appointed...Arthur Lee.

Arthur Lee, fifth son and eighth child of Thomas and Hannah Lee of Stratford Hall, Virginia, was born in 1740 and was sent by his family to Eton in England for elementary education, followed by matriculation at the University of Edinburgh, for medicine.[358] At that time Edinburgh was arguably the single most prestigious medical school in the world. Graduating in 1764, Lee would practice medicine for only five years before becoming weary of it. He entered the Inns of Court in London in 1770 and was accepted to the British bar by 1774. At that time, he was retained to assist Franklin as agent for the colony of Massachusetts. When Franklin returned to Philadelphia in March 1775, Lee accepted the role of primary agent for the colonies in London.[359]

Lee was fully dedicated to his family at Stratford Hall, to Virginia, and to the colonies, in that order. To that end, he was advised toward the end of 1775 that a French agent, Beaumarchais, was attempting to arrange a secret shipment of weapons, uniforms, and supplies to the American colonies in support of their insurrection. At that time he was unaware of the source of the capital supplying this gift; he [360]was advised that the French Crown had *no* role in this gift and would disavow any knowledge of its existence. Lee was, of course, unaware of the inner circle of Franklin, Pownall, Fothergill, and Barclay. But he was more than happy to advance a claim of responsibility for negotiating this gift.[361] John Jay of New York was most impressed with this diplomatic *tour de force* from the Massachusetts agent from Virginia and would subsequently insist that Lee be given diplomatic status in France. Jay would remain a devoted supporter of Arthur Lee for the next ten years and absolutely insisted that he replace Jefferson in France.

Now, in fall 1776, Franklin assessed his status in the role of minister to France. The inner circle had presumed that this would be a solo appointment, and now Franklin would have to take ownership of this development and revise the plans to funnel materiel to the colonies. It was clear to the inner circle that *no one* in the American colonies had yet grasped the impossibility of the ministries to the various nations and crowns of Europe by the revolutionary patriots. As yet, they were only beginning to accept the concept of a "United States of America." They lacked a formal leader, with Henry Laurens eagerly serving as president of the Continental Congress, but with unclear authority. Therefore, there were no "diplomatic credentials" to be issued to the various ministers. There was no national currency with which to negotiate grants and loans. There were no authorizations for the incurring of debt by the ministers. There was no national seal with which to ratify treaties and alliances with European nations. And in the end, the divers ministers were seeking financial support for an effort to, well, to *overthrow a European monarchy*. What European monarch would contribute millions for such a cause? Of all the citizens in the American colonies at that time, there was precisely and uniquely *one* person who carried the prestige, the charm, the negotiating skills, the awareness of the challenges of European diplomacy, the sophistication, and the self-confidence, to successfully navigate these treacherous waters during this treacherous time. And he did not need the assistance of two inept "ministers" to assist him.

Silas Deane was a man of meager resources, and his loyalty could be easily purchased for security in the French foreign service. Arthur Lee would be more problematic: he was loyal to a fault but was young, extraordinarily imperious, and inexperienced in the ways of European diplomacy in that era. Furthermore, his personal proclivities made him perpetually suspicious of the potential for betrayal by those with whom he worked. It would prove a miserable way to live his life and would make him quite susceptible to duplicity and plotting against him. Franklin had recognized this weakness when the two men were yet in London. In 1773, with no other "takers," Arthur Lee proudly arranged for the appointment of his older brother William to replace Sir William Plomer in the office of "Sheriff of London." Little did he realize at the time that Franklin, Pownall, and the Club of Honest Whigs were laughing hysterically behind his back at this development.

"Sheriff of London" was the legislated prerequisite for anyone seeking the subsequent office of "Lord Mayor of London." Thus it was something of an obligatory post for those commoners seeking access to the halls of Westminster, but it was a terrible position: upon being elected or appointed sheriff, the dupe was immediately forced to swear an oath of loyalty to the Crown and to *pay* a surety bond, which was invariably forfeited, of £300 to the same Crown. From there, the poor individual was expected to retain at least six assistants, out of his own resources, as he would be tasked with procuring defendants to appear at Court in the Old Bailey upon subpoena, financing their daily upkeep while they were held in custody, and bearing the expenses of all this transportation and gaol supervision. It was a financial sinkhole, and according to court records dating back centuries, no one ever served a second term as Sheriff of London. They simply couldn't, and wouldn't, afford it. For a post that paid £200 *per annum*, it typically cost at least three times that much to perform properly. And in the end it held no *guarantee* that the office holder would indeed rise to the office of Lord Mayor.

So, by Franklin's arrival in Paris in December 1776, he knew precisely what he needed to do. Deane would serve a perfect foil and cover for Franklin during the first year of the revolution, but he would need to be recalled. Lee would need to be embarrassed and his incompetence exposed to the American government in order to accomplish his recall from Paris as well. Both tasks were well within Franklin's purview and within his control. Franklin spoke with his secretary, Edward Bancroft; he needed one favor from Bancroft and another from Barclay's friends in London.

Chapter 23

E dward Bancroft was born in Westfield, Massachusetts, January 20, 1745.[362] His father would die in the following year from a seizure. Five years later, his mother would remarry; the young family would move frequently within Massachusetts, but by 1759, they were living in and operating a tavern in Hartford, Connecticut. There they would solicit the services of a tutor for young Edward, a recent graduate of Yale College named Silas Deane. This acquaintance would rekindle eighteen years later, in France. By 1760, the family was in Killingsworth, with Edward apprenticed to a physician named Benjamin Gale. He would subsequently run away to Barbados, never completing his training. From Barbados, he went to Suriname in South America, where he wheedled a job as "plantation surgeon" just long enough to give him some savings in silver. He then embarked upon studies in tropical botany and zoology in the area, and with carefully compiled notes, he would later produce a noted textbook of his observations. Perhaps more importantly for his later life, he also developed a yellow dye from the bark of black oak trees specific to South America, which he styled "quercitron." This would become his "get rich quick scheme." which would rule his financial status for much of the remainder of his life. For the most part, his expenditures in bringing his miracle dye to the linen draping industry in Great Britain would leave him chronically tipping at the brink of bankruptcy and at the risk of debtors' prison.

By 1767, he was sailing for England, where he would maintain residence for the remainder of his life.[363] In 1769, he produced *An Essay on the Natural History of Guiana* and signed it Dr. Edward Bancroft. He would keep the title for the remainder of his life as well. One section of his zoological observations was devoted to the torporific, or *electric* eel, and Bancroft would observe for the first time that the shock could occur by touching the fish with an iron rod, or conversely, by touching another *person* who was touching the fish with an iron rod. Indeed, the eel was self-generating electricity. The "electricians" world was fascinated by this discovery.

Soon after the appearance of this text, he would apply as a pupil to St. Bartholomew's Hospital under the tutelage of Dr. William Pitcairn.[364] It was during that time that he would make the acquaintance of Franklin and Pownall, and, encouraged by their tutorials on the American colonies of his youth, he would produce his *Remarks* in direct challenge to the opinions of Knox and Grenville. This would provide him notoriety in London political circles for the ensuing ten years. In August 1774, Franklin recommended Bancroft as a reviewer of scientific books and articles to one Ralph Griffiths, editor of the London *Monthly Review*.[365] This popular publication allowed the erudite readers of London the opportunity to read reviews of various new works, of which they might otherwise have been unaware. And Bancroft was a skilled writer and reviewer. Within four months, he was being published and quoted in the streets for the *Monthly Review*.

At this time, Bancroft invested in the "Vandalia Company," land speculators in what is now West Virginia, including Franklin, Thomas Walpole, and Samuel Wharton of Philadelphia. He also invested heavily in his personal project regarding the production of quercitron. He had forwarded significant funds to his brother Daniel to secure bark from the South American trees to send by ship to London. Unfortunately, 1775 would prove an extremely volatile time in the shipping industry due to Parliamentary actions far beyond Bancroft's control (the *Intolerable Acts*, v.s.). By 1776, he was severely in debt and had a wife and three children he was struggling to support. Franklin had gone back to

America. Pownall was involved with his own wife and newly acquired family. Bancroft was suddenly vulnerable to speculators that needed his assistance.

For over two hundred years now, Edward Bancroft has been the subject of extensive speculation and suspicion as to his role in the American Revolution. In 1889, over one hundred years after the revolution, Great Britain revealed for the first time that Bancroft was a "secret agent" for the British government. This was immediately interpreted as "spying against his home colonies," but this has been an over-reaching conclusion, not supported by the evidence at hand.[366] While it is not our purpose to speculate on Bancroft's role in Franklin's French enterprise, suffice it to say that in a nutshell, Franklin was well aware of the source of Bancroft's subsistence while he lived in Paris/Passy in the company of Franklin. Bancroft was approached in late 1775 by Paul Wentworth, a British agent born in New Hampshire who had come to London and was fully supported by Lord Suffolk in exchange for divers "favors" in defense of the Crown and in opposition to the American colonies.[367] Wentworth could truly be considered a traitor to his home colonies and was an active recruiter for informants in London. Lord Auckland and Lord Weymouth would approach Bancroft, offering him cash in exchange for any information he could provide, in a timely fashion, on the American colonies. "What kind of information?" Ships departing for the colonies from the European mainland, the nature of the cargo, the nationality of the ship and crew, the date of departure, all these were of value to some degree. The extent of the degree of value was negotiable with each transaction. Bancroft saw no concern in this type of transaction, since the information was readily and openly available to anyone who wished to take the trouble to gather it, and readily agreed.

William Eden, Lord Auckland, would henceforth consider Edward Bancroft an agent for the British government, and, as his passage of information was to be directed only to Wentworth or to Eden, it was, of a sort, "secret." And therefore, Bancroft could be considered a…"secret agent."[368] But only insofar as he was an agent of Great Britain selling secrets. Beyond that, Bancroft kept none of his activities secret from Dr. Franklin.[369] Indeed, Franklin would readily advise personal friends, when asked, that Bancroft was a "spy for the

Crown." He seemed to find it rather amusing, as it afforded him a secretary for whom he had to pay no regular stipend; George III was providing that service for him.

Furthermore, Bancroft did not hesitate to agree to Franklin's two requests: information on British military strategy against the colonies that might prove timely enough to allow Franklin time to advise Washington (anything to occur within the ensuing two months or less could not be relayed with a sufficient time allowance for a response); and a diplomatic *faux pas* directed against Arthur Lee that would provide embarrassment sufficient to necessitate his recall to Philadelphia.[370] Bancroft promised to see what he could do. Both proved quite doable, and Bancroft delivered with remarkable promptness. The Arthur Lee debacle was choreographed by the British foreign ministry to a "T." It left Lee with a black mark on his diplomatic record, which would prove insurmountable, and in the end would afford Franklin the justification to have him sent back to the colonies.

Franklin's other pressing issue, however, proved to be Silas Deane. Deane was the first agent sent to France by the Second Continental Congress, having appointed him on March 2, 1776. He departed that summer for France, six months ahead of Franklin, and with Deane aboard ship was the French minister Joseph Matthias Gérard de Rayneval, who would volunteer to assist Deane as interpreter; it seems that Deane, hastily appointed as agent to France, spoke absolutely *no* French. During the voyage, Deane and Gérard discussed and disputed the cause of the American colonies. Gérard also advised Deane that there was money to be made in the diplomatic service of any nation in Europe. Indeed, as to this day, many of the "deals" between nations were accomplished by bribery and subterfuge, and in that realm, the ministers were first in line as recipients of the largesse of other nations. In the end, Gérard would give Deane wagering odds on the long-term viability of America. Deane, in a vulnerable moment, accepted the odds *against* American survival. This regrettable decision would impact the remainder of Deane's life.

Silas Deane was born January 4, 1738 in Groton, Connecticut, son of a blacksmith also named Silas Deane.[371] Deane was a bright student and was able to "pension" (obtain a scholarship grant) to Yale College, graduating in 1758. Shortly thereafter, he was retained by the Bull family to tutor a stepson, Edward Bancroft; this was the beginning of a life-long friendship between tutor and student. Subsequently, Deane was admitted to the bar but soon garnered greater success as a merchant and as a bridegroom. He would marry, and be widowed, twice, both times to a widow with significant financial resources from a first marriage (in this, his life would echo that of Thomas Pownall to a remarkable degree!). By 1776, he had served as a representative in the Connecticut Assembly and as a delegate to the First Continental Congress. There he would enter into a dispute with a fellow Connecticut delegate, far more politically connected and personally domineering, Roger Sherman, over the appointment of Israel Putnam to Washington's military staff. Turned out from Congress as a result by the Connecticut Assembly, Deane's consolation prize, at the insistence of John Jay of New York, was the agency to France. Once again, Jay had inserted himself into the discussion of foreign ministry appointees, as a self-styled "expert," but more bluntly as a Franklin wannabe. His presence in Congress would prove a vexation for Franklin and his colleagues for the remainder of the revolution.

Deane arrived in Bordeaux, France on June 6, 1776, and immediately sent a dispatch to his former student Bancroft in London, praying him to come to Paris to assist in the affairs of the American colonies.[372] He enclosed £30 in British coin to defray travel costs. Anticipating this action, Franklin had already advised Bancroft of Deane's impending arrival, so Bancroft had made provisions to respond promptly. Bancroft arrived in Paris on July 6, Deane on July 7, and the two met for strategic planning on July 8. By July 11, they had been whisked to Versailles to meet with the French secretary for Foreign Affairs, le Comte de Vergennes, and his under-secretary Conrad-Alexandre Gérard de Rayneval, the brother of Deane's recent acquaintance on the Atlantic crossing. Deane mostly listened (remember, he spoke no French); Vergennes was direct and blunt. France would not recognize the American colonies but were disposed toward assistance, provided it was discreet and not traceable to the French Crown. Further, Deane was never again to talk to Vergennes.

All correspondence, verbal and written, was to be addressed to Gérard only. Finally, Deane was warned that Lord Stormont, British ambassador to France, had spies everywhere, and Deane had to maintain strict discretion and encrypt all correspondence.

Deane was, in a word, overwhelmed.[373] With no diplomatic experience and no ability to speak to the French in their own peculiar idioms, he was at a loss as to how to proceed. He contacted Arthur Lee in London, who was, at that time, only the agent for Massachusetts; he had no status with the Continental Congress. But Deane was frantic for American assistance and conversations in English. He also sent notification to Dumas in The Hague as to his arrival in Paris, because Dumas was at that point the only other official "minister" in the American foreign service.[374] Now Gérard stepped in to aid Deane: he put Deane in touch with Jacques-Donatien Le Ray de Chaumont and Pierre-Augustin Caron de Beaumarchais. Le Ray was a wealthy merchant and landowner, as well as minister of Blois; Beaumarchais was, well, it's complicated. Beaumarchais was, by parts, a magician, a seamstress, a stand-up comedian, a playwright, a statesman, a politician, and a self-confessed charlatan. In a word, he enjoyed intrigue.[375] And the American cause was the single most intriguing issue he had ever encountered. He was fascinated, and sworn to assistance, by whatever arcane route he could devise. And he deliberately made the pathway to assistance so complex as to avoid detection throughout the revolution. He had mastered the art of sleight-of-hand; it would prove a valuable tool for Franklin and his colleagues.

Through some method of unseen pulling of strings, finances had suddenly appeared readily available. Beaumarchais was afforded one million livres in French gold coin, handed to him personally, to conceal in his home. He was assured that that mysterious source was going to provide another one million livres in *Spanish* coin in the coming month, somehow arriving from Madrid. These were to be used to purchase French muskets and powder, shipped in unmarked crates, to the West Indies. Beaumarchais created his own black-market company for this industry, giving it a French/Spanish flair: *Roderigue Hortalez et Compagnie*. The name reeked of Beaumarchais. At the same time, he arranged a scrap metal drive for old and unusable muskets and other firearms, the rustier and more broken the better. These too were crated and marked with Beaumarchais's new company stamp and sent for shipment to Portsmouth, Virginia, and Baltimore, Maryland. Beaumarchais and Gérard were in full expectation that that shipment would be intercepted by a British blockade, and in that they were not disappointed. When the Brits off-loaded the shipment just outside the American coast, they discovered the condition of the contraband firearms, which would be the source of ridicule directed by the British toward the Second Continental Congress for many months. They laughingly repacked the worthless firearms and allowed them to be transported to their destinations. Congress was mortified at the condition of this "gift"; Adams registered his outrage.[376] The unmarked shipment was directed to St. Eustatius and Havana, to the attention of Oliver Pollock. From Havana, Pollock would take the new weapons through New Orleans and on to Fort Pitt.

Deane by that time had received responses from Arthur Lee and Charles Dumas. Lee advised Deane, with the sniff almost discernable in the letter, that he was "predisposed by important business in Westminster and could not depart for Paris until some later time." In actuality, he was doing little more than assisting his brother William in their endeavors as sheriff and alderman of London. Dumas was more evasive, simply advising Deane that he was already providing essential aid to the American colonies through his contacts in The Hague and would continue all conversation by encrypted correspondence. Deane's only friend during that summer was Edward Bancroft. And in August, Bancroft left Deane in Paris and returned to London.[377] Shortly thereafter, Wentworth pounced upon Bancroft, drawing him into Eden's web of artifice.

Chapter 24

Whn Deane, and Lee independently, advised the Second Continental Congress of the success with procuring arms and ammunition, Franklin decided that it was time for him to book departure from the colonies, both to carry out the French mission and to avoid British confrontation in, and possible extradition from, the colonies. By October he was aboard an American packet ship headed to Cherbourg, along with two grandsons: seventeen-year-old William "Temple" Franklin (the illegitimate son of William Franklin and an unnamed mother) and seven-year-old Benjamin "Benny" Bache, son of Richard Bache and Franklin's daughter, Sarah Franklin Bache.[378] Benny would soon be safely placed in school; Temple would prove invaluable to his grandfather in his massive correspondence and the perfect alternative to Bancroft for the most secret personal messages. The next step would be up to Bancroft, the "British spy."

By the time the Franklin contingent arrived in Paris, to enormous fanfare and festivities, on December 21, 1776, Deane was already in receipt of a massive letter from Bancroft in London.[379] But the correspondence was not filled with meaningless blather; rather, it was a veritable treasure trove of inside political information about the British designs on the colonies. He spoke of the peace effort by the Howes, both in London and again with Franklin that past summer of 1776, in private discussions. He then advised Deane that Franklin had insisted on nothing short of independence as the pivot of negotiations with Richard Howe and that that stance had of course been rejected. He went on to advise Deane that Burgoyne's army was being fortified with Hessian mercenaries in anticipation of a drive from Canada toward Albany and then to New York City, to cut New England off entirely from the other colonies, as the first step in severe punishment of Boston. But, Bancroft continued, it was already late in the year, and as was the British wont in that era, the invasion would likely not begin until the following year.

Upon reading that section, Deane nearly fell backward in his chair! *This was precisely the information that Dr. Franklin had been so desperately seeking!* And here was Edward Bancroft discreetly but directly handing the Americans the very solution they needed to bring the French into the revolution. When Franklin had participated in that horrid mission to Canada earlier that year, he had perceived firsthand that 1) Benedict Arnold's American army was disheveled and in general disarray, and in no shape to wage battle, and 2) Burgoyne was fully aware of the desperate appearance of the enemy.[380] Clearly, Burgoyne would anticipate an easy stroll down the Hudson and the end of Massachusetts in the war. Here was the opportunity for the Continental Army to school the British invaders.

But Bancroft's letter went on, unabated. Deane was advised that his presence in Paris had stirred up a flurry of activity and opposition in Parliament, led by Lord Grafton. Then, astonishingly, he began naming British spies that Deane needed to avoid: Dr. Hugh Williamson, Col. George Mercer of North Carolina, and Lord Stormont, who was the British ambassador to Versailles.[381] Bancroft urged Deane to use encryption and any subterfuge he could glean from his French colleagues.[382] He went on to press the need for France to aid the American cause as soon as possible, since the Americans alone could not withstand the British military. And then, quite curiously, he advised Deane that while he, Bancroft, could not pay informants, he nonetheless had a valuable information source very close to Parliament and to the Privy Council. In all the correspondence Bancroft would later send to William Eden, Lord Stormont,

Paul Wentworth, and various other "British intelligence," he would never, not once, mention Thomas and John Pownall. Curious behavior for a purported "spy."

Deane could scarcely wait for Franklin's arrival to show him the letter from Bancroft. The next morning, in Franklin's quarters, Temple would fire off a letter in Dumas's curious encryption, to Washington by way of Benezet in Philadelphia, advising him of the planned Burgoyne invasion.[383] That letter would arrive in Washington's hands, completely unmolested, on March 1, 1777. The plan of defense of the Hudson against the Burgoyne invasion ensued. Bancroft had checked off Franklin's first task; now it was Arthur Lee's turn.

When Franklin arrived in Paris, Deane immediately moved him and his two grandsons to his hotel, where Franklin would have three rooms and an enormous backlog of mail, some dating back to the previous August.[384] Franklin, by this time, would routinely receive over fifty pieces of mail and parcels of varied sizes per *week*. Into the impromptu study in the hotel were delivered over one hundred pounds of letters and parcels. The three Franklin men (including Benny) and Deane proceeded to open and hastily read the correspondence, rapidly cataloguing each piece as either "urgent" or "defer." The stacks rapidly grew; it was clear that Temple would have to serve as a full-time secretary. It was at this time that Arthur Lee, summoned by Deane from London, appeared on the scene.

Lee was enormously egocentric, and with some justification: he held a medical diploma from perhaps the most prestigious school on Earth at that time and had been accepted into the British bar. But his self-importance was equaled by his inexplicable insecurity.[385] And he would, for the remainder of his life, hide his insecurity behind indiscreet criticism of his peers, as well as of total strangers. There were few people who met Arthur Lee who did not detest him within thirty minutes (John Jay was a notable exception; Lee's older brothers were most assuredly *not*). Franklin and Deane were no different. And so Lee entered Franklin's study with the three adults in study of letters and with Benny opening correspondence rapidly and indiscriminately, and Lee flew into a rage of righteous indignation: "How can you all be so careless with confidential letters? What is the matter with you? Dr. Franklin, did you learn nothing from Alexander Wedderburn in the Cockpit? Can you not control this child? What makes you think you have any comprehension of the importance of each letter?"

On he went, until Franklin sighed and in a firm but even tone said, "Enough!" He went on, "Dr. Lee, we have but recently arrived, and with the backlog of letters to the American ministry in Paris, we feel it is essential that we review, catalog, and then reread the notices from diplomats, statesmen, and ministers of the various monarchs of Europe. Filing of correspondence can wait until we have achieved a system of identification and cataloguing of all these letters. You are most welcome to assist; you are most assuredly *not* welcome to criticize the voluntary labor of my family." Lee stalked out of the room.

Deane and Franklin exchanged stares, shrugged, and returned to their work. Without comment, they both realized the depth of a problem now revealed. Bancroft had already been in direct correspondence with Deane; now Franklin moved to enlist Bancroft as his secretary in Paris and to direct a personal favor regarding an immature and almost certainly incompetent diplomat in the American ministry to France. Before the end of January, visitors to Dr. Franklin would include Le Ray, who, upon surveying the chaotic piles of letters everywhere, immediately charged his esteemed host with departure from Paris for the more friendly, and far more commodious confines of L'Hôtel de Valentinois in Passy, Le Ray's home estate.[386] Franklin, with the assistance of his grandsons and professional movers, could not uproot quickly enough. For the next eight years, Passy would be the immovable home for Benjamin and Temple Franklin; initially, Deane would stay behind in Paris.

At this time, the Second Continental Congress decided that Franklin, being the best-known of the three American ministers in France, should be the natural designee to move on to Madrid to treat with the court of Carlos III.[387] Franklin initially responded by denying receipt of this directive; Lee, therefore, took it upon himself to plainly declare that Congress wanted Franklin to move on to Madrid. Franklin, of course, had much more business to transact in Paris and had no intention of abandoning his life-long mission for some silly diplomatic trip, and he advised Lee that he was simply too old and too tired to relocate yet again. When Lee persisted, Franklin bluntly told him that 1) he, Franklin was *not* leaving Paris for Madrid or anywhere else for that matter, and 2) that he, Arthur Lee, under threat of insubordination, *was* hereby directed to proceed directly to Madrid, to treat with the court of Carlos III. Lee sighed deeply and once again stalked out.

When Lee arrived at the Spanish border in the foothills of the Pyrenees, he was promptly refused entry to Madrid.[388] Carlos III was in no position to move against Great Britain, and especially not in support of revolution against a monarchy. After all, Spain at that time was the ruling monarchy of over one *dozen* colonies in America, none of which needed a blueprint for pursuit of independence. But unbeknownst to Lee, the Spanish Crown had already agreed, through Vergennes and Barclay, using the subterfuge of the church in Vitoria and the Abbé Desnoyers, to provide ₶1,000,000 in Spanish gold, to procure weapons, powder, and capital to the American colonies through New Orleans and Oliver Pollock.[389] A court adviser met with Lee in the border town of Vitoria to advise him that the Crown had agreed to facilitate, but not to contribute to, secret aid through Havana and bade him go back to Paris immediately. Lee was only too happy to accede to this directive, thinking this diplomacy business was not so difficult. He remained clueless.

Returning triumphantly to Passy, his mission an incredible success, Lee was confronted by Deane, now living with Franklin at the L'Hôtel des Valentinois, and with, not surprisingly, no extra space left for Arthur Lee.[390] Lee would ultimately find lodging in Chaillot, but this was three miles from Passy, and he was most assuredly the "odd man out" in the ministry now.[391] Franklin provided no access to foreign correspondence in his study for Lee; rather, he advised Lee that since he had demonstrated such facile success in Madrid, he was now to depart for Berlin, the capital of Prussia. An agent of Eden named William Carmichael (one of Edward Bancroft's closest friends!) agreed to accompany Lee.[392] Bancroft was now in Passy and serving as more or less a volunteer secretary to the American ministry.[393] He wrote to Eden, *Lee will not leave Paris till towards the end of the week. Till he is gone, Franklin and Deane deal only in generals. They don't like him nor his connections on your side of the water. Lee and Carmichael set out for Berlin. There is really some business,* but the absence of Lee is the chief object *[emphasis added].*[394] The sting was on.

At the last minute, perhaps due to insecurity about traveling alone with Carmichael, Lee asked Stephen Sayre, a friend, to come along to Berlin.[395] Sayre was an odd selection for this task, as his reputation in London had to have preceded him. It is unclear whether Lee was aware of the "Sayre Plot" to kidnap George III. If so, it is clearly the strongest affirmation of the absolute cluelessness of Arthur Lee. Further, prior to the alleged plot, Sayre was, like William Lee, recipient of the political "Old Maid Card" of London, an appointment as sheriff. If Lee *was* aware of Sayre's rather checkered background, he was affording Sayre an incredible amount of trust in a most challenging mission. The trio arrived outside Berlin on June 4, 1777 and secured lodging at a local hotel.[396] Lee then headed for the Court of Prussia, producing diplomatic papers from the United States of America. An undersecretary looked at Lee, looked at his documents, looked at Lee yet again, promptly told him to go away, and slammed the door to his office. Odd, thought Lee, that this was *not* the reception he had received in Spain. The following day, he tried again, and again to no avail. Lee would persist over several days without success. Lee simply could not grasp that "the United States of America" was a nonentity outside of the confines of the Second Continental Congress and that *no* European nation was in a position to recognize the credentials of a rebellious rabble.

In the meantime, the British ambassador to Prussia, twenty-five-year-old Hugh Elliott, took special interest in this inept and awkward would-be American diplomat.[397] He had been advised by Eden that Lee carried a diplomatic pouch with him at all times, the contents of which might be of value to the Crown. How *great* a value was to be determined. Pass keys were secured, and on June 26, 1777, with Lee and Sayre out for supper, Elliott entered the hotel, and then Lee's room, unlocking a bureau and finding the diplomatic papers and Lee's journal. He went out a back alley to a room in an adjoining building, where four professional copiers (men who served as an eighteenth-century Xerox of a sort) immediately set about dividing the papers and copying them as quickly and accurately as possible. Elliott then proceeded into another neighborhood, greeting maîtres d'hôtel at several establishments to affect an alibi, and then returned to Lee's hotel. To his horror, there were Lee and Sayre at the front desk, securing their room key. Elliott intercepted them and, introducing himself, proceeded to blather on about Berlin and anecdotes about his life in the city. This charade droned on for two hours, at which time Lee begged off, heading to his room. Elliott briskly exited and went back to the copy room, where the packet had been repackaged, the copying duly completed. But Elliott still had to get the packet to Lee's bureau.

As Elliott headed into the front door of Lee's hotel, he watched in horror as Lee came shrieking down the staircase, "I've been robbed! My room has been violated and my papers purloined! This is an outrage! Call the marshal!"[398] Elliott panicked and dropped the packet, with Lee's name conspicuously on the frontispiece, in a prominent location near the doorman, and fled. Within less than five minutes, the doorman, without seeing Elliott, retrieved the packet, and it was back in the hands of Lee. But Lee was having none of it. His papers had been stolen from his locked room, from a locked bureau, and *both* had been resecured. He called for the maître d'hôtel and insisted at that late hour upon a full enquiry. Lee was seething. Sayre calmed him down, and they sat together in the lobby. Thinking through the events of that evening, it became clear that the impromptu visit by the British ambassador was most peculiar and most incriminating.

The following morning, after a sleepless night, Arthur Lee strode back to the Prussian Court and this time *demanded* an audience with a law enforcement official.[399] And this time, the Prussian government was listening. Investigators were sent to the hotel, where house staff confessed that representatives of the British embassy had indeed secured keys to Arthur Lee's room and bureau under the directive of "official business with a British subject." Elliott was summoned to the Court and admitted that he had acted alone in the confiscation (not theft!) of Lee's documents. The Prussian Crown recommended his recall to London, and this was ultimately done. Elliott was recalled, to be replaced in Berlin by Morton Eden, the brother of William Eden. Elliott was publicly reprimanded for his malfeasance, upon his return to London, and then privately given £1,100 for his service.

Lee remained in Berlin only long enough to pack and to secure passage for his return to Paris; he conspicuously excluded Carmichael from his itinerary. Sayre begged off and would subsequently depart Berlin, heading east to St. Petersburg and the Court of Catherine the Great. Lee felt he had been personally disgraced: he had betrayed the American cause to spies in Berlin by inadequate security and begged Franklin and Deane to forgive this lapse.[400] Franklin was especially critical, and Lee would henceforth never again be considered worthy of discussion of financial arrangements with the French Crown or private sources. For his part, Franklin could privately smile; Lee was on his way out. Another mission accomplished. The largest was yet to come.

Chapter 25

William Carmichael, with no further business apparent in Berlin, went to The Hague, where he had been advised to confer with Dr. Charles Dumas, the linguist/encryptionist, who had been assisting in arranging loans to the colonies from the deep pockets of the United Provinces.[401] There he was advised by Dumas that there was essentially no chance of obtaining a loan from any of the provinces at that time due to fear of interference with the business of Great Britain. In a nutshell, the United Provinces feared and respected the British, and any agency that carried any appearance of disloyalty to the British Crown would be met severely with violence, confiscation of shipping, and possibly even blockade of the Dutch ports. In that climate, securing loans from the wealthiest traders in the United Provinces was out of the question. But Dumas was not totally dismissive; he advised Carmichael that the relationships between the Provinces and Great Britain were quite malleable and fungible, especially if and when the colonies achieved recognition as a nation by one of the Crowns of Europe. He promised to keep Carmichael advised.

Carmichael then returned to Paris, and Dumas resumed his ongoing correspondence with Passy.[402] This was originally all directed to Dr. Benjamin Franklin, but in the more recent six months, he had engaged Temple Franklin personally, more often, and through him David Barclay. By increments, Dumas and Barclay, with Temple as the mediator, would arrange many European loans and gifts, including those of the French and Spanish Crowns, directed toward the colonies. They would prove the most effective fundraisers of the revolution, and with Morris and Salomon in the colonies, would provide a network of laundering funds that would keep Washington's Continental Army in the field through 1782.

Paine's editing of the *Pennsylvania Gazette* would not survive 1776; by the end of summer, he was carrying a rifle as a volunteer for the Pennsylvania division of the "Flying Camp," the brainchild of Thomas Pownall.[403] This lasted only a short while; he subsequently joined Nathanael Greene's force in Fort Lee, New York. There he would participate in the evacuation of the fort and the retreat to Newark in November. Things were starting badly for Washington. His army was grossly deficient in uniforms and supplies, and there were multiple desertions. Paine began writing the first of a series of sequels to *Common Sense,* titled *Crisis,* during this low point early in the revolution. He was side by side with Washington outside Newark, serving as an aide-de-camp and carrying a musket. His first sequel was the pamphlet that begins with the stirring words: *these are the times that try men's souls...* Indeed.[404] Rushed to publication by December 18, Washington would have Paine read it to his army. It was read in statehouses all through the colonies and before Congress. And hearts were notably stirred. In perhaps the greatest gambit of the entire revolution, Washington took his army from Pennsylvania into New Jersey on Christmas night and surprised the Hessian army encamped at Trenton, New Jersey in the early morning, routing them from their camp.[405] It gave the American "Continental Army" a huge morale boost, and the Hessians retreated, immobilized.

Paine would remain encamped with Washington until January 1779, producing six subsequent essays of the *Crisis* series while serving full-time as a soldier and aide. In a unique journalistic role, Paine was envisioning the role of the "G.I. journalist" 170 years before Ernie Pyle.[406] It provided him a unique vantage point, while at the same time he provided an inspiration to the soldiers around him. No "sunshine patriot or summer soldier," he was literally walking the walk. The fatigued, chronically poorly outfitted, poorly equipped, and poorly fed recruits of Washington's Continental Army could dissolve into self-pity or watch Paine enduring and inspiring, sigh and shoulder their loads and carry on. They typically chose the latter. Franklin could never have dreamt of this degree of devotion to his cause; in the recounting of Paine's exploits to him after his return to America, he could only marvel and dissolve in emotion.

In the wake of Washington's triumph at Trenton, Paine took to pen and ink yet again, this time addressing *Crisis* specifically to Lord Howe, who was circulating a rumor, based upon intelligence from William Eden, that Paine was nothing more than a "hired gun" from an unnamed but world-famous colonial sponsor now living in Europe (the reference being obvious to all who heard the rumors). To this, Paine responded as only he could write:

What I write is pure nature, and my pen and my soul have ever gone together. My writings I have always given away, receiving only the expense of printing and paper, and sometimes not even that. I never counted other fame or interest, and my manner of life, to those who know it, will justify what I say. My study is to be useful, and if your lordship loves mankind as well as I do, you would, seeing you cannot conquer us, cast about and lend your hand towards accomplishing a peace. Our independence, with God's blessing, we will maintain against all the world; but as we wish to avoid evil ourselves, we wish not to inflict it on others. I am never over-inquisitive into the secrets of the cabinet, but I have some notion that, if you neglect the present opportunity, it will not be in our power to make a separate peace with you afterwards; for whatever treaties or alliances we form we shall most faithfully abide by; wherefore you may be deceived if you think you can make it with us at any time.[407]

To what "notion" was Paine referring? Clearly he was aware that Franklin was already in negotiation, through Barclay, with the French ministry in Paris and Versailles, and was expecting an announcement at any time. Unfortunately, this announcement was yet a year away.

In that regard, Howe likely interpreted this edition of *Crisis* as "Yankee impudence."[408] But developments in Pennsylvania would dispel any thought of

Paine as insincere; he was appointed secretary to the commission treating with the Indigenous peoples of western Pennsylvania on January 21, 1777, and sent to parlay with them in Easton, Pennsylvania, the following month. Then, on April 17, 1777, Paine was elected secretary to the Committee of Foreign Affairs, as the reformulated Committee of Secret Correspondence would henceforth proudly be known.[409] Paine was therefore, *de facto*, the first true "secretary of state" for the new nation, trumping Thomas Jefferson by twelve years. Unlike Howe, the members of the Second Continental Congress were already fully aware that Paine was indeed no "hired gun"; he was contributing *all* profits from *Common Sense* and his *Crisis* series to the war effort, and the profits were not insubstantial. He would prove a major contributor to the military and would receive relatively meager compensation in the end. Howe took occupancy of a mansion at 524 Market Street in Philadelphia, the former home of Thomas Penn's son, in righteous indignation against Paine's ascendance; twelve years later, Washington would occupy that same mansion as the nation's first White House.[410]

The massive problems of waging war from three thousand miles distant with primitive (by today's standards) communication would rapidly become apparent to Great Britain during 1775.[411] There was simply no effective way to direct "cause and effect" between London and the American colonies. In the best of circumstances, round-trip communications packets required a minimum four months. But critical political decisions could not be made in an instant, or even in a week. The sclerotic deliberations of Parliament and the Privy Council almost guaranteed that a final decision from the government could take four to six months, and that only if there was little controversy and little discussion. A debatable issue might require as much as a year or more.

Franklin and Pownall, the most experienced of the inner circle in the impact that distance could cause for transportation of messages, were made acutely aware of this problem as early as 1755. Pownall could recite the circumstances of his arrival in New York with Governor Osborne, Osborne's ghastly conclusion to his life within the week, Pownall's notification of the demise of Osborne, and his simultaneous request for reassignment by the Board of Trade. While his message was sent by packet ship to London in November 1755, it was not until May 1757 (!!) that his new assignment of lieutenant governor of New Jersey would be in Pownall's hands. Granted that Pownall's various political appointments were likely not atop any agenda or consent calendar in London in that time frame, nonetheless, it had taken eighteen months to finally attain a response.

But in the months and years after December 1774, the delays in responses to stimuli on both sides of the Atlantic would become more and more apparent and would more critically impact the inability of Great Britain to make any coherent war policy in North America.[412] Strategies therefore had to be dictated by military leaders on the fly, often with disastrous results. In the end, one could readily ascribe the ultimate loss of the American colonies to this straightforward but insurmountable dilemma. And through it all, Franklin would take full advantage when he could and continue to trust the planning and innate ability of Washington when he could not. The outcome would speak for itself, and both Franklin and Pownall were assured of this likelihood by 1776. It would require but one major victory by the American army in the field; all of Europe was waiting with growing impatience to join in the assault upon the powerful British war machine.[413]

Chapter 26

I f one were to peruse a present-day map of the United States and identify the confluence of borders among the three states of New York, Massachusetts, and Vermont, and then measure twenty miles due northwest of that point, one would be more or less pinpointing Saratoga and Saratoga Springs. While Saratoga Springs has been the perennial playground of the East Coast for the past two hundred years, prior to the American revolution it was Saratoga and Schuylerville that would be the hub of activity in that small part of the American colonies.

Originally founded as Fort Vrooman by the Dutch in 1689, Fort Saratoga was rebuilt by Col. Philip Schuyler in 1702, just above the inflow of the Hoopic River into the Hudson.[414] Settlers moved into the area in the subsequent decades, forming the small town of Schuylerville. During King George's War, the French, with support from Indigenous tribes of the Iroquois Nations, conquered Fort Saratoga and pillaged Schuylerville, killing or capturing over a hundred settlers. In an irony of history, it was this rout that immediately drew the attention of Philadelphia printer Benjamin Franklin and started the entire undertaking of the fortification and establishment of a militia in Pennsylvania. At the conclusion of the French and Indian Wars, with the Treaty of Versailles, Fort Saratoga, now Fort Clinton, was considered the defender of Albany from northern invasion. Armed with Bancroft's intelligence directed through Deane and Franklin to Washington, it was decided that Saratoga would be the point of confrontation against the British invasion from Canada.

In late 1776, the British army, with the leadership of Lord Germain, Lord North's secretary for the American colonies, plotted a strategy to defeat the rebel Americans as promptly and brutally as possible. Feeling that the major source of the rebellion had come from the Adamses in Boston, Lord Germain decided that a force from Quebec, joined by a force from New York City, could effectively control the Hudson River, through Lakes George and Champlain, right up to the Richelieu River, thereby isolating New England.[415] Once New England was cut off, loyalists in the other colonies would prevail, and attention could be brought to bear against the rebels in Massachusetts. It was a sound plan; the execution, as predicted by Pownall, would prove far more problematic.

First of all, the British army in Quebec was under the direction of General Guy Carleton, and he and Germain were already at odds over Carleton's declining to attack Benedict Arnold's American force as they withdrew from Canada following the Franklin debacle of the previous spring. Into this dispute, General John Burgoyne privately entered discussion with Germain in London on February 28, 1777, describing a detailed approach to invading New York down to the Hudson; after deliberating about a month, Germain approved this plan, recalled Carleton, and bade Burgoyne commence arrangements. Part of Burgoyne's plan involved a secondary force across Lake Ontario, directed against Fort Stanwix.[416] The other part involved pressing General William Howe to move simultaneously from New York City up the Hudson toward Albany. With Germain's approval in hand, Burgoyne boarded a ship to return to Canada. Two weeks later, Germain received a letter from General Howe advising him that Howe felt his army could rapidly control the Middle Atlantic colonies by moving his army to Philadelphia.[417] Inexplicably, Germain *approved* this action but reminded Howe of his responsibility to Burgoyne in New York as well. Howe would receive this approval by June, the year now nearly half gone. Oddly, Howe had decided to attack Philadelphia from the Chesapeake Bay; clearly the British were not using the maps of Evans and Pownall.

Unaware of Howe's dithering in the middle colonies, Burgoyne went on with his preparations. Carleton had delayed his return to Great Britain, as he was being feted as the governor of Quebec. In a show of vindictiveness toward Burgoyne's scheming behind his back with Germain, Carleton pressed his quartermaster corps to hold supplies in Canada, assuring them that Burgoyne could secure materiel from Ticonderoga, and food and supplies from northern New York. He then departed for London with no provision for countermanding his orders as governor, thereby leaving Burgoyne's army grossly undersupplied, with no authority to ameliorate the situation through the Quebecois. By June 14, Burgoyne was as prepared as Carleton's schemes would allow for the invasion of New York, anticipating Howe's arrival from New York City in a massive pincer movement to culminate at Albany.

Washington faced a true quandary: was this the opportunity that Franklin, Barclay, and Pownall had assured him it would be? Did he have the resources, especially the manpower, to withstand the British army coming down from Canada? Col. Benedict Arnold had failed miserably the previous year, and his army was left in disarray. Whom could he count upon to lead the American forces? He was reticent to move that far afield from the critical three cities of the northern colonies, Boston, New York City, and Philadelphia, but at the same time he was reluctant to relegate a mission of this importance to a general officer less experienced, and perhaps less inclined, in Fabian strategy of warfare. Further, he was not yet convinced whether Britain would once again approach by land or by sea. Either approach was a reasonable concern, and the pathway for defense would be remarkably different, based on the answer to that question. In the end, Washington decided to trust his Fabian defense, along with Lord Loudoun's and Thomas Pownall's "Flying Camp," spreading his troops along the Hudson. As part of his strategy, he would leave Ticonderoga with a force of local militia under General Arthur St. Clair. It would prove a fateful decision.

The influence of Franklin and various of his confidants would become patently obvious during the "Saratoga Campaign." While the story is relatively well-known and need not be recounted here, there are a few fine points that reflect Washington's adoption of Fabian techniques, perfectly executed, along with concepts from both Pownall and Henri Bouquet. Burgoyne headed south in the waning days of June, clearly now headed overland toward Ticonderoga. This news was sent promptly to Washington through his remarkably efficient spy network in the New York and New Jersey area. Astonishingly to Washington, and to historians forever after, Howe moved his New York British Army toward New Jersey, skirmishing against a small force led by Benjamin Lincoln, but then maneuvering his primary army to Somerset Court House (now Millstone, New Jersey), where he awaited attack from Washington. Here Washington almost had to be thinking, *Of all the bloody stupid arrogance of this man, to abandon Burgoyne and attempt battle against me.* Recalling Franklin, Washington of course declined to engage an entire entrenched army of British regulars, whereupon Howe loaded his army on ships. Now, whence Howe's army? Washington was willing to maintain his flying status in case Howe reversed north to the Hudson River. But after days of observation, it became clear that Howe was headed south—but where?

At this point, Washington directed his adjutant, Horatio Gates, to take as many troops as he could muster toward Saratoga. Washington was still unsure if Howe intended to punish the Virginia planters or Franklin and maintained his mobility back in New Jersey, awaiting Howe's arrival at Cape May, New Jersey, by sea. His intelligence network was watching.

Meanwhile, Burgoyne was moving his army and a relatively large train of up to 1,200 women, children, and civilian support staff, due south toward Fort Ticonderoga. Seized by Ethan Allan and the Green Mountain Boys two years previously in a raid somewhat embarrassing to the British, the fort was defended by St. Clair and a modest force, but concerns had already been raised early in 1777 that the fort was ill-positioned for the terrain and therefore highly vulnerable to expert engineers and artillery. While the opinion was far from unanimous, St. Clair remained alert to the possibility that his brigade might be forced to abandon Ticonderoga, just as the enemy had done previously. Ultimately, the British artillery engineers would indeed solve the vulnerability of Fort Ticonderoga, placing cannon on the heights above the fort, where it would be an easy target for bombardment and full destruction. Fort Ticonderoga had been rendered indefensible, and both Burgoyne and St. Clair knew it. As St. Clair led his men in silence out of the fort under protection of a new moon, he quietly advised them, "I can lose our lives and save our reputation, or I can save our lives and lose our reputation. I have chosen the latter."[418] In so doing, he, like Washington so many years before with Braddock, managed to lose a battle while saving an army. Furthermore, although the abandonment of Ticonderoga did not forestall Burgoyne significantly, it did allow for the flying army of Gates to move into position, while alerting the American forces at Fort Stanwix, under Col. Peter Gansevoort, that the British campaign was moving from Canada over land rather than water.

At that same time, a western British army under Brevet-general Barrimore ("Barry") St. Leger was headed to reinforce Burgoyne from the western side of Lake Ontario. Anticipating little American resistance in his path after the routing of the American army in 1775, he was surprised to find Fort Stanwix heavily garrisoned. Initially, he attempted a siege of the fort, which would fail, and then a flanking maneuver, which would also fail, due to a skilled counterattack from General Benedict Arnold. Ultimately, St. Leger would break loose long enough to achieve Fort Ticonderoga in the latter half of October 1777. By that late date, Saratoga was out of his army's reach.

Washington, for his part, was more than happy to play Fabianus against Howe in Pennsylvania and could execute this strategy like few military leaders of his time. After Howe finally arrived at the northern extent of the Chesapeake Bay in August, he and Washington would play a cat-and-mouse game all the way to Philadelphia, with Washington engaging Howe's army at Brandywine Creek, and then again at Germantown, before withdrawing once again to Valley Forge. Howe, for his part, was initially quite proud of his triumphant entry into Philadelphia by September 26, 1777, but was far too distant, and far too late, to provide any assistance to Burgoyne in the upper Hudson Valley.

Thus, Burgoyne was left to his own devices as he approached Albany from the north. Having occupied Fort Ticonderoga, Burgoyne would reconnoiter his army at Skeenesboro and reassess his status during the last days of June. He would then move south toward Saratoga on the path to his goal of Albany. The American general, Philip Schuyler, still had surprises in store, as his military felled trees across the roads, burned granary stores, and overall made the path to Saratoga far more difficult; it was not until the end of July that the British would arrive at Fort Edward above Saratoga.

On August 3, a small band of skirmishers sent by General Howe gave General Burgoyne a message: *I am departing by ship to engage Washington at Philadelphia. Will come to New York once this objective is accomplished.* Burgoyne looked at the note, the ground, and then crumpled the note and tossed it into his campfire. His staff would not learn the contents of the letter until many months later, during an inquiry. It was clear to Burgoyne now that Howe was not coming; St. Leger was not coming. It would be up to him alone to engage the American army under Gates and Arnold.

Burgoyne now made a serious underestimation. Without reinforcements, he felt that his army needed fresh horses. Loyalists in the area advised him that farmers in the territory of "The New Hampshire Grants" (now Vermont) and western Massachusetts possessed healthy draft horses for the taking. Burgoyne dispatched Colonel Friedrich Baum and a thousand Hessian troops to "round up some horses." He would never see this regiment again. Wandering into the New Hampshire Grants and finding the horses far more scarce and more difficult to acquire than advertised, Baum would be met by an army of two thousand "Green Mountain Boys" under John Stark, who would summarily rout Baum's army, and in the "Battle of Bennington," Baum would lose his life, four thousand miles from home.[419] Burgoyne's situation was becoming more ominous by the day. It would take the entire month of August for Burgoyne to entrench along the Hudson. He then had to make a critical decision: press for Albany or retreat to Canada for the winter. Remaining overconfident, he chose the former.

But during this delay, the Americans were not at leisure.[420] Daniel Morgan's rifles were directed by Washington to "fly" from Pennsylvania to the Hudson. Likewise, Benedict Arnold hastened from Fort Stanwix, and Benjamin Lincoln's army cut off the northern communication lines of the British between

Skeenesboro and Ticonderoga. Burgoyne's army was rapidly and unwittingly being swallowed by a far superior American force. Gates, not nearly as popular among the army regulars as Washington, arrived on the scene in mid-August and began assembling his staff. The site for optimum fortification was argued by the Americans until Count Tadeusz Kosciuszko, a gifted military strategist and engineer who had come from Poland to aid the American cause, arrived on the scene, directing the American engineering corps to Bemis Heights.[421] The fortifications he directed there would, just like Fort Clinton/West Point, and many of his other American revolutionary defenses, prove impregnable against the British. As the impending battle ground developed in October, Benedict Arnold would direct the American right, with Gates in the center and Lincoln on the left.

Burgoyne would first attempt to circumvent Arnold's flank, but Morgan's long rifles would thwart this attempt, with a brutal loss of British lives. Burgoyne would then attempt an assault directly in the center of the American line, and this would be turned back as well. On October 13, 1777, Burgoyne realized that his army, totally demoralized, malnourished, and surrounded, was done. His staff sued for peace but refused to allow the terms "surrender" or "capitulation" to be used in what he would refer to in Parliamentary inquest as a "convention." The official surrender was accepted by Gates on October 17.[422] Word was feverishly passed to Washington and Paine, and thence to a waiting confederacy of four men in Harpur Street and Passy.

Chapter 27

T homas Pownall had suffered some political reversals in the two years
prior to Franklin's departure from London. While Pownall maintained
his regular attendance in meetings of the inner circle, including the
early meetings after Paine's entry into the group, he was finding his pathway
in Parliament far more circuitous, and as a result, his political reputation
suffered. His seat in Parliament with the Whig party was based on his election
in Tregony, Cornwall in 1767. In the election of 1774 he was "turned out" by
the political forces of Lord Falmouth, and at a crucial time in the plans of
the inner circle, he was desperate to maintain a voice in Commons.[423] Lord
North offered him the seat from Minehead, Somerset. This of necessity created
a serious conflict for Pownall; Minehead was a *Tory* seat (not unlike a staunch
Democrat or Republican in the U.S. today losing a Congressional seat and
turning around to run for a sure victory representing the opposing party). But
in desperation, and with a desire to maintain both his standing and his efficacy
in the inner circle, Pownall acceded, knowing full well that he would have to
shoulder the calumny and derision of this decision. He needn't have waited
long. Thomas Hutchinson, of all persons in London, laughed that Pownall,
having sown the seeds of radical governance of the colonies, was now reaping
that harvest. Hutchinson would never know that it was Pownall who had leaked

his personal letters, through Franklin, to the Boston press, and therefore, in a moment of candor, had to admit that through this decision to accept a change in party Pownall was "making himself of some importance" in Whitehall.[424]

One of Pownall's most difficult confrontations with this change would prove, naturally, to be his subsequent meeting with the inner circle. Franklin was at once amused and mock-critical; had Pownall somehow lost his zeal for the American colonies? Would he prefer now the shameless peace-mongering of Lord North? Pownall advised the inner circle that this could culminate in his being named to a commission from the Crown to seek a peaceful resolution with America.[425] Franklin advised Pownall, with equal candor, that 1) Pownall lacked at that point the political loyalty to achieve such an appointment, and 2) Pownall lacked the zeal to sell such a concept to the likes of Washington, Adams, and Hamilton. The entire situation left Pownall in a lurch; politically, he looked as if he were attempting to cleave himself in half. In conference with Lord North, he would concede that peaceful negotiation with America would be henceforth his politically expedient approach.

In his fifth edition of *The Administration of the British Colonies,* now in two volumes due to the extensive and complex political arguments proffered from varying sources, he would describe the difficult relationship between Colonies and Crown:

I had conceived an idea of our colonies as shoots which the old tree, in the vigour of its health had put forth. I viewed them as spreading branches of the same organized plant, advancing in its natural vegetation; but I found, alas, this system to be a mere vision... The parent tree begins to view these shoots as a separate plant, *and with its over-topping branches casts over them a shade rather of jealousy and mistrust, than of its old affections; the young shoot in its exuberancy* feels itself as a separate plant, *and begins to find the old connecting layer as rather curbing and cramping, than as supporting its increasing vegetation [emphases sic].*[426]

Therefore, Pownall averred, the correct solution for this dilemma was an Imperial Parliament made up of seats from both Great Britain and her colonies, with some limitations imposed upon the colonies in terms of political powers.

Barring this, he concluded more timidly, Great Britain would have to accept an American union. In Parliament, Lord North proposed a conciliatory bill that would remove colonial taxation in exchange for colonial defense funding from colonial coffers. Pownall would now find himself sitting opposite Burke, Barre, and the other Whig leaders, and as a result in vicious debate and heated exchanges against his former political friends and allies.[427] In the heat of the moment, Pownall walked out onto the tightrope:

"Parliament must necessarily have a right to interfere, and I think should so far interfere, as to examine, to settle, and to give the several colonies once for all, such a constitution as is fit for such dependent communities within the empire [such as Scotland]; by settling with them and for them, such articles, terms, and conditions as may be confirmed by act of Parliament, in like manner as was done in the union of the parts of the present kingdom, which articles when once confirmed by Parliament, cannot, according to the law of nations, of justice and policy, be altered without the consent of the parties." This was Pownall's mediation offer of February 1775.

Before the American colonies could hear of this proposal, the embattled farmers of Lexington and Concord, Massachusetts, had fired upon British soldiers, killing dozens. There would be no action on Lord North's bill. By November of 1775, on the heels of Franklin's departure from London to America, the Crown had urged military preparations by General Gage in Boston.[428] As a Tory, Pownall had no choice but to concur. But then oddly, as a parting gesture in Parliament later that same November, he rose to argue for peace and reconciliation one last time. This time he would receive no other response than raucous laughter from Tory and Whig alike, led by Edmund Burke. Burke would then counter with his own famous conciliation plan, which included retention of the *Townshend Act* as to the taxing of trade. Pownall argued vehemently against *any* retained taxation on the colonies, realizing that all colonies north of Maryland would find that stance unacceptable at this late date. He then awaited a supporting voice from Lord North; that supporting voice would not be forthcoming. Although Burke's bill would also fail, it was clear that Pownall was no longer of a voice with Lord North. Peace was a forlorn hope.

The British Parliament of the time of the American Revolution faced multiple accusations of "corruption." Parliament had evolved in England from the time of the Norman conquest of 1066 CE. The French-speaking William the Conqueror in that year solicited the bishops and landowners of England to enjoin together into an "advisory council to the Crown" (French: parlement) to keep his hand on their heads and at the same time to keep his ears open to the intrigues of a foreign nation. In 1215, the Royal Advisory Council/Parliament of King John forced him to agree to assess and collect no further taxes without their consent. This was attested in the Magna Carta, from which the House of Lords could legitimately claim an origin. While the Parliament of that time remained clergy and land holders/nobles, over time it would be opened to a rising, wealthier middle class that would demand a voice despite being prevented from land acquisition. Much of this occurred during the reign of Edward III in the fourteenth century. During that time, knights and burgesses, who had first come together at the request of Simon Montfort in opposition to Edward II, began to meet regularly in what they self-described as "The House of Commons" to distinguish themselves from the "Upper Chamber" of nobility and clerics.

By 1430, the right to vote was established as the "Forty Shillings Law" that stated anyone holding land worth at least forty shillings could vote in elections of members of the House of Commons. (These non-nobility landholders of the middle class comprised only about three percent of the populace at that time; land ownership by anyone other than nobility in England was then, as now, a relative rarity. As previously noted, these individuals were legally designated as franklins). By 1485, in the reign of Henry VII, laws could not be introduced by the ruling monarch, but only by members of either Commons or Lords (the official title "House of Lords" would not become law until 1544). Thus, the monarch had to solicit a member of his Privy Council if he wanted a given bill introduced into Parliament. The power of the monarchy was already waning by the time of Henry VIII. But it was far from a democratic assembly; as noted, only three percent of the male population of England in 1548 owned over forty shillings of property. Most of the property at that time, and in some areas even until today, was in the hands of the nobility. Thus, the small number of voters could easily be influenced by their local lord to vote for whomsoever the lord wished them to vote.

One hundred years later, during the middle of the seventeenth century and the British Civil War, the modern concept of Parliament began to take shape. While Cromwell united the English and Scottish Parliament for a brief period, it was not until 1707 that the two would be permanently fused as "The Parliament of Great Britain." By then, the House of Commons had risen in prominence, being allowed to function independent of the wishes of the monarchy. But as of 1770, the House of Lords was still exerting considerable influence on the operation of the British government. While Great Britain is reluctant to admit to this, it was Franklin and the American Revolution that would change this construct entirely; after the American Revolution, the power of the House of Lords would dwindle rapidly in the next century to that of a stamp pad and a bottle of ink.

There were two major areas where the Lords stood guilty of corruption. The first was the entire idea of male primogeniture, a stillborn concept of Salian law that declared the first male down a mother's birth canal would be the heir apparent of the noble title and its lands and privileges, regardless of ability, wisdom, or experience. In the case of first-born twin sons, this event could be nearly akin to a derby, as it were, with huge stakes; something of a "Breeder's Cup." As a result, there were numerous examples through one thousand years of English nobility where the legal heir proved a blithering idiot. But short of murder of the idiot, there was nothing to be done for this but to bear it in grudging silence.

The second was the concept of "rotten boroughs" (also referred to as "pocket boroughs," since the outcome of all votes in these boroughs was based on the pocket or purse of the lord owning the borough), areas where a seat in Parliament had been established sometimes as early as the twelfth century and not uncommonly with less than five legal voters in the district. This would set the stage for anyone with enough capital to become a member of Commons. More often, the local lord would instruct, by force or bribe, those five voters whom they were to elect. And therefore neither Lords nor Commons was a true representation of the will of the British people. This would all change rapidly, *after* the American Revolution.

And so it was that Thomas Pownall, now a shadow of his former revolutionary self, due to his having been forced to accept a Tory seat from a rotten borough in order to maintain a presence in Commons, strode into the House of Commons, having heard about Saratoga the previous week, and announced on December 2, 1777, that the American revolution was over, that Great Britain had lost, and that the American colonies were never again to be considered anything other than an independent nation.[429] The response was a mixture of cheers, jeers, and yawns from the members gathered. Pownall shouted above the din.

"I now tell this House and government, that the Americans never will return again to their subjection to the government of this country... I now take upon myself to assert directly...that your sovereignty over America is abolished... forever. The navigation act is annihilated." Now other members of Parliament broke out of their private discussions to listen to Pownall.

"All the treaty that this country can ever expect with America is federal and that, probably, only commercial. In such treaty, perhaps, you may obtain favorable terms; but exclusive terms of trade you must never more expect. They are determined to maintain their independence at all events."

Pownall's response was by far the earliest and most audacious public declaration of the significance of Saratoga. But all the members of the inner circle grasped it immediately, along with their colleagues. No one could have been more enthusiastic than Charles G.F. Dumas, who was downright giddy now, and in December 1777 he literally ran from ministry to ministry in The Hague, offering one nation after another "favored nation status" with this new jewel in the western Crown, the United States of America. Countries from France to Spain to The United Provinces [The Netherlands] to Italy to Prussia to Austria were now ready to listen to Dr. Dumas. And suddenly doors at The Hague were flung wide open to admit the little minister for America. He would never again pay for a meal in the United Provinces.

Barclay adopted a mood of strict business; he and Vergennes had heard the news almost simultaneously and now met with Necker in preparation for a visit to Versailles and the Court of Louis XVI. He knew that Louis would also be extremely excited with this opportunity to goad George III and avenge two previous French defeats at the hands of Great Britain in the previous thirty-five years. Barclay talked now in terms of millions of livres, military engineers, and naval support to make America a reality. With a financial command unequaled in Europe, he drew at once the attention of Necker, Grand, and his own banking partners.[430] America now represented an investment potential of untold wealth, and Barclay was determined to be present at its inception.

Franklin would also meet within days with Vergennes.[431] He would need to brush Deane and Lee aside now and set up his own private American ministry. The silly games with Lee were over; both those ministers needed to be humiliated and sent home. In fact, the official notification of Deane's recall had already been formulated and would be received in Passy by the end of February. Lee likewise needed to be recalled or sent elsewhere. Franklin advised Bancroft to see to it. He then began arranging talks with the French Foreign ministry; he wanted this alliance accomplished by January 31, 1778 [in actuality, it would be delayed until February 6 due to the illness of Vergennes's secretary]. Temple Franklin would leap into encryption of his grandfather's correspondence, using the simple but baffling approach of Charles Dumas and rejecting the complicated, almost ridiculous method of Massachusetts secret agent James Lovell. Lovell was rarely able to provide correspondence from his own hand, in his own encryption method, without multiple errors.[432] For Benjamin Franklin's purposes, it simply wouldn't do. Bancroft was, by mutual consent with Temple Franklin and his grandfather, eliminated from these exercises and never shown the Dumas code. Not a single Bancroft letter would ever be produced in the Dumas method. But at the same time, Bancroft fired off a copy of the treaty to Eden through his usual network of intrigue.

By far the most intimate vantage point regarding the Saratoga victory would come from Thomas Paine. He literally had an identical viewpoint to that of Washington, as he was yet serving in Washington's army. At the same time, due to his appointment as secretary of the Committee of Foreign Affairs, Paine was placed in the position of near-constant travel between Washington's camp and Congress in Philadelphia. Paine took both roles very seriously; he corresponded with the colonies in the Caribbean about the status of the British colonial revolt, while maintaining regular meetings with Washington. He would be with Washington at Brandywine Creek, and again at Germantown. He personally took possession of a chest of government documents when the British seized Philadelphia on September 26, barely evading capture and hiding the chest in Trenton, New Jersey. On October 30, 1777, he was already versed in the surrender of Burgoyne at Saratoga and was able to send a most remarkable piece of correspondence to Richard Henry Lee, older brother of Arthur Lee and adjutant now to Washington. In this, he addresses the "capitulation of Gen'l Burgoyne" while addressing his concern about the trustworthiness of terms that would exact a "promise" from Great Britain not to employ the captured troops once they were released back to their country. He pointed out that the terms were too generous, raising a new issue that no one, including America or Great Britain, at that time could know: whether the United States had already been recognized by a European monarchy such as France or Spain. If so, this could be an ultimate betrayal: sending British troops back to England at just the moment when those nations were declaring war.[433] Well-schooled at the "Franklin College of International Affairs" in Craven Street, Paine was rising to new heights in his understanding of all issues from multiple points of view and literally directing the American Second Continental Congress in foreign affairs. Paine closed his letter to R.H. Lee by advising him that he, Paine, was traveling to Fort Mifflin to assess the status of the British artillery in that area.

Just below Philadelphia, where the Delaware River begins to widen into Delaware Bay, Fort Mifflin stood on the Pennsylvania side and Fort Mercer on the New Jersey side. From September to the first of November, the Americans held both forts, preventing the British navy from provisioning Philadelphia from the sea. Several unsuccessful attempts had been made by the British on Fort Mifflin. Washington had charged General Nathanael Greene to lead the defense of the Delaware River, and seeking intelligence on the status of both forts, he directed Paine to go first to Fort Mercer, and then to Fort Mifflin.[434] Fort Mercer in the first weeks of October was secure, but as Paine and Col. Christopher Greene (a third cousin of Nathanael Greene) were crossing the Delaware in an open rowboat, the British shelling of Fort Mifflin was taking place. Paine and Greene made their reconnaissance with the fort and then crossed back to Fort Mercer amid the bombardment. Ultimately, both forts would fall to the British by November 7, but Paine would be hailed as the "hero of Fort Mifflin."

In the fallout of the simultaneous victory of Saratoga and loss of Philadelphia, Washington would be subjected to criticism out of the protective reach of Franklin, within the Second Continental Congress.[435] But Paine was already pointing out the issues with the "Convention of Saratoga" (recalling again that Burgoyne would not sign a document containing the words "surrender" or "capitulation"), and the relatively poor negotiations of Gates on behalf of America, with terms that looked almost as if America had lost. He then rose above the controversy with a ringing *Crisis* that asserted that through a team effort had come the defeat of an army from the largest military force in the world. He praised Gates and his officer corps and then pointed out that the Fabian tactics of Washington against the inevitable occupation of Philadelphia had converted that town, for Howe, from "a conquest, to a trap." Indeed, Howe would winter in Philadelphia but would be gone within the year. This was the first affirmation in print, from any author, that this was the way that Washington, and the American army, would conduct the war against Great Britain, and that this tactic would prevail. The stable flies were indeed winning.

In Passy, Franklin was all business in the closing days of 1777, and his rooms at L'Hôtel de Valentinois became a veritable hornet's nest of activity. On the heels of Saratoga, secret negotiations were underway, with Vergennes serving as mediator and facilitator between Franklin on the American side, and, well, on the French side, no one was willing or permitted to state how high on the food chain their directives arose, but it was clearly far above that of Vergennes to affirm or refuse. Franklin would at times grow quite frustrated by "let me get back to you on that issue," repeatedly from Vergennes. But then he would remind himself that Vergennes and his little coterie, so dismissive only a year ago, were now clearly listening carefully to the lists of American needs and demands and providing hints of acceptance at every meeting. Furthermore, by the mere fact that Vergennes was no longer free to respond to negotiations on his own, Franklin realized that there were power brokers in Versailles, perhaps even at the level of Crown, that would brook no misunderstanding in the wording of any treaty.

Franklin would also, per Barclay's request, continue to demonstrate "the spendthrift" to any and all who came to visit Passy. Glorious, generous meals, endless cases of wine, finely dressed men and women almost constantly moving through his quarters. This appeared to be a minister of unlimited budget and unlimited generosity. Behind the scenes, Franklin was plotting with Temple and with Bancroft. Bancroft continued to be a rich source of information to the British crown, but with all missives approved by either Franklin or his grandson, or both, prior to shipment. All three knew full well that there was precious little that Great Britain could or would do about endless lists of French, Dutch, and Spanish ships laden with cargo to the West Indies, as long as these European nations were officially classified as "neutral." Until a given European nation had signed an alliance with the American rebels, no European ships could be subjected to detainment and search at sea without risking charges of breach of the Consolato del Mare and the *Navigation Acts*. And so, through 1777 and on into 1778, the British navy watched helplessly as ships sailed from Nantes, Cherbourg, L'Orient, Bruges, Amsterdam, Cadiz, and other ports bearing God-knows-what to God-knows-where. At the same time the Brits were forced to pay Bancroft, and through him, the American ministry in Passy, for all this information. With great irony, Franklin had ensured that the cost of his deluxe board in Passy would be borne by George III!

But Franklin, through Wentworth's interception of his correspondence, was simultaneously advising the French that he was in secret negotiations with the British to preserve the British *Navigation Act*, even with American independence, in order to save this rich source of trade between those two nations.[436] And the French were, of course, in a position where they could not reveal their awareness of this secret correspondence, or challenge Franklin about it, for fear that they would lose their conduit of secret information through the porous communication of Wentworth. Franklin had quite deliberately figured a way to play Great Britain and France off one another, while maintaining the persona of the "doddering old man." It was diplomatically brilliant. And now the French understood what the Americans and British had known for twenty-five years: they were playing in the diplomatic stratosphere now, and in Franklin they were dealing with the shrewdest and most literally intriguing politician of the eighteenth century. They would keep their guard more carefully moving forward.

Vergennes at this point, in late 1777, was not yet able to proceed to drafting and signing any alliance. The Spanish throne was no longer Habsburg; it was Bourbon, just like that of the *Ancien régime* of France.[437] The two nations had signed a "Bourbon Family Treaty" earlier in the eighteenth century at a time when international treaties were being signed and broken almost yearly. It stated that neither monarchy would sign a treaty with any other nation without first offering the other Bourbon monarchy at least notification, if not cooperation. But now Spain, in great financial straits, still trying to maintain a far-flung empire of colonies, and perhaps now in total distrust of Franklin, chose to bow out from the negotiating table; France was on her own. And here Franklin decided to take his pressure one step further: he went to the French press and submitted for publication an article discussing the American ministry's peace negotiations with...the British. Now Vergennes, clearly becoming warmer toward the American ministry generally, and Franklin in particular, pressed over the ensuing forty-eight hours for agreement with the articles of French alliance.

After some arguing between Arthur Lee and Vergennes over the trade of molasses between America and France, the alliance was formalized on February 6, 1778. Franklin immediately gave his copy to Edward Bancroft, who had a copier prepare an enumeration of the points of alliance, which he then forwarded to William Eden in London.[438] This would comprise one of the last messages Bancroft would send to Eden as his "secret agent" in Passy; Eden had been appointed by the British ministry to the Carlisle Commission, to be sent to America in April, 1778 to treat for peace. During his time in Philadelphia, Eden would be replaced as undersecretary to Lord Suffolk; never again would he be involved in the procurement of information from his "secret agents." By the end of 1778, Bancroft would be the last British informant left in Paris, and Franklin's board would suffer.

But the alliance was a major diplomatic coup for Franklin and for the United States of America.[439] The following month, Deane received correspondence from Philadelphia that he had been recalled from the French ministry due to his poor effort in recruitment of French officers and engineers in 1776.[440] He would advise Franklin, who in turn would encourage Deane to "stock up" on French gold specie.[441] Franklin knew that Deane would need this; he was returning to a hostile Congress that would be asking difficult questions, the answers to which Franklin had never shared with him. And with the recall, Franklin was relatively sure that Silas Deane's political career was nearing its terminus. In the end, Deane would load over £2,000 in French gold into his pockets, his seams and his luggage, and prepare for his return to America. He and Franklin would deliberately delay this exodus in order to allow Deane the honor of attending a formal celebration of the Treaty of Alliance at Versailles with the full Court of Louis XVI in attendance. When Arthur Lee learned of this insubordination to Congress by Franklin and Deane, he was furious.

Franklin, unable to change the fate of Deane in his recall to Congress, now moved with Bancroft to drive the final nails into Arthur Lee's diplomatic coffin. He first contacted Sam and Joseph Wharton, old Philadelphia friends and brothers, now doing "war business" in London. He then pressed Lee to retain John Thornton as his personal secretary while in Passy. With a natural trepidation toward Franklin, Lee cautiously agreed, and Thornton then volunteered to travel to London to "scout out the American 'prisoner of war' issues" in order to allow Lee to prepare a report to Congress. No sooner had Thornton arrived in London than he was approached by the Whartons, who subsequently reported to Franklin and Vergennes that "a Thornton, claiming to be a private secretary of Dr. Arthur Lee, is leaking state secrets to London agents of the Crown." Franklin feigned outrage and swore that he would charge Congress with the immediate recall of Arthur Lee. The plans of the inner circle would now continue unabated.

Chapter 28

William Lee, Arthur's next oldest and significantly "slower" brother, had arrived with Ralph Izard in Paris in early 1777.[442] Lee was appointed minister to Prussia and Austria and Izard to Tuscany. Lee spoke not a word of German or French and was uncertain of the language of Austria (which was German, except at court, where it was French). Izard was unsure of the location of Tuscany and was uncertain of its language (which was Italian). He of course spoke not a word of Italian and was under the misconception that the capital of Tuscany was Rome (it was Florence). Franklin and Le Ray were privately much amused at the nearly impossible mission of these two American "diplomats." Franklin advised them that the three target nations were always willing to provide interpreters for foreign diplomats and that their negotiations should go quite well. He neglected to advise them that none of those nations would be willing to admit a minister from a rebellious colony with no recognized diplomatic credentials. And his comments about interpreters were deliberate deceptions designed to humiliate the Americans. Izard never got to Florence. Thinking better of it, he ultimately decided to stay in Paris as he realized that he truly had no idea what he was doing. William Lee, however, proceeded as far as Frankfurt and requested an audience with the Court of Berlin (Prussia) and the Court of Vienna (Austria).[443] Finding lodging in Frankfurt, he then awaited admission to one or both courts. And waited. And waited. And waited. After several months in Frankfurt, it finally dawned on Lee that 1) no interpreters would be provided by either court, because 2) neither court had any intention of admitting him for an audience.

He then took it upon himself to shift his focus from Frankfurt to Amsterdam, for which he had neither diplomatic credentials nor congressional authorization.[444] Through Jean de Neufville, the private agent of Engelbert François van Berckel, the pensionary [ruling authority for foreign treaties] of Amsterdam, Lee succeeded in securing a "treaty" using the identical language that Bancroft had provided the British crown. De Neufville was in his own right a wealthy banker and merchant in the United Provinces and saw recognition of the United States as little more than an opportunity to move into a closed market owned by the British, whom he hated with a passion. It never occurred to Lee that 1) he was not an authorized diplomat to the United Provinces and 2) Amsterdam had no power to finalize international treaties (that authority in the United Provinces resided in The Hague, through the diplomatic mediation of the official American agent Dumas, not Lee, and van Berckel, not de Neufville). Dumas got wind of the problem from his contacts in Amsterdam and attempted damage control but arrived too late. Lee was so excited that he forwarded a copy of his "treaty" to the Second Continental Congress; this would subsequently prove disastrous for the United Provinces, as we shall see. Dumas fired off a letter to Philadelphia, warmly criticizing the unauthorized negotiation by Lee with a Dutch individual likewise lacking appropriate credentials. It was a general debacle, and clearly few members of Congress understood the depth of the idiocy at that time, but it was to become all too clear within two years.

For Thomas Paine, 1778 would prove to be an eventful year, but not in a very good way. The recall of Deane was somewhat beneficial to Franklin; in July 1778, Franklin would be named "diplomat plenipotentiary to France," meaning he alone would be empowered to negotiate with the French Crown. Arthur Lee and John Adams (Deane's replacement in Paris) were out. Once again, Lee was infuriated. Adams of course was outraged.[445] Lee would never plumb the depths of Franklin's international and congressional influence, and in the end his frustration likely contributed to his progressive madness and untimely death. But Deane's return to America in May 1778 would prove difficult for Paine.

Over the previous two years, factions were developing naturally within Congress. The Second Continental Congress would be the sole government of the United States throughout the revolution and was naturally unwieldy due to the size and diversity of residence of its constituent representatives. It was clear to all that the division of Loyalists/Tories v. Patriots was primarily one of Boston, New York, Philadelphia and the coastal south v. everybody else. It was also clear that at any given time, the population of the British colonies was about 33% Loyalist, 33% Patriot, and 33% "other," including individuals whose loyalty could be bought with words, deeds, or cash. Governing this nation was an ongoing challenge, and arguments in Congress were frequent and sometimes vicious. To Congress, Deane returned and was almost immediately attacked for the military proposals he had attempted with European nobility.[446] Charged with securing capable military leaders, he had proposed Charles William Ferdinand of Brunswick (commonly "Prince Ferdinand of Germany") as a likely General of the Army to replace Washington (that concept seems highly unlikely to have been considered, insofar as Prince Ferdinand, as Deane must not have been aware, was the brother-in-law of George III of Great Britain).[447] Another name mentioned was Charles-François de Broglie, the patron of Lafayette, and one of the secret contributors to the French gift to America in December 1776. De Broglie would also have also been named "Generalissimo," placing him above Washington. Congress would never pursue these ideas, considering them both fantastic and insulting to the Virginia delegation. But in the mention of de Broglie came the topic of the "French gift."

It seems that this near-miraculous gift, delivered under mysterious circumstances after the secret meeting of Achard with Franklin and Jay in December 1775, had been a source of concern and frustration for Congress for the ensuing two years.[448] Delivered by Beaumarchais as a "secret gift from France," it was unclear at the time what was implied by the term "gift."[449] In

September 1777, Lazare-Jean Théveneau de Francy, serving as an agent for Beaumarchais, addressed the Second Continental Congress regarding the French "gift" and promptly presented a collection notice for the entire one-million-livre "gift," which he described as a "loan" under the direction of Beaumarchais. It was this specific request that had prompted the recall of Deane to address this. Deane had claimed responsibility for negotiating this "gift" when in reality he of course had nothing to do with it. (The gift had been negotiated between Barclay, Vergennes, the Court of Louis XVI, Jacques Necker, and Robert Morris, by Charles G. F. Dumas in The Hague.) Deane's false claim would culminate for him in real trouble: it was at that point in time critically important to the French court how that gift was defined.

Then as now, the concept of a gift is just that: no strings attached, no expectation of reciprocal favors.[450] On the other hand, a *loan* of one million livres, as claimed by Théveneau for Beaumarchais, had a completely different meaning. Any suggestion of a *quid pro quo* transaction that involved the French court would imply that the French court was expecting some sort of repayment or return on an investment. But if the loan was given to the Second Continental Congress, *who* thereby was expected to repay it in gold or in kind? The obvious answer would be the Second Continental Congress. But that created a diplomatic dilemma of global consequence. The Continental Congress can only be a responsible debtor if it represents an established and recognized independent body, namely the United States of America. Therefore, the French court, by virtue of this loan, not gift, was tacitly recognizing the sovereignty of the United States. And therefore, France would be in breach of treaties all over Europe, including with Spain and Great Britain, and those nations could demand satisfaction for this action. Almost certainly without realizing what they had done, Beaumarchais and Deane, through nefariously attempting personal profit from the French "gift," had created an international incident that left the Court of Louis XVI reeling.

By the time Deane had answered the recall from Congress, France had already signed the Treaty of Alliance with America, which at face value would appear to render the issue moot. But Congress was still on the hook for a possible one million livres in French gold to Beaumarchais and needed Deane to make account of the real source of this financial bonanza. Deane appeared before Congress in July 1778, nine months after his summons, with no records, no affidavit, and really nothing but a feigned outrage over his recall to America. He then asserted once again that he was a responsible party in securing the gift and was due at least some consideration from Congress as a result. Paine was quite adamant in his public response to this claim and pressed the point that the gift was just that: a gift. Thus, no "consideration" was due to Deane, Beaumarchais, or anyone else.[451] By this time John Jay, a long-time friend and supporter of Deane, had succeeded Henry Laurens as president of Congress and demanded of Paine some supporting documentation of his assertion. And here Paine would make a crucial error. He wrote in response, *Those who are now [America's] allies, prefaced that alliance by an early and generous friendship.* Paine would forever assert that his reference to 'allies' and 'friendship' were personal, rather than national, and declined to name names (which would have included Barclay, Grand, and Necker) due to obvious sensitivities during that volatile political time. But Jay and Deane pounced upon that statement, asserting that Paine had admitted that the French Crown was indeed the source, and thus, if it were a loan, as stated by Deane, then France had indeed recognized the United States as early as December 1776. Jay immediately demanded Paine's resignation as secretary of the Committee of Foreign Affairs, citing libel of the French crown by a private citizen. Paine requested a hearing before the entire Congress, and Jay refused. Reluctantly, Paine tendered his resignation on January 8, 1779.

When Franklin got word of the harsh treatment of Paine by Jay, he was furious. Paine had been treated shabbily by both Deane and Jay, and Franklin needed Paine's inscrutable reputation to remain intact to fulfill the plans of the inner circle. Although he had sent an overly generous reference letter with Deane to provide to Congress, he vowed to have nothing further to do with Deane, and over the ensuing two years, as Deane pressed for a return for his efforts in the French gift and begged for Franklin's support, nothing was forthcoming from Philadelphia or Passy.[452] In poverty and humiliation, Deane would move to Great Britain to live out a relatively lonely life. Paine would move on as well, still mindful of his charge from Franklin and still bound to support the American Revolution.

The year 1777 would be even more crushing to Thomas Pownall on a personal level: his beloved wife, Harriett Fawkener, died during that year after a protracted illness.[453] Pownall would remain a participant in Parliament, but far less vocal after his bold statements in response to Saratoga. Through 1778 and 1779, his input would lessen, and by 1780, he had declined to consider another term in Parliament.[454] Writing in encrypted correspondence to Franklin and Barclay, he admitted that his years in Parliament had left him disenchanted with his homeland, and he expressed repeatedly a hope to return to America after independence had been achieved. Further, as a Tory member of Parliament, he feared that his statements in Commons were now generally an ongoing subject of ridicule as the political chasm between him and his party of record grew ever deeper and wider.

He turned to the private sector thereafter, publishing *A Memorial Most Humbly Addressed to the Sovereigns of Europe,* which was widely publicized and well received.[455] Although published anonymously, it sounded so much like *The Administration of the Colonies,* now in six editions in London, that readers readily guessed its source. In this treatise, he predicted the imminent loss of the New World empire of Spain and the rise of the United States as a world power due to its innate ingenuity and rapidly expanding population. He saw the American Revolution as only the first of many and postulated that ultimately the world would warrant an international Congress of nations, as well as a World Court for judicial administration.

The wording was regrettably so much Thomas Pownall, so awkwardly phrased and confusingly illustrated, that two American writers felt compelled to publish *A Translation of the Memorial to the Sovereigns of Europe upon the Present State of Affairs…into Common Sense and Intelligible English.* This anonymously published edition of 1781 proved equally popular and was snapped up in America.[456] Pownall could almost see his two colleagues winking at him, their identities given away by the term *Common Sense* in their title. Pownall was feeling much better personally by that time and immediately produced an itemized peace proposal, which he sent to Lord North and the Court of George III. Both copies were returned to him unopened.[457] Throughout the American Revolution, some things would never change.

❦

Chapter 29

O n January 17, 1779, Franklin turned seventy-three, and by that time was feeling all of those years. Already carrying perhaps fifty pounds more than he needed, on legs and feet broken down by years of gout and worsening circulation, he was becoming more and more immobile with every passing month. Queen Marie Antoinette had given him the loan of her "carriage mobile," a litter carried by four men indoors or two mules out of doors, utilizing two stout poles threaded through brass eyelets on either side of the padded chair, in parallel lengthwise. This he would use more frequently now when he had to venture anywhere outside his quarters in Passy, and the sight had grown commonplace in that neighborhood.

With age he also found himself less amused by the awkward behavior from his critics; he was still living with two of them at that time,[458] while John Adams was running interference.[459] Now Adams received the recommendation from Congress that Franklin be "minister plenipotentiary" for France,[460] and oddly (or perhaps deliberately; Adams was never the most popular man in any crowded room in his life[461]) no mention of further assignment for him in Europe. So the referee was leaving, and Arthur Lee and Ralph Izard would still be around, two insufferable gnats in Franklin's parlor, and nearly as useful.[462] Well, if they were planning to stay in Passy, Franklin would make sure their sojourn was as uncomfortable as possible; in this he was able to readily enlist the cooperation of Vergennes and the French foreign ministry. If anything, they hated Arthur Lee more than Franklin ever could; Lee made constant demands that would horrify Franklin and would inexplicably expect that His Royal Majesty King Louis XVI would do whatever Lee demanded. Ultimately, with the loss of status for both Lee and Izard, the political climate would finally overcome the free board and accommodations they had enjoyed for the previous eighteen months, and both would reluctantly depart. But that departure was yet a year away.

Franklin was still driven to maintain his efforts to support Barclay in his negotiating the financing of the American cause. To the chagrin of the inner circle, no other nation had, up to 1779, officially provided financial support, which forced Barclay to continue surreptitious efforts throughout western Europe. Spain and the United Provinces were still amenable to entertaining Barclay's demands, with a promise on return of free trade. But they had not yet recognized any American diplomats. John Jay had been sent to Madrid after the recall of Arthur Lee, but with no diplomatic skills, no language skills (not a word of Spanish), and insistent demands, rather than requests, for financial support, he too would find himself spending his days in the Pyrenees rather than Madrid. With but one exception, the American foreign ministry had proved an unmitigated disaster throughout the revolution. But the worst was yet to come.

The United Provinces (referred to, today, as "The Netherlands") were, in the mid to late eighteenth century, one of the strongest trading nations in the world. They maintained a huge merchant marine, supported by a modest military navy. They traded globally; they invented the "colors" to be flown on every Dutch ship. This message to the world was that the ship was from the United Provinces and had come in peace. In time, every nation would embrace the concept, in order to aid with identification from a distance at sea. But their economy had suffered significantly with the rise of the British navy. Once the rival of the old "Hanseatic League" in the North Sea and Baltic Sea, they were more and more supplanted by British trading vessels with military escorts.

But despite being forced to take a second chair to Great Britain in maritime affairs, their investors, political leaders, monarchs, and people still depended upon world trade for much of the Dutch economy. Because of this, the Dutch were, by 1775, deferential to the British, and wanted no part of any hostility, or suggestion of hostility from their neighbor across the North Sea. Thus they interpreted the efforts of the American colonies to treat with The Hague as an unwelcome overture to break an uneasy alliance with a gentle giant.[463] The Dutch ministers in The Hague would greet Dumas, Franklin, Barclay, William Lee, Carmichael, and anyone else who bothered them from America with "What part of 'no' do you not understand?" They left official negotiations there. At the same time, under the table, Barclay was succeeding in freeing up funds from the United Provinces, as well as Prussia, Switzerland, the Palatinate, and Brunswick. But outside the inner circle, there were likely less than five people on Earth who were aware.

Now, the Second Continental Congress, hearing from Arthur Lee and Ralph Izard that Franklin was at the least now senile and quite likely a British spy, and with Adams corroborating the former while rigorously refuting the latter, decided that if they wished to finally approach the United Provinces for funds in 1780, they should retain a new minister for that purpose.[464] Inexplicably, they chose South Carolina representative and former Second President (after John Hancock) of the Second Continental Congress, Henry Laurens, for that role.[465] But Laurens had lobbied hard for the position and seemed almost frantic to obtain international support for the colonies in order to maintain the war. Admitting that he spoke no Dutch, Frisian, Flemish, French, or German, he steadfastly assured the Second Continental Congress that he would achieve financial support from the United Provinces and that this could be accomplished through the able assistance of Franklin's polyglot agent in The Hague, Charles G.F. Dumas. The various delegates were surprised at Laurens's undue interest in this role but agreed to provide the appropriate letters of introduction.

As Laurens prepared for his trans-Atlantic sojourn to the United Provinces, he was provided the usual diplomatic packet, including the recommended Plan of Treaty, and then someone in Philadelphia inexplicably resurrected that old treaty William Lee had negotiated in Amsterdam in 1778 with de Neufville, while he was nothing more than a private citizen. Without giving it so much as a thought and thinking that it might provide Laurens with negotiating leverage or at least a language template, some unknown secretary for the Committee of Foreign Service added it to his diplomatic pouch. Laurens set sail from Philadelphia in August 1780, but his ship was subsequently overtaken by a British frigate off the coast of Newfoundland before they really got into the high seas.[466] Laurens reacted by pitching his diplomatic packet into the sea, but alert British sailors were able to "hook" it (a commonplace maneuver for a seasoned sailor armed with a gaffing hook to retrieve lost items or shipmates). The officer on deck, leafing through the packet, thought, *How well the Board of Trade can use this information*, and believed himself in the direct line for a handsome reward. Then he noticed an older, folded document.[467] Removing this from the packet and looking it over, he struggled with much of the vocabulary in French. But he was well able to sort out "les Provinces Unis" and "les États Unis" and the date from 1778. Now his eyes grew wide. He ordered the arrest of Henry Laurens for high treason against Great Britain, and against His Majesty King George III. After relieving the ship of much of its supplies of food and water, the Brits released the crew to the ship. But Henry Laurens was staying aboard the British frigate as a special guest, headed for London. Once arrived in London, Laurens was consigned to the Tower of London to await trial, and upon translation of the Lee-de Neufville document to the Privy Council, Great Britain promptly declared war on the United Provinces, based on the apparent recognition of the United States by the "Lee-de Neufville Treaty."[468] William Lee had unwittingly struck yet again and had single-handedly created a war.

David Barclay continued to assert his ambition for Franklin's goals in the financial sectors of Europe. He would insist that Robert Morris become finance minister for the United States. This would be made official in 1780. By ongoing access to the treasury of France, and now receiving funding from Spain and the United Provinces, Barclay was able to wheedle loans and refinancing of loans repeatedly, but by 1781, Jacques Necker was becoming notably frustrated with the ongoing war effort in America. He had steadfastly refused to recommend to the French Crown a tax levy to support the war, but the economy of France was teetering on the brink of insolvency. Through the eyes of Necker, the American Congress, along with Franklin and Vergennes, seemed financially insatiable. Spain had never been an eager participant, and now the United Provinces were about to be drawn into a direct confrontation with the Brits.

Dumas, Franklin's "man in Amsterdam," now recovered from the dustup with William Lee over the "Lee-de Neufville treaty," had actually taken up copies of that document and distributed them discreetly among the various diplomats and politicians sympathetic to the Patriot Party in Amsterdam. The situation between France and Great Britain was becoming warmer with every passing week, and the United Provinces were drawn directly into the center of the impending storm.

The oceanic trade of Europe over the course of one thousand years had been governed more or less passively and by mutual understanding through the "Consolato del Mare," a document produced in Barcelona during the thirteenth century that stipulated that unless any two nations were at war with one another, their ships could pass through the Mediterranean and the Atlantic, and later, by passive acquiescence, the North and Baltic Seas unmolested.[469] This would hold internationally enforceable unless a nation at war was carrying contraband to a neutral nation, or likewise a neutral nation was carrying contraband to a nation at war. Every nation seemed to accept and understand the "rules" and was generally content to live by them. The easy rule of thumb thereby became "free ships/free goods." But as Europe's warfare became more commonplace and more mechanized, and as international treaties became more complex and malleable, the definition of "contraband" became harder to define.

By 1750, the British, with at that time the most powerful navy in the world, defined "contraband" to include "naval stores." Today, "naval stores" refers primarily to products derived from pine resin used in rendering ships water-tight, but in the "age of sails" in the eighteenth century, the definition was far less water-tight and could include timber for deck planking and masts/spars, as well as roping and canvas. The largest European trader in that definition of "naval stores" was the United Provinces, with their massive merchant marine.[470] Great Britain adopted the stance in 1778 that all exports of naval stores from the United Provinces to France, were by maritime law subject to confiscation by the British navy, insofar as France was no longer considered neutral. France, in turn, frantically trying to treble the size of their navy, cried "foul!" asserting that timber was not contraband and that the Brits had no right to molest honest trade between France and her trading partners in Europe.

For Dumas in Amsterdam, it came down to whether the ports of the United Provinces were going to 1) continue to ship naval stores to France with the military assistance of Dutch warship escorts (termed a "convoy") or 2) shut down their ports from export of naval stores entirely, since the ongoing search and seizure of Dutch trading ships by the British was becoming expensive. The "Anglomanes," the pro-British and dominant party in The Hague, were vocally in favor of stopping that trade completely, while the Patriot party in Amsterdam prayed that the government of the United Provinces provide convoys. But that decision was more complicated than a simple yes or no. If plan 1 were adopted, the Brits would respond "Why do you need convoys to ship neutral goods? Either you are violating the international trade laws of the past one thousand years, or you are wasting military vessels and funds." And they would consider this to be an act of war against Great Britain. But if plan 2 were adopted, the French would respond, "Why are you acceding to the wishes of the British, with whom we are at war? Are you a British ally?" And so the United Provinces, in their effort to maintain neutrality, had reached a diplomatic crisis.

Their initial response, as so often happens with smaller, neutral parties, was to wish it away.[471] Through January and February 1779, the States-General for the United Provinces debated the issue without taking definitive action. Amsterdam continued to trade with France in an excruciatingly round-about fashion, through Statia [St. Eustatius] in the West Indies. The other Dutch ports effectively shut off shipments of naval stores. More and more Dutch merchants were approaching Dumas, as the American minister, to press for favorable trade status. British influence in the United Provinces was waning quickly.

At this point, at the urging of Franklin, Dumas submitted a petition to the Second Continental Congress in Philadelphia to officially appoint him as *chargé d'affaires* for the United States at The Hague.[472] Clearly, he had already been providing this service; a title would be of great benefit to all concerned: *My request, at the commencement of this letter, has for its object the service of the United States of America, as much at least as the proper care of my fortune, of my family, my honor and credit, my character and safety. The earliest of your agents and correspondents, Gentlemen, in Europe, out of Great Britain, has risked all these things from the time he received and accepted this honor, with a confidence equal to that which it was offered.*

By May, Amsterdam had loaded an exhaustive shipment of neutral goods, along with ships' timbers, and a convoy was promised by the Dutch admiralty. But now, the courage of the Dutch and French governments wavered, and they encouraged the Amsterdam merchants to go on without the timbers or the convoy. The merchants, with Dumas leading the charge, refused to debark under those circumstances, insisting on both convoy and timber shipments. This standoff would last well into the summer.

⚜

Chapter 30

A curious mission from Franklin and d'Estaing suddenly jumped to first priority in the United Provinces that summer.[473] Franklin had sensed from the time of his being singled out for opprobrium and accusation by the Fourth Earl Sandwich in Parliament on February 1, 1775 that this was done out of Sandwich's mortal fear of what Franklin thought, schemed, and connived in the back alleys and publick houses of London. Armed with this knowledge, and with the fact that as lord of the British Admiralty, Sandwich controlled all military ship movements for the British Navy, Franklin conceived of a somewhat sophomoric method of neutralizing the most powerful navy in the world. He would simply have d'Estaing and French naval vessels feint and shift, move on the North Sea this month, the English Channel the next, the Irish Sea the month after, occasionally stopping and seizing packet ships and pleasure craft showing the British colors, firing on minor coastal fortifications, and otherwise simply being a nuisance to the British shipping industry.

Inexplicably, this strategy proved almost incredibly effective; the feared British blockade on American eastern ports was seriously hobbled throughout the war by virtue of Sandwich's constant recall of ships to Great Britain for coastal defense. Thus European ships, while still working the Mississippi corridor with Oliver Pollock, found that the blockades of secondary ports like Portsmouth, New Hampshire and Portsmouth, Virginia, were surprisingly easy to "run." Quite simply, there would never be sufficient British ships to provide for the American blockade, or perhaps ultimately of greater import, to provide for the defense of the British army.

Franklin sent Bancroft to leak information to the British Crown about a planned French and Spanish invasion of the British mainland in summer 1778. There remains serious doubt that this strategy was ever sincere, but with the cooperation of Kings Carlos III and Louis XVI, ships flying the colors of each nation appeared in the westernmost edge of the English Channel, opposite Plymouth, in apparent reconnaissance of the British coastline. Sandwich immediately recalled over half the British navy from America, and ultimately the blockade would not be effectively restored for over nine months. Franklin then recommended Bancroft report that Victor-François, 2ème Duc de Broglie [sometimes mistakenly cited as "Broglio"] had collected an army at Calais for imminent invasion of Great Britain. Of course, this was pure bluff, but once again, Lord Sandwich was calling for ships to return to the English Channel to defend Great Britain. The game had become almost laughable in Versailles and Passy. And then a more serious opportunity beckoned.

John Paul Jones was born John Paul on July 6, 1747 on Arbigland estate, on the southwest coast of Scotland.[474] With the sea in his blood from birth, he was apprenticed to a ship's captain at age thirteen, sailing out of Whitehaven, Cumberland, and regularly traversing the Atlantic. His older brother William had emigrated to Fredericksburg, Virginia, and John visited him on occasion. During the 1760s, he served as a mate on several vessels and gradually worked up to captain. This culminated in two regrettable issues, one involving a seaman flogged for insubordination who subsequently died, and on another vessel, a seaman threatening mutiny over disputed wages, whom Paul stabbed to death. Fleeing from the British maritime industry, Paul ended up in Fredericksburg, where his older brother had by then died. At that time Paul was able to find trading vessels in need of expert seamen and worked up and down the Chesapeake. Soon he became well-known to the various plantation owners there. And it was there that he would append the name "Jones" to his surname "Paul," presumably to avoid identification and extradition by British naval authorities.[475]

In 1775, with war against Great Britain looming, the Virginians encouraged him to travel to Philadelphia to introduce himself to the Second Continental Congress. With a letter of introduction from Richard Henry Lee, he was retained on the spot and appointed first lieutenant assigned to the ship *Alfred* out of Philadelphia. Over the next two years, he would serve the military faithfully, transporting troops and staging raids on British merchant ships. Unfortunately, he still carried with him a lifelong love of privateering (the utilization of privately owned but armed ships that could be retained by any nation more or less for piracy against the trading ships of enemy countries), and as a result, even with military ships, often did not understand or would not accept, that he could not simply steal cargo and retain it as personal treasure. Repeatedly, this would get him into difficulties with the more organized military and keep him from attaining significant leadership grades.

By December 1777, the Second Continental Congress felt that Jones might be better served in Europe than in the colonies, where he was no longer as well received (and Jones felt it in his better interest to avoid the British military authorities patrolling American waters), and so it was mutually decided that he should travel to France and see where he might be of assistance with Franklin's ministry. It would prove a wonderful holiday gift for Franklin. Jones would find accommodations in Paris over the winter and spend many days in Passy. Franklin would introduce him to the various political and military figures of Paris and make sure he was well fed and entertained. In early 1778, Franklin and Jones hatched an idea.

Jones was able to secure command of small French packet ships and frigates during 1778, after the Treaty of Alliance had been signed.[476] With these he would harass British merchantmen in the Irish Sea, and ultimately, as captain of the ship *Ranger* under American commission, he would attack, board, and overtake HMS *Drake*, a British war sloop, and carry it back to Brest. The public relations disaster of the British losing a ship of that namesake to Jones, and right under His Majesty's nose, was enough to draw British defenses to England and Ireland. Jones and his crew were at odds by the time they arrived at Brest, and it would require Franklin and Adams to separate the American combatants over arguments about prizes and compensation. Franklin kept Jones with him while Adams sided with the crew in the arguments. Franklin had more important issues than credit for the *Drake* and brought Jones to Versailles at the end of the year. Louis XVI had a personal gift for Jones as the naval hero of the Irish Sea: the *Duc de Duras*, a large merchantman that could accommodate forty-two guns, making it by definition a "man-o-war," a step below a "ship of the line" (sixty-four guns). The ship was thus refitted, and Jones then rechristened it *Poor Richard* (Fr: *Bonhomme Richard*) in honor of the best-loved *nom de plume* of his American benefactor, host, and friend, Benjamin Franklin.[477]

Now Franklin arranged a modest fleet of four French ships to accompany *Bonhomme Richard* into British waters to harass British ports again during the planned (?) French and Spanish invasion of Cornwall (which would never actually take place).[478] Jones took his fleet up the western coast of Scotland, crossed to the south of the Orkney Islands, and returned down the east coast of Scotland and England. Off the Yorkshire coast in the gathering evening of September 22, 1779, they encountered two British ships, HMS *Serapis,* a man-o-war, and a hired privateer sloop, *Countess of Scarborough*, escorting a large British merchant fleet to the Baltic. Engaging the two ships, Jones ran into stiff resistance and ultimately decided to entangle and board *Serapis*. Drawing friendly fire from the French ships, the two ships' crews engaged in direct combat for hours, until the *Bonhomme Richard* started taking on water, and despite the efforts of Jones and the crew, it ultimately sank. During the intense fighting between the crews of the two ships, the British officers entreated Jones to surrender, which prompted his most famous response: "I have not yet begun to fight" [Jones was fully aware throughout his service in the American Navy during the Revolution that were he to surrender to a British force, he would be summarily hanged]. And with his own ship dipping beneath the waves, Jones and his crew indeed had to fight their way to success aboard *Serapis*. Ultimately, *Serapis* was overtaken by the Americans, and *Countess of*

Scarborough then surrendered to the French ships.[479]

Jones commanded the British *Serapis* now and with the four French ships headed to port for much-needed repairs of the several ships, as well as medical care for many injured French, American, and captured British seamen. But curiously, at the specific prior directive of Franklin, he headed directly for the Texel, as the port for Amsterdam was known, in the neutral United Provinces, rather than a French port.[480] Franklin was already aware of political and financial issues in France and the United Provinces. France was chronically bereft of ready finances for ship repairs, and it was not unusual for ships to be in "dry dock" for months awaiting materials essential for repairs. The United Provinces on the other hand had the craftsmen, the materials, and the finances necessary to render a wreck sea-worthy in less than a month. Furthermore, with Dumas's negotiations in The Hague at an impasse, the United Provinces might need a small "nudge" in the direction of the Franco-American alliance. *Serapis* limped into the Texel at the end of September, bringing the conflicted loyalties of the United Provinces to a crisis.

The "Texel affair" would culminate in the ascendancy of the Patriot Party in the United Provinces and an end to their alliance with Great Britain. Initially, Jones sought repairs for *Serapis* in the shipyard at the Texel,[481] and the British ambassador to the United Provinces, Sir Joseph Yorke, immediately filed an official protest,[482] insisting that Jones be evicted from the United Provinces while returning *Serapis* to the British crown. The States-General were unwilling to take sides at this point and stalled for time. Jones requested medical care for the wounded as a humanitarian gesture. This of course caught Yorke off guard, and he was, under unrelenting political pressure from *both* the Patriot Party and the British Party, forced to accede to this request. This bought Jones considerably more time. By November, even Jones had grown anxious to depart, with his new prize ship nearly repaired. But at that time the United Provinces were advised of the presence of a British fleet just outside the Texel, waiting to seize Jones upon his departure.[483] Those ships would wait aimlessly for another two months, again forestalling their more valuable deployment to America.

Finally, in the last week of December, with the British government and Sir Joseph Yorke howling in protest on a near-daily basis, Jones slipped out of the Texel, leaving the *Serapis* as a decoy, evaded the British, and returned to Brest. Now commanding *Alliance*, originally a French ship, but with Jones commissioned by the American Continental Congress, and under an American flag, he had won the Dutch public over to the American cause and would report his success to Passy.[484] Within weeks, the United Provinces would recognize the sovereign nation of the United States of America. Dumas had negotiated almost this entire effort behind the scenes on behalf of his benefactor and idol, Benjamin Franklin. The Dutch for their part were anticipating 1) American victory and 2) "favored nation" status in the trade agreements with this most dominant new nation in a new hemisphere. It would be the successful culmination of Dumas's efforts as the first American minister in the United Provinces. And the coffers of the United Provinces opened for Barclay.

Chapter 31

Over the first five years of the American Revolution, Franklin had labored almost without interruption in the diplomatic affairs in Versailles, in France generally, and throughout Europe. And during that time, it seemed that the Second Continental Congress was more enemy than friend. The "aid" they had dispatched to his ministry more commonly became serious stumbling blocks in Franklin's efforts to achieve for America the recognition by European nations so desperately essential to maintaining her financial base during an ever-lengthening war. The years were by then starting to take their toll. Franklin had struck up flirtations with Mme. Brillon and Mme. Helvetius in Passy but was most assuredly of no physical ability or inclination to achieve requital of their affections. With every new minister sent to his home in Passy would come new aggravations and delays as Franklin struggled all the more to keep these inexperienced and uneducated "diplomats" apprised of the progress he had made, while deploring their inability to move the process more rapidly. By 1780, with the British "Southern strategy" in full flower, with the British Privy Council and Board of Trade more confident that their Crown would still prevail, and with Barclay struggling mightily to find any further European funds from the private sector, Franklin was simply running out of energy.

From the time that he was advised by Barclay of the death of Thomas Penn, the question for Franklin would be periodically raised: "Are you still of a mind to proceed with separation from Great Britain?" The question would arise from various sources, not limited to the members of the inner circle, but also from friends in London, in Paris, in Philadelphia, in Boston. Was it necessary now to wrench Pennsylvania from the grasp of the Penn family proprietors? Was the Crown an adequate surrogate for the proprietors? Would Franklin survive the initiative and potential delay in achieving separation of all the American colonies, just to free Pennsylvania? How would he maintain his coign of vantage as age crept into the equation ever more frequently? First addressed in the inner circle, Pownall had raised the blunt issue (Pownall never lacked for bluntness) that the neighboring colonies of Pennsylvania such as New York, Massachusetts, and even New Jersey, now Crown colonies, did not seem to enjoy any greater freedoms, any better quality of life, any political advantage, over that of Pennsylvania. Therefore, there truly was no benefit in wresting Pennsylvania from the proprietors, only to deliver it to the Crown. No, the liberation of Pennsylvania would *have* to be the liberation of America; anything less would improve nothing in the lives of the citizens of the colonies.

With this unshakeable argument finally ingrained into Franklin's thinking, he would pursue a healthy dislike for the nation he had so desperately sought to love.[485] From 1765 to 1775, Franklin had lived the life of an American Anglophile: he had cultivated the best friendships of his life, enjoyed the best music and theater, the libraries and coffee houses, and initiated some of the greatest political debates in Edinburgh and at Westminster that he would ever experience. Now, in order to cultivate his ambition for a successful conclusion of the revolution, he would likewise need to cultivate a healthy revulsion of everything British.

As it turned out, it really was not much of a reach. The harsh military tactics of the Southern strategy would cost the British and the Indigenous peoples dearly in reprisals for decades to come (v.i.). The behavior of Parliament would be unforgiven for over a century. Not until well into the twentieth century would Great Britain regain a modicum of the trust that its American subjects had once afforded it. Franklin made a point of obtaining and reading in detail the American gazettes and letters describing the treatment of American soldiers, prisoners of war, and civilians at the hands of British military officers, most commonly of the nobility. *Barbarians, bastards, beasts, cruel, inhuman, philistine* would all appear in Franklin's correspondence during the war. To the regret of his British friends in the inner circle, this burning hatred would bubble to the surface in correspondence with them. It appeared that the war was taking a severe toll on the overall disposition of Franklin, much to the concern and amazement of those with whom he corresponded.

But for Franklin, he simply could not, at his advanced age, afford to relent in his passion for independence. He would consider himself right up until 1783 the primary inspiration for liberty in America, and in that role he felt that he had to be an unending source of encouragement for those at home who dealt first-hand with the privations, the tragedies, and the loss of human life that the revolution brought. By the summer of 1780, with the heady days of Saratoga long past, and with the British moving almost unchallenged and unabated through the Carolinas, Washington and his staff were reaching a new depth of discouragement.[486] Washington would press to Franklin that *this cannot go far longer. We are unsupplied, starving, and without powder. The army is dissembling on a daily basis. By winter we shall be finished.* He prayed for renewed financial support. At this point, Franklin turned yet again to Vergennes, requesting the stratospheric figure of twenty-five million livres. Vergennes's one-word response would completely deflate Franklin: "Impossible!" Just before Christmas, 1780, Franklin dictated his resignation from the American ministry in France to Temple.[487] The dream was over; he simply could go on no longer.

Barclay and Pownall, in other parts of Europe, could only share Franklin's despondency. Barclay cancelled financial appointments in The Hague and Vienna. Pownall focused his attention on his antiquities research. They were all finally ready to pack it in. They had all done their part and were simply at an impasse. Perhaps the British opposition was insurmountable after all. Perhaps their assurances of success had been miscalculated. Perhaps the *Somersett* decision and the Hutchinson letters would be forgotten. They had all reached the end of their inspiration.

But two people in America had clearly not yet, like John Paul Jones, begun to fight. And two people still burned with the zeal of a dream of liberty for all mankind. Thomas Paine wrote secretly to Vergennes, asking him for nothing. Rather, he informed Vergennes that he would be in Paris by March 1781 to *collect* seven million livres from the French treasury.[488] For Paine, it was simply a done deal and the right thing for a military partner to provide. Vergennes, upon receipt of this letter in January, decided to see what he could still arrange. Thomas Paine without trepidation arranged for passage to France by packet ship. But Paine would not provide the true spark to drive the American cause successfully across the finish line. That role would fall to yet another aide to the American cause who had arrived from Europe.

Marie-Joseph Paul Yves Gilbert du Motier, Marquis de Lafayette, was born September 6, 1757 in Chavaniac, Auvergne Province, into a minor family of nobility, who were career soldiers.[489] He was educated in a military school where he was entered into the officer corps at age thirteen. From the untimely death of his father and uncle during his youth, young Gilbert du Motier had already inherited the title of marquis. And while this carried the promise of secure income for life, Gilbert accepted the responsibility to make himself into an effective military leader through the personal acquisition of martial skills, as well as an extensive education in military tactics. He would be named a member of the King's Musketeers by age fourteen and captain in the Dragoons at age eighteen (a French "flying army" corps). By that time, he could ride a horse like a Cossack and handle firearms like an American frontiersman. Officers ten years older than this boy were intimidated by him in combat games. He would marry at age sixteen to Marie Adrienne Françoise, aged fourteen, and would become father to Henriette at age nineteen. By that point, he was restless for service and anxious to display his military abilities and became smitten by the American conflict.

The "Age of Enlightenment" was not limited to Scotland or even to Great Britain; it was pervading philosophical circles throughout Europe. In the cause of the United States of America, men like Jefferson, Franklin, and Paine had convinced Europe that here was a new nation with a new concept about the rights and equality of all men. Young Gilbert, not yet twenty, realized by 1776, with the publication of the Declaration of Independence, that he simply had to go. He was living in Versailles at that time, in the shadow of Marie's father, the Duc d'Ayen, and went to see Silas Deane, the American agent, in the fall of 1776. Deane recommended that he go to Philadelphia, present himself to the Second Continental Congress, and apply as an adjutant to General George Washington. When the Duc d'Ayen heard of the plan, he raged at Deane for attempting to enlist this boy, his son-in-law, for a futile cause, and sent young Gilbert to the Duc's brother, the French ambassador to London, the Marquis de Noailles. The marquis likewise forbade Gilbert to go to America but failed to appreciate his financial status: when, against the wishes of his father-in-law and uncle, he appeared at the London docks to board the packet *Victoire* bound for America, his embarkation was blocked under the order of the Marquis de Noailles. Gilbert du Motier then calmly asked "How much for the ship?"[490] The captain was initially taken aback, but responded, "£112,000," whereupon Gilbert signed a note for that amount on the spot and bade the captain cast off, under the authority of the ship's new owner. Laughing, the captain did just that, and on March 25, 1777, Gilbert was off to Philadelphia bearing the gift of a packet ship for his new country.

He was commissioned a major general by the Second Continental Congress July 31, 1777, for which he promised to serve without pay, as he was already heir of a marquis title, with an annual income of ₶120,000. Congress assigned him to Washington's staff for guidance, protection, and development as a true general. Headstrong, but brave to a fault, he fought at Brandywine Creek, where he was shot in the leg but was able to organize an American retreat in orderly fashion, as his mentor had done at Fort Duquesne so many years before. Fearless under fire, Lafayette caused Washington grave concerns over his potential for serious injury or worse, but the men rallied around "Le Garçon Guerrier" in skirmish after skirmish. Lafayette would consistently implore Washington for a command of significance, and Washington would urge patience. In 1780, Lafayette decided to redirect his appeals, choosing to return personally to Versailles, to the French Crown. In response, Louis XVI approved the deployment of an army under Le Comte Rochambeau and a naval force under Admiral de Grasse. Help for Washington was clearly now on the way.

Returning to Washington's camp with the good news, he was finally assigned a division by his commander, who instructed him to move his force to Virginia's southern border. In December he was ordered to join with Baron von Steuben, who was bringing his troops up from North Carolina after he and Nathanael Greene had just won the Battle of Cowpens. Lafayette refused to be sent away from New Jersey, where he hoped to meet the French army due for arrival any day; Washington assured him quietly but firmly that great things were about to transpire in Virginia.

By 1780, the British military had stumbled into a false economy on the North American front by utilizing American loyalists to fight American patriots. While this was not winnable in New York or Massachusetts, it was proving surprisingly effective in Georgia and the Carolinas, where the rural population was far more sparse, more poorly provisioned, and highly unorganized. From the base of the Chesapeake Bay all the way to Savannah, there were plenty of loyalists who had made a nice living in the port cities of the South loading cotton, indigo, molasses, and rice for the ports of Great Britain. They had built warehouses, town houses, and country mansions, and did not relish losing this to the rebels from the North. For their part, the British military had learned that they really needed to provide only an officer corps to organize the loyalists, and the loyalists would do the rest. And tragically, the officer corps, being eighteenth century British, were more than happy to also teach the loyalists some of the most brutal and loathsome field tactics of combat ever devised.

By using this "Southern strategy," as it became known in London, the British were able to effectively compete with Washington in this war of attrition. In battles during 1780, including Camden and the Waxhaws, it is estimated that both the Patriot army and the British army were comprised of over ninety percent native-born Americans. Charles Cornwallis, leading this strategy, hoped to bring the individual colonial governments into loyalist hands and still salvage the colonies. If he could secure the southern British colonies, he and Lord Germain felt that Europe would quickly lose interest in this rebellious "cause," and a successful reconciliation could then be negotiated.

One corollary of the British victory at the Waxhaws came on the heels of the administration of the final United States president to have been a veteran of the revolution, Andrew Jackson. At the Waxhaws, he was about aged seven and witnessed the brutal deaths of several neighbors and family at the hands of the British and their Indigenous allies. As a result, he learned early in life to hate both groups with an insatiable and unrelenting zeal. The British would feel his wrath first, at the Battle of New Orleans in 1815, after the close of the War of 1812. That battle would end in the worst rout in the history of British/ American warfare, with the near-total destruction of an entire army. General Andrew Jackson watched the slaughter of over a thousand British soldiers and dozens of officers as he recalled the British officer who had beaten him on his back with the flat side of a sabre when Jackson was seven years old. Emotionless before his men, he was breathing deeply. For the Choctaw, Chickasaw, and Cherokee nations, their punishment from Jackson would wait until 1830, with the *Indian Removal Act*. Over the ensuing ten years, this law would be carried out by the Jackson and Van Buren administrations with unrelenting zeal, culminating in the "Trail of Tears." Thousands of Indigenous persons from the three tribes perished during a forced march from the Carolinas to Oklahoma, and again, all Jackson would think about was how many of his family and neighbors had died at the hands of these Indigenous allies of Tarleton's British troops so many years before.

But in the fall of 1780, Nathanael Greene and Daniel Morgan (with "Morgan's Rifles") arrived in western North Carolina to shore up the battered Patriot volunteers. At King's Mountain, Greene accomplished the first patriot victory since the British strategy had begun in Savannah. In early 1781, at Cowpens, the patriots would win the day yet again, and Cornwallis would withdraw, retreating to the Carolina coast at Wilmington. There he hoped to be replenished with supplies and fresh troops to carry the strategy back into North Carolina. At that point, two curious developments changed Cornwallis's mind, and thereby the entire "Southern strategy." Skirmishers led by this young officer named Gilbert attacked the flank of Cornwallis during his retreat to Wilmington and then hastily withdrew to the north.[491] It seemed most odd to Cornwallis. But then a few days later, it happened again. And then again. This young French officer seemed to know where the most vulnerable points of attack lay within Cornwallis's exhausted troops. The American forces would materialize, attack, and be gone. Nathanael Greene, with the best teacher on Fabian strategy that the eighteenth century would produce (George Washington), had in turn shared this colonial strategy with his young colleague. Gilbert was in turn exploiting it to dual advantage. While Loyalist casualties mounted and Loyalist zeal for warfare waned, it became clear within six weeks that Gilbert's retreats would invariably be north, and soon Cornwallis was lured to the base of Chesapeake Bay.

The second development was based upon the first: Cornwallis, also well aware of the potential for delay by requesting a strategy permission from the British ministry, decided that if this (Gilbert) be the only defense of southern Virginia, perhaps it was time to take the "Southern strategy" there.[492] Whether from ego (of which Cornwallis was certainly not lacking), expediency (because of minimal relief of his army at Wilmington), or opportunity (because of poor intelligence as to the implication of this adventure), Charles Cornwallis impulsively decided to move on tidewater Virginia. It was a decision that would end the American Revolution and launch a new nation.

It would be difficult to overstate the emotions of at least two dozen political leaders from Virginia over the notion of a British army with a reputation for savagery marching on the James River in their absence. One could start with Washington, the entire Lee family, George Mason, Thomas Jefferson, James Madison, a young adjutant of Washington named James Monroe, Patrick Henry, Edmund Randolph, Charles, Robert, and Benjamin Harrison—the list was endless. And their families, their land, their livelihood were all being jeopardized by this arrogant barbarian from Great Britain. Washington and

Hamilton could barely constrain these Virginia patriots, but had to do so. This assault was the second British error of the war (Howe and Saratoga being the first), and if Washington could convince the cavaliers of Virginia to remain calm and listen to his plan, the war could finally be brought to a conclusion. It would take some careful coordination with the French, whose naval delay in New Jersey had cost the Americans a crucial opportunity two years before. And he was determined not to lose yet another. This time, he had an adjutant who spoke fluent French, that same Gilbert, whom he considered a son, and whom he addressed in meetings as simply "Lafayette." Communication with the French military under Rochambeau and de Grasse was no longer a stumbling block.

In early February 1781, Paine boarded a packet ship in Boston, bound for L'Orient, France, joined by John Laurens, the son of Henry Laurens. Henry was now a guest of the British government in the gaol of the Tower of London thanks to the ineptitude of William Lee. John was joining Thomas Paine to collect the demand Paine had made upon the French treasury. Paine bore no concern of failure in this mission: Washington needed the funds, Lafayette needed Washington's army, and the French Crown needed Lafayette to succeed. With this clear connection, Paine was assured that Vergennes had no choice but to deliver. John was recovering from a failed personal relationship with Alexander Hamilton, which had persisted over three years, but finally was ended by Hamilton's decision to marry. Laurens would find solace in the arms of Paine during their Atlantic crossing, and the pair would spend a pleasant cruise together.[493] At that same time, a packet ship travelling west was carrying a letter from Passy to Philadelphia and the Second Continental Congress, announcing Franklin's resignation and plan to come home. Their passing was momentous.

When Paine and Laurens arrived in the office of Vergennes on April 17, Laurens boldly announced, "We are here to collect the seven million livres and have not a moment to lose. Where is it?" Paine turned five shades of scarlet, and Vergennes responded with screaming in French that the interpreter refused to translate for the Americans. Who was this child? And how dare he come to this

Court and make demands of this nature? Paine almost immediately fell all over himself, at once shushing the ineptitude of Laurens and begging forgiveness from Vergennes. Vergennes spat on the floor in front of them and walked out of his own office. Paine turned to Laurens. "Not another word! Not one, not until we are away from Versailles. Say nothing to anyone. Hold your hat in your hands and look at the floor. Do not smile. Do not speak. If someone speaks to you, bow. Do not respond. Never, ever, again, address an officer of the French court in this fashion. Are we quite clear?" Laurens was already gazing at the floor. He nodded.

Paine knew that, as they were yet in the office of Vergennes, that if they stood in place, he would eventually return. After about thirty minutes, he did. Paine, through the interpreter, offered, "My deepest and most sincere apologies, my lord. This man is recovering from fever. No, he is not contagious, but he is still delirious. He attempted to attack a cat on our way to your office. I fear it was the crossing. Please do not judge him harshly. He is a harmless and stupid person. He will not address you or anyone in Versailles further."

At the "stupid" comment, Vergennes smiled broadly. Paine had won the day for America. Vergennes then gave the duo the bad news: there would not be seven million livres for America. And then the good news: there would be six million. Paine now grinned broadly, kissed Vergennes's hand, and then pulled Laurens by his collar out of the office. Vergennes's secretary would emerge about thirty minutes later with the bank notes and specie.[494] There would be a celebration in Passy that evening!

Amid the wine, the rich food, and the laughter at L'Hôtel des Valentinois that evening, Franklin rendered his own bad news.[495] He had resigned the American ministry to France the previous week. He was awaiting orders from Philadelphia. Paine protested. This could not happen. They were too close now. They could not shut this down at this point. Franklin assured him that this would not impede their mission but only his role. Paine again protested and realized that now he really did have to hurry home.[496] There was damage to mitigate in Philadelphia, and their names were Lee and Izard. For months, Lee and Izard had bombarded the Second Continental Congress with prevarications about the diplomatic incompetence of the "poor old doctor of Passy" and assured the Congress that the revolution would fail if Franklin were not immediately replaced.[497] It was then Robert Morris who reminded Congress that without Franklin, there would be no French involvement whatsoever, dating back three years, and without the French, there would be no revolution, now or ever. Congress tabled the resolution to recall Franklin.

Paine's return to Philadelphia could not have proved more fortuitous. Bearing six million French livres, which he publicly handed to Washington, he assured Congress that Rochambeau was receiving four thousand French regulars to his encampment in Rhode Island that summer as reinforcements, at Washington's disposal, and that de Grasse and a large military fleet of over one dozen ships of the line was on the way to the West Indies, and finally that Dr. Franklin had given him a terse message to deliver to Congress: "You are most welcome." In the ensuing stir from various members of Congress, it would fall to Gouverneur Morris, no friend of Franklin or Paine, to rise, gravely holding up Franklin's resignation letter, look over the group, and then slowly and ceremoniously begin ripping it in two, a smile spreading across his face.

"Mr. Paine, do inform Dr. Franklin that his resignation has been *refused* by this august body, as we require his presence in Paris to draft the British Capitulation Treaty assuring our independence."[498] Spontaneous cheers erupted.

Washington, enthusiasm now resurrected by French livres and French muskets was absolutely champing at the bit to plan the liberation of New York from Sir Henry Clinton's British army. Heading into the summer of 1781 with assurances of a superior force, he felt that New York City was within their grasp. Here Rochambeau, with forty years' military experience but no desire for personal gain, reminded Washington of how America had arrived at this day, and how easily it could be stolen away. Listening, Lincoln and Hamilton whispered between themselves, examined the floor carefully, and then Hamilton looked up at his commander and said only, "The stable flies, general." The unanimous voice of Rochambeau and Washington's staff was that

Virginia would be easier and far less destructive to both America's military and to the civilians involved. They feared that to attack New York City with the full brunt of the artillery of Henry Knox and French Colonel d'Aboville would leave the city nearly leveled, and not a worthy war prize for anyone (unbeknownst to the command post of the Continental Army, much of New York City was already in ruins due to an uncontested fire in Manhattan two years before). Washington looked across the room and his jaw tightened into a grimace, not in anger but rather in acquiescence. For a fleeting moment, he had let personal vengeance against Howe because of all the setbacks and defeats of the previous five years get the better of his Fabian judgment. On the bright side, this meant that he could also deflect war away from the plantations of the east coast of Virginia and thus away from Stratford Hall, and of course, his beloved Mount Vernon. He looked slowly around the room at his young military staff, and said one word, "Virginia." They would begin the plan to bring Lafayette north and call for the French navy from the West Indies.

The Yorktown "siege," perhaps more accurately a demonstration of withering artillery bombardment and gradual encroachment of infantry from all sides, between October 9 and October 17, would resemble to a degree Saratoga almost exactly four years before, but on a far grander scale.[499] With de Grasse now holding the Chesapeake from the British navy, there would be no possibility of British escape by sea, and with the Virginia militia, smarting from skirmishing defeats throughout the summer, now holding the York peninsula at its head, there would be no possibility[500] of British fighting for a land egress. The only two infantry engagements would be at British "redoubts," earthworks in advance of the actual British fortifications. One assault was under the command of Lafayette, the other under the command of Hamilton.[501] Prior to Hamilton's assault, Washington drew him aside and urged him to be forthright and courageous, for "I can assure you, Hamilton, that Lafayette intends to drive the British into the Shenandoah at this point." Both assaults would achieve their intention with little resistance.[502] Thus Cornwallis, like Burgoyne almost exactly four years previously, was bottled, the cork was secured, and the label affixed. His army had lost, and so he pressed for terms on October 18.

Per the directive of Lord Germain, Cornwallis chose not to "surrender or capitulate" and instead hid in the ruins of his Yorktown headquarters. His adjutant, Brigadier General Charles O'Hara, appeared with the remnants of the British force at 2:00 p.m. on October 19, 1781, on the open ground outside Yorktown, marching between the French on one side and the Americans, with Washington at the van, on the other. O'Hara brought the ceremonial "sword of surrender" to Rochambeau, who looked at him and crossed his arms. "Monsieur, your army has been defeated by the army of 'Les États Unis d'Amerique' and to them your sword shall be delivered."

And then nodded toward Washington. O'Hara sighed and walked over to Washington, who inquired, "Where is Cornwallis?"

"Sick in his headquarters."

Washington had already sensed this insult from the vanquished Brits, crossed his arms, and told him flatly, "The adjutant of the vanquished seeks the adjutant of the conquerors."

And he nodded toward General Benjamin Lincoln. O'Hara flushed, sensing the return of the insult, and finally found a willing hand in Lincoln.[503] It was done. The war itself was not.

Chapter 32

In London, the news of Cornwallis's surrender of a British army in Virginia was greeted with a new resolve by the Privy Council to fortify Sir Henry Clinton's defense of New York. But in Commons, the now constant harangue from Burke, Barre, and the Whig party generally was nearly too much to bear. Lord North was brought to tears. Millions of British pounds sterling had been poured down this rabbit hole in America, and the British had achieved little more than international embarrassment. This was the first example to the world of the near impossibility of trying to wage "war at a distance," in this case three thousand miles. Without rapid communication from "headquarters" (London), without a supply line that could respond within days, rather than months, without a public stake in defense (Great Britain, after all the silliness between Franklin, Earl Sandwich, Jones, Broglie, and the French-Spanish "invasion," was never forced to defend its homeland from attack), a war of attrition that Washington, Franklin, and Pownall executed to near-perfection, was simply and bluntly unwinnable. This was the first, but it most assuredly would not be the last: the same lesson would be learned by Napoleon at Russia, Hitler at Russia, and the United States through the second half of the twentieth century. Month by month, the British desire to maintain a losing war effort was waning, and with it financial support and ultimately political support.

By March 1782, Lord North's government had collapsed, and he was given the bum's rush from 10 Downing Street.[504] Lord Rockingham took the reins and then promptly died in July. Lord Shelburne, a far more sympathetic ear to America, then walked into a firestorm of opposition and was gone by February 1783. The final government to negotiate the independence of the United States would be led by a tenuous coalition of Lord North (again!) with Charles James Fox. Four governments within the year would be the British legacy from Yorktown. The message to the ministry from Commons was now clear: end this!

In France, the response was somewhat muddled. Franklin knew almost immediately that this "second Saratoga" was the end of his rainbow, and his mood changed correspondingly. Initially moody and brooding at the dawn of 1781, now with the message from Congress refusing his resignation and with Yorktown, he was giddy and his old delightful self at dinners and theater with his French entourage as the year came to a close. But behind the diplomatic scenes there was a much darker and complex array of negotiations developing.[505] The British were most anxious to break the Franco-American alliance apart, fearing that their island could be a ready target, and at the very least that their economy was at high risk of losing their number one trading partner (America). So the British requested and received an audience for secret negotiations for "a separate peace" with the United States. They could then deal with the French and Spanish through land reparations.

But then the British blundered horribly once again. It was becoming clear to all now, what Pownall had been saying all along: "The corruption of the British government had come from the head, and the only cure is decapitation." The ministry of Britain entered negotiations with Franklin with an idea of keeping the United States within the British Empire as a sort of "Western Scotland." In that regard, they had simply turned a deaf ear to Franklin and Paine and twenty years of American politics. To initiate the negotiations, they had sent the son of George Grenville, twenty-seven-year-old Thomas, whose presence was clearly intended as an insult to the American delegation. Franklin had come to the table with a totally different offer: ceding Canada to the United

States.[506] "You will never develop a populace in that frozen land that will create a trading partner. You will have to pay for its defense as you were supposed to be paying for ours. You *will lose Canada*. It is only a matter of when." The British were certainly not in a mood to discuss land reparations with America. Canada would be reserved as a chip for the French table. Franklin then could just as well have opined, "What part of the word 'independence' do you not understand?" But now, holding the entire trump suit, he chose diplomacy, making it clear to the British diplomats that their efforts had to culminate in one absolute certainty. And here, once again, Pownall's statement to Commons in 1777 would prove prophetic: "The Americans never will return again to their subjection to the government of this country. Your sovereignty over America is abolished."[507]

Washington was in a completely different situation as the siege of Yorktown ended. There was no clear-cut suggestion that Great Britain would, at that point, totally capitulate to the new nation.[508] And so, with Virginia secured, and with the "Southern strategy" now in tatters, Washington moved the bulk of his forces back toward New York. The largest remaining British army in the colonies remained there, under the ongoing command of Sir Henry Clinton, and he appeared unready to push out of the city into the area around New York City, or to cede his position. At the same time, skirmishers of the Loyalists would remain in the Carolinas for the ensuing twelve months, which would prove tragic to the cause of America.

Henry Laurens's son John was born October 28, 1754 and would be the eldest son surviving infancy.[509] By that time, Henry and his partner George Austin, of "Austin and Laurens," had become the most prominent slave-trading house in America. Moving to Europe in 1771 at the insistence of his father, John would attend school in Geneva, Switzerland until 1774, when he moved to London to enter Middle Temple at the Inns of Court to study law. At that time, he began seeing Martha Manning, whose brother was a banking officer and member of Parliament. In 1776, learning that she was pregnant, John agreed to marry her. Shortly thereafter, in December, he returned to America specifically to enlist in the military, leaving the pregnant Martha in London.

He would never see her again and would never meet his young daughter.

Arriving in Charleston in April 1777, John would travel to join his father at the Second Continental Congress. There he advised Henry that he was joining Washington's army; Henry used his political pull to have John named an "aide-de-camp" there, joining the other young aides, Hamilton and Lafayette. He would see action in September at Brandywine and would remain with Washington until his deployment as a diplomat to Paris with Thomas Paine in 1780. Returning to America in May 1781, he would claim credit for the six-million-livre French loan, and Paine would exercise discretion and not tell of the diplomatic faux pas that his young colleague had created in Versailles. John finally rejoined Washington outside Yorktown, Virginia.

By this time, Henry was the guest of honor in the gaol of the Tower of London, courtesy of William Lee and George III. Richard Oswald, once based in Africa as an employed agent for Henry's slave-trading business, and now a businessman and bureaucrat in London, heard of Henry's plight and brought him food, clothing, and newspapers regularly.[510] Richard then initiated negotiations at the Court of George III for Henry's release (Henry by then was fifty-seven, and gaol was a most unhealthy domicile, even in a warder's apartment at Byward Tower). At the end of 1781, the American rebels came by a bargaining chip to aid in Richard's negotiation. On the last day of 1781, New Year's Eve, Henry was released in a prisoner swap for…General Charles Cornwallis, at the time held in Philadelphia. Henry hastened on to The Hague, a year late.

After Yorktown, John left Washington's army and returned to South Carolina under the command of Nathanael Greene, to aid in the defense of the rural west against the British army still occupying Charleston, South Carolina.[511] On August 27, 1782, ten months *after* Yorktown, a regiment of British regulars dispatched from Charleston to forage for food came upon Laurens's brigade. In the ensuing skirmish, Laurens was shot and killed. He was twenty-seven years old. Henry returned late in the year to bury his son on the family plantation. On November 30, just over three months after the death of John Laurens, Benjamin Franklin would apply his signature to a peace treaty with Great Britain, negotiated for Great Britain by that same Richard Oswald, ending the American revolution. For Henry, it was three months too late to save his only son.

Having succeeded in an agreement to terms with Great Britain that would guarantee American independence by November 1782, the American delegation of Franklin, Jay, and Adams had broken a trust with Vergennes, which forced Franklin to come with hat in hand, begging forgiveness, and at the same time, with typical Franklin chutzpah, seeking yet one more loan for the American cause.[512] Here Vergennes was cool, not angry. He was clearly hurt that the Americans had gone so far as to actually sign the private treaty with Great Britain; it fell to Franklin to assure him that their bargain still stood and that until Great Britain had successfully treated with both the Bourbon Crowns, there would be no public acknowledgment of American peace. For Franklin this was no shallow promise; he would not feel total confidence in the successful conclusion of his lifetime goal until France and Spain were satisfied.[513] The previous year had brought reversals for both those nations in battle with the Brits: the French navy under de Grasse had been scattered in the West Indies, with many French ships now war prizes in Plymouth, England; and at Gibraltar, the Brits had repulsed a Spanish force attempting to turn them out of this strategic piece of property and had roundly defeated them. Only a British defeat in India, 4,500 miles from home, had blemished their record during 1782, and they were in no mood to cede vast blocks of colonies in their empire.

In the end, Great Britain would lose the United States, keep Barbados, Antigua, Jamaica, and the Bahamas, lose the "Northwest Territory," keep Canada, keep India, and keep the all-important Gibraltar, which they hold to this day. Vergennes would reluctantly provide yet another loan to America, tilting France yet one more step toward bankruptcy and revolution of its own, and the Treaty of Paris would be officially signed September 3, 1783.[514] Franklin wore his old blue velvet jacket one last time for the occasion; it was the jacket he wore nine- and one-half years previously for a less auspicious event in the Cockpit. After he had affixed his signature one more time to an historic document, he removed his newest invention, his "double spectacles" (later known as bifocals), looked up at the august delegation around him, and declared, "Gentlemen, there has never been a good war or a bad peace," and smiled. He had seen his dream to its conclusion.

On the heels of the Yorktown triumph, Thomas Paine took time to send a lengthy letter to "His excellency, George Washington," about his present state of extreme poverty.[515] The Silas Deane affair had tarnished Paine's reputation before Congress, at the hands of John Jay, and Paine prayed that Washington would provide aid in rebuilding it. He went to lengths to point out that in London at the present time, October 1781, Silas Deane was debasing the Americans to British audiences while through correspondence debasing the British to American audiences. He went on to point out that he, Paine, had tried to advise Congress of the treachery of Deane, but that Jay had refused to hear him out. He hoped that with the loan that he, and not John Laurens, had negotiated for the American cause from France in November 1780, he would once again be held in esteem in his adopted country.[516] Ultimately, what he truly hoped was that Washington would intercede on his behalf before Congress to secure him immediate funds with a promise of an annuity. Everything in the letter was factual; much of what he wrote was typically factual. And in the end, the state of New Jersey would award him a generous plot of land just across the Delaware from Philadelphia in Bordentown. For the remainder of his life, Thomas Paine would consider this home.

In Virginia, the state assembly would discuss Washington's petition on behalf of Paine, and a bill was introduced to provide £2,000 for him from the sale of a plot of public land. The bill presented in their senate failed by one vote. That vote would be cast by…Arthur Lee. For Lee, any man that bore the taint of Benjamin Franklin was a man not to be trusted and therefore not worthy of compensation for any service, no matter how just. John Dickinson in Pennsylvania proved far more receptive to the plea from Washington; he would personally guide a bill through the Pennsylvania assembly that would award Paine £500. That sum would leave him in a comfortable position for the remainder of his life. The Second Continental Congress finally responded on

September 27, 1785, two weeks after the return of Franklin to Philadelphia, awarding Paine $3,000 in continental dollars. Now financially comfortable, Paine turned to his inventions and a plan to return to visit his elderly parents at Thetford, East Anglia.

Thomas Pownall would greet the Peace of Paris with an almost overwhelming sense of relief and near-total exhaustion.[517] He wrote to Franklin [the spelling is all Pownall]: *I wish that events of warr and uncorresponding issue of peace may at length teach the civilized part of the world that warr is a bad way of adjusting claims and rights and that treaties must settle them at last. I will hope at least that the two seperate dominions and governments are settled in a permanent peace—our holy book says, blessed are the peace makers but referrs them for their reward to heaven—you must feel the reward in the heaven, you are in possession of, your own mind.* Pownall was most assured that his work with Franklin was now completed. He would continue a brisk correspondence with both Franklin and James Bowdoin over the ensuing two years. He would revise his topographic maps yet again, including the Lewis Evans map, and he would publish an essay entitled *A Memorial Addressed to the Sovereigns of America*. And then he would marry a second time, to a wealthy and attractive British widow, Hannah Astell, in 1784. He was sixty-two. The Pownalls decided to "honeymoon," such as it was, with a grand tour of the Continent, beginning in August and lasting over nine months. In the end, Pownall had to hurry back to Great Britain in time for the departure of Franklin in the summer of 1785.

Charles Dumas had become totally overwhelmed with the responsibilities as proxy minister for the United States to the United Provinces following the Texel affair and the departure of John Paul Jones. With Franklin now minister plenipotentiary of France, the Second Continental Congress decided that John Adams should pursue a similar role in the United Provinces and should press them for official recognition of the independent United States of America as a sovereign nation.[518] To that end, Adams headed for Amsterdam the spring of 1781 to treat with Dumas and with the various Provinces. Here the two would meet roadblock after roadblock, as the Grand Pensionary of the United Provinces was in no hurry to antagonize the British government by recognizing the United States.[519] After door after door had been slammed in their faces, Adams and Dumas decided to relax and wait for negotiations between Great Britain and the United Provinces to develop. At that point, Congress advised Dumas that henceforth the Committee of Foreign Affairs would be designated the Office of Foreign Affairs, with Robert Livingston of New York its secretary and Dumas's superior.[520] Thus, all further correspondence to Congress should be directed to Robert Livingston.

Livingston was fortunately not Dumas's paymaster; fortunate for Dumas, because nothing he was doing seemed to satisfy Livingston. Livingston would now discover first-hand what Franklin and Pownall had known for twenty-five years and could have told him: over 95% of European correspondence arrived too late to allow for any timely action to take place. Therefore, one had to instruct the ministries of Europe in what to do, as *chargés d'affaires*, and then trust the ministers to act in the best interests of the United States. But Livingston was naive and would berate Dumas for "fresher and more timely information." He told him to "go to the wharves with new correspondence and determine the next ship to depart and place your correspondence with them." The directive was, for all experienced correspondents in Europe and the United States, by parts ridiculous and useless. A given ship could slide out of the harbor and then sit for days or weeks, awaiting favorable winds, to achieve departure to the high seas. Some Atlantic crossings could be affected in as little as four weeks; others took four months. And the wharves were simply not a place where this transit time could be reliably predicted. But Dumas, as was his wont, assured Livingston that he would do his utmost to improve his performance; his approach would be, as it always was, an absolute blizzard of correspondence sent out at least five times per week. Robert Morris was the paymaster, and during this time, Dumas would be chronically destitute.[521] Compensation would come through Franklin, of all odd systems, and Franklin would, as much as possible, quietly supplement the money passed on to Dumas.

The news of Yorktown hit the United Provinces by storm in February 1782. Within one month, the United States of America was recognized by the United Provinces as a free and independent nation, and in April, Adams was credentialed as minister plenipotentiary for the United States in The Hague.[522] The America House was purchased by Adams, with Dumas serving as real estate agent; it would prove only the third free-standing embassy in The Hague, following those of France and Spain, and the first dedicated American embassy in history. Adams now felt as if he had "arrived" and was a bit less prone to outrage. He would be called to Paris in late 1782 to sign the secret Peace of Paris and to aid in formal peace negotiations between France and Great Britain, and from that point, Dumas would assume the proxy role of *chargé d'affaires* at The Hague.

David Barclay was still negotiating grants and loans from Spain and the United Provinces through 1782 to 1784. In this he would remain successful, providing Franklin's new nation a reasonable base of funds with which to cover their cost of government. But Barclay was becoming an international master of political science and the financial basis of nations through an ongoing correspondence with David Hume's old friend and colleague, Adam Smith. Barclay was growing ever more frustrated with the Second Continental Congress, most of whose membership he would never meet, and to whom he would never write a single piece of correspondence. It seems he was most unimpressed with their lackadaisical approach to finances and advised Franklin that without a radical change in governance, America could never survive. Barclay was never one to mince words, and his enchantment with America was fading by the month. The source of this disenchantment could be summarized in a single word. He and Thomas Paine, with the legacy left from Dr. Fothergill, were of a mind that the abolition of American slavery should be addressed sooner rather than later. And they were concerned that with the Peace of Paris of 1783, the topic was suddenly pushed into the background. Both men were well aware of the role that the abolitionists had played to secure the independence of the American colonies. Now, as Paine had pursued recompense of finances he felt were justifiably due, Barclay felt precisely the same way about abolition. It was time for America to deliver on its promise from Jefferson's Declaration of 1776. He was waiting, but quite impatiently.

Chapter 33

By the closing days of November 1782, with not only peace, but also peace with independence nearly assured, Franklin resumed a clandestine correspondence with Pownall and Barclay. From Passy, he advised the other two members of the inner circle that the time had come, the time to initiate the essential, and necessarily secret, process of obliterating the "tracks" of evidence of his ingenious and remarkably comprehensive scheme. They had already realized in 1774 that were their plan successful, it would yield a most unfortunate legacy not only for the makers of the plot but truly for all the principals involved: the use of *Somersett* to lure the southern colonies, the theft and publication of the Hutchinson letters to warm the northern colonies by tying that correspondence to the "Boston Massacre," the authorship of the "Intolerable Acts" to punish Boston and draw in New York, the punishment of Arthur Lee for, well, for being Arthur Lee, the use of the Roman Curia and its "Peter's Pence" in France, Spain, the United Provinces, and Baltimore to launder funds, the mischievous and shameless manipulation of the Fourth Earl Sandwich to keep the British navy out of North America, the Texel episode and John Paul Jones to draw the United Provinces into an alliance and away from Great Britain, and the bankruptcy of the Court of Louis XVI to finance it all. In the end it was a terrible story, with terrible consequences for prominent people in at least three established countries, and one newly minted. No, it could not be told; it could *never* be told. The correspondence, the evidence, all needed to be destroyed while the three surviving original members of the inner circle were still healthy and capable of the task.

It is estimated that of all the correspondence of the eighteenth century, we likely have little more than ten percent.[523] Many letters contained the admonition: "Burn this" or "Burn this after reading" or "Destroy this" or similar dictates. Franklin was notorious for using this directive in much of his correspondence, and we have a few letters from his hand where the phrase has been preserved on a letter. This would, of course, imply that by and large, his colleagues respected and complied with his wishes in that regard. Other correspondence was simply lost or left in large bundles, crates, or files as legacies or estates, as in the case of Barclay, where descendants were proscribed, by Barclay himself, the task of editing and collating, and just like Martha Washington with the personal letters from her beloved husband George, the heirs destroyed them en masse.[524] Fires wiped out entire libraries of correspondence, sometimes accidentally and sometimes through arson, as in the case of the entire home of Lord Mansfield eight years after the *Somersett* decision, including his legal library and all his personal notes from the Court of King's Bench (this act of violence occurring during the "Gordon Riots" of 1780 by Protestants against the Roman Catholic aristocracy in London).[525] And so it was that all three surviving original members of the inner circle commenced a unique approach to starting fires in their furnaces and stoves during the winter of 1782–83. (Interestingly, Thomas Paine adamantly refused to participate in the willful destruction of *his* correspondence and personal papers and would carefully compile and protect them from destruction for the remainder of his complex life.) The older and more debilitated Franklin pressed Temple, his grandson, into the task, as the two continually waded through stacks of correspondence and copies, saving those deemed innocuous while commending the sensitive standouts to the flames. The true ratio of the difference will never be known; both Franklin and Temple took that information to their graves.

In the end, Pownall likely suffered the most from this hastily achieved conclusion to their plot. His legacy was by far the least assured, and within two generations, few outside his family would recall that he once authored the final draft of the Albany Plan of Union with Franklin, convinced Franklin that the only path toward severing Pennsylvania from its hated proprietors was a revolution by *all* the American British colonies, and purloined the "Hutchinson Letters." His meteoric rise to prominence in the American colonies, including the governorship of Massachusetts and South Carolina, and lieutenant governorships of New Jersey and New York, his rejection of the governorship of Pennsylvania, all unprecedented in American history, would be relegated to a footnote.[526] His brother John would accept full credit, or blame, for the "Intolerable Acts," although the brothers equally conspired in preparing them for Parliamentary vote to punish the American colonies, in order to secure an equally vengeful response from those same colonies, in 1774 and 1775. And other than the resolution of the "Corn Laws" in Parliament in 1772, exactly during the arguments at the Court of King's Bench over *Somersett,* he would be remembered in Parliament as the Whig who had to become a Tory in order to keep a seat in Commons, a most embarrassing development in 1774–75.

But at the same time, Pownall far exceeded his confidants in matters of the heart, successfully and successively courting *two* attractive and wealthy widows, Lady Fawkener and Hannah Astell, who provided him a far more comfortable life than any impoverished Lincolnshire scholar had a right to anticipate.[527] And in this, Barclay and Franklin could only observe in wonder and envy. In affairs of the heart, Pownall turned out to be the undisputed champion of the trio and would never worry about finances or companionship again.

Franklin's legacy had long been secured, and he would have an unimaginable seven more years of political triumph to seal this, without ever confirming his complete role in the making of a nation. He would live long enough to see President Washington running the affairs of state, under the directives of a document from the hand of Jefferson's cousin, James Madison, that of course being the Constitution of the United States of America. But he and Temple would work hard during those years to create an image of superficiality, totally incongruous with the real picture of the scheming, conniving, ever intriguing

Benjamin Franklin that the people of Philadelphia, London, and Paris knew so well. Franklin would, in the end, be the quiet philosophical grandfather of a country, full of literary witticisms but never a militant or a revolutionary. During that time, he would also cast himself, fulfilling the vow he had made to Barclay and to Dr. Fothergill, as an ardent abolitionist.[528] Even though he had once owned at least five slaves of whom we are aware, he would preside over the Pennsylvania Abolitionist Society for its first three years of existence.

Barclay, the great financier who so deftly compartmentalized his life between dealing in military ordinance, developing one of the most successful banking establishments in world history, and at the same time providing philanthropic endeavors such as manumission with Pennsylvania homesteading by former slaves and founding Quaker schools in Great Britain and America, would go to great extremes to avoid drawing attention to himself.[529] Truly self-deprecating to a fault, he would never reveal the mechanisms whereby he had successfully raised and delivered funding of the American Revolution. By his Quaker reckoning, he had provided millions of pounds sterling through Jacques Necker and George Grand and passed it through the Roman Curia into the hands of Robert Morris via Haym Salomon, a truly ecumenical sleight of hand. And once the Treaty of Paris of 1783 was concluded, he would simply distance himself from any acknowledgment of his pivotal role in that outcome.

And so in the end, by 1785, the tracks had been effectively covered, and while rumors abounded throughout Europe, and especially in Great Britain and France, of a covert conspiracy to free the American colonies from their British overseers, no confirmation would ever be forthcoming.[530] Franklin, exhausted, nearly eighty years of age, supervised the packing of his personal effects in Passy and prepared with his two grandsons to return home one last time.[531] Pownall, with his newlywed, wealthy wife, was on the "grand tour" of Europe, cost be damned. They had money, and life was waning away; the only thing to do was to spend it luxuriously, and so they did.[532] Barclay had attended the deathbed of the dear friend and original member of the inner circle, Dr. Fothergill. Fothergill had passed quietly of heart failure during the revolution, on the day after Christmas, 1780.[533] In 1779, Barclay had travelled with the aging physician to High Ackworth to organize the Ackworth School for Quakers. In keeping a promise to his surrogate father, Barclay would secure the financial status of that school, still in existence 240 years later. So it was that Pownall and Barclay prayed Dr. Franklin return one last time, to Southampton, before leaving Europe forever behind.

July 27, 1785: Dr. Franklin was the center of attention at a farewell party aboard the ship in dock at Southampton.[534] The ship was scheduled to embark at dawn for New York, and Dr. Franklin knew that he would not be returning to Europe. It was simply time to live out his life at home. Many of his remaining old friends from Great Britain, and a few expatriates from America and France, were in attendance and sharing in the revelry. Among the guests present were none other than David Barclay and Thomas Pownall. Barclay was most assuredly no reveler, and that night Pownall would also feel more reserved and somewhat more melancholy than festive. He had just returned with his new bride from their grand tour of Europe and was coming to the realization that his life no longer held his goal of returning to America. And so they asked Dr. Franklin out onto the deck for their last goodbyes, the final meeting of the inner circle.

After a cordial embrace with Pownall, Franklin pulled his coat closer in the late night damp and said, "Is it not curious, in the end, Thomas, that all through the revolution, half of us were fighting to end our slavery, and the other half were fighting to *preserve* it?" Then he chuckled a bit.

To which Pownall, buttoning his coat, and heading for the gangplank, responded, "And in the end, Dr. Franklin, is it not curious that every one of you got precisely what he wanted."

And he smiled and waved as he walked down the dock, leaving Franklin and Barclay behind. Barclay then paused, looked down for a moment, and looked directly into Franklin's eyes. "And in the end, Dr. Franklin, not a one of them got what they needed."

Franklin was quiet, thinking, and then said, "I am not sure I apprehend your meaning."

Barclay peered into Franklin's eyes one last time, squeezed his shoulders, and responded, "My dear, dear Dr. Franklin. Thou must finally understand that not one of us will be free, until all of us are free."

And then David Barclay backed away, stepped down the gangplank, and faded into the fog of the night.

Epilogue

David Barclay watched anxiously over the ensuing ten years as the Americans established their Constitution for the United States of America, hoping that they would address the issue of abolition of slavery of Black Africans. Franklin had vowed to Fothergill and Barclay his dedication to the cause of abolition once independence of the United States was assured, but in the final seven years of his life, other than presiding over the Abolitionist Society of Pennsylvania in Philadelphia, no further progress ensued. In reading the Constitution, Barclay fixed upon Section I Article 9, noting that the final compromise called for solving the issue by 1808, twenty years after the document was signed. Furious, Barclay crumpled his copy on the spot. After the death of Franklin, and with no positive action taking in place in America toward abolition, Barclay called his family together in 1792. With his voice rising, and with rare hints of emotion, he directed them: "The Americans continue in this vile and hideous sin against humanity and will not consider abolition. Mr. Paine, Dr. Fothergill and I worked for years to assure the American emancipation from Great Britain. We were assured that abolition of enslavement of Black Africans would follow soon thereafter. The roads of America are already awash in the blood of their African brothers and sisters. Now they endeavor to pass the sin on to their children. For how long? My patience is at an end now. I forbid any of thee to endeavor a biography of my years of work for America. I have destroyed all my ledgers, correspondence, and notes prior to 1785. I will support no effort to memorialize my work on behalf of America. This family will have no business dealings with slave owners. Ever. I pray for, and pity, the children of these bestial men, for they will be washed in the blood of their bondsmen, and their end will be brutal and tragic. America has chosen to isolate itself in this transgression from Europe and from the civilized world. They shall not be able to maintain this blot forever. But we can have no further part with the slave owners of America. I forbid it! And henceforth, I will never again broach this subject in this company. I thank thee all for thy loyalty to thy family name." And so David Barclay would be known as a staunch Quaker abolitionist and an adept, honest, and hardworking banker. As a clandestine conspirator, he would never be betrayed by his family.

But the words of Barclay to his family were perhaps overly harsh. Franklin's Pennsylvania had indeed pursued the concept of abolition while Franklin was in France, enacting legislation to ensure the gradual manumission of African slaves within the timeframe of the American Constitution. Massachusetts had "one-upped" Pennsylvania in the year of the Treaty of Paris as the one state that would consider absolute and immediate abolition of slavery through the *Quock Walker* trial in 1783.[535] The territory of Vermont would follow the lead of Massachusetts in 1786. The political developments in New Hampshire regarding abolition remain almost too tortuous and arcane for even today's expert historians, but by 1800 there were no slaves in New Hampshire. The other states north of Pennsylvania were more inclined to follow the path laid out by Pennsylvania, with progressive manumission of slaves over the ensuing generation, but with a finite ultimate end to the practice built into the legislation. With fits and starts, this would extend up into the 1840s, but for all points from Pennsylvania north, the practice was unusual after about 1826.

Pennsylvania has referred to itself as the "Keystone State" now for over two hundred years, and yet if one were to enquire about the origin of this nickname, one would hear a panoply of explanations that have developed as rather a "folk etymology" over the course of that time. In actuality, it applies specifically to abolition and the role that *Somersett* played during the American revolution. All the states south of Pennsylvania (including Delaware) relied heavily upon slave labor for their economy, while all the states north of Pennsylvania (including New Jersey) did not. The Pennsylvania instigator of the American revolution would rely upon *Somersett* to encourage revolution for one leg of the colonial arch to the south, and upon the "Hutchinson letters" to accomplish the same for the other leg to the north. Pennsylvania would be considered the "keystone" in this economic and political model, anchoring the two sides during the revolution, while remaining more inclined toward the goal of federal independence and less inclined toward dealing with specific issues dividing the colonies. Once independence was won, Pennsylvania would spearhead the effort for progressive manumission, but only one half of the "arch" would follow suit.[536] The six southern colonies would maintain the institution for one more war. And the original source of the designation, "Keystone State," would of necessity be blurred by posterity into an unrecognizable explanation of sorts.

Upon Franklin's return to Philadelphia in the fall of 1785, he took stock of all that he had missed during his past nine years in Europe. Many of his friends and colleagues had not survived the war years. He was aware of the loss of John Fothergill and of Margaret Stevenson, his landlady in Craven Street, London. He now learned that abolitionist Anthony Benezet had died the previous year in Philadelphia; prior to his death, he had urged Franklin to take up the cause of abolition of slavery in his place.

On the heels of Pennsylvania's law to initiate the gradual abolition of slavery and manumission of its many slaves, problems had arisen due to the simple fact that Philadelphia remained the national capital throughout the 1780s. This in and of itself had created "issues" for the Americans from the south who were now involved in the day-to-day work of the government. While the law of 1780 had excluded members of the Second Continental Congress from the initiative of manumission, it did not address others involved in the federal government. Therefore, members of the executive and judicial branches of government who were slave owners, especially after ratification of the Constitution, faced automatic manumission of any slaves they kept in Philadelphia for over six months. This left them either accepting the manumission rule or "swapping out" their personal servants every six months. Regrettably, more took advantage of the latter than accepted the former. The first American president would be one of these.[537] Pennsylvania would move to correct this problem in 1788, and thereafter, the state judiciary would vigorously defend the right of freedom for slaves brought to Pennsylvania. Through Franklin's Abolition Society, aggressive litigation would send a message to travelers from the West Indies and the American south: do *not* bring your slaves with you to Pennsylvania. They would be liberated via writs of habeas corpus and expensive lawsuits.

None of the states south of Pennsylvania would ever achieve legislative manumission of slaves, and abolition of slavery, prior to the American Civil War. Delaware would vote on the issue in 1792, 1793, 1797, 1803, and 1847; it would finally pass in their House in 1850, but in their Senate it would fail by a single vote. And so for Delaware, as for all the states to her south, the words of Barclay would prove prophetic.

David Barclay, true to his word, would drop back into the role of "silent partner" in his bank, disgusted with the ongoing willingness of his partner, Bevans, to continue financial support of slave owners in the American south and West Indies. He would be named an honorary member of the Pennsylvania Society for Promoting the Abolition of Slavery and for the Relief of Free Negroes Unlawfully Held in Bondage (which practicality would reduce to Pennsylvania Abolition Society by 1790) in 1787 at the behest of its new president, Benjamin Franklin. By that time, Barclay was also an active member of The London Meeting [Quakers] Addressing the Sufferings in the Slave Trade (it was the traditional stance of the Quakers that the slave trade oppressed not only the Black African slave, but all whites involved as well, due to the duress it created in their own consciences). In 1795, he would receive through a failed security bond a small plantation in Jamaica, which came completely supplied with…Black African slaves. Barclay was naturally appalled and moved to divest himself of ownership of the slaves as quickly as possible.[538] Here he would learn that manumission was not so simple as saying, "Let them go." When he advised Alexander McLeod, the agent in Spanish Town for the Barclay family, to manumit the slaves, McLeod responded that this measure "would prove highly unpopular on this island" and countered with a trial manumission of one couple, Hamlet and Prudence, paying them for their labor on the plantation. Barclay reluctantly acceded to this offer, but within the year, McLeod would declare the couple "relaxed in their labor" (not working at the level of the slaves around them) and would turn them out. Barclay then insisted on providing the couple a yearly support of thirteen guineas in perpetuity; they would live out their lives with Hamlet working as a horse breeder and wrangler and Prudence as a laundress.

Barclay was not finished with the issue. Later that same year, he sent one William Holden from Great Britain to Jamaica with the instructions to free the remaining slaves on the plantation, and in deference to McLeod and the slave owners of Jamaica, to remove them to Pennsylvania in the United States, where they would pursue free work and free lives. Holden found two elderly house slaves whom he refused to manumit, as he felt they would not stand the hardship of transport, but agreed to take the others through Kingston, Jamaica, to Philadelphia. At Kingston, the slaves rebelled and insisted on returning to the plantation; they wanted to take a stand in defiance of the slave owners around them. A single slave treated with the defiant slaves and finally convinced them to complete the relocation to freedom, for fear of being "taken up" and executed or returned once more to slavery on another plantation in the British West Indies. They would finally agree and accept relocation on free land in Pennsylvania. This endeavor was considered a reasonable success.

Barclay would continue his efforts at philanthropy and abolition full-time for the remainder of his life and would die quietly in Walthamstow, Essex (now in North London) in 1809.

Thomas Pownall would spend the years after 1785 immersed in his studies and writings on British antiquities and the role of agronomy in the new world of manufacturing. He remained involved in studying the relationship between the European powers and the emerging movement toward self-determination throughout the Western Hemisphere. And then an individual who had embraced the latter issue stepped into his life.

Sebastián Francisco de Miranda y Rodríguez de Espinoza was born March 28, 1750, in Caracas, Venezuela into a family with relative wealth and influence in the colony of Venezuela, but periodically involved in the intrigues of Spanish society in South America. Accused of being a "impure white" by the upper class, Miranda's father was forced to obtain a legal genealogy report, duly notarized, to maintain his family status and personal wealth. From that background, Miranda would seem to have a sixth sense for 1) survival, while 2) backing the losing side. This would follow him throughout his life and long career as a soldier for independence.

His initial military experience occurred in Morocco, where Spain was attempting expansion to surround and besiege Gibraltar. Despite apparent success in the campaign, Miranda was recalled ignominiously to Cadiz, and then sent to Cuba, where he would participate in the siege of Pensacola during the American Revolution. Subsequently, he would participate in campaigns against Jamaica and the Bahamas. At that point, he would be accused of spying for the British against Spain and summoned for recall to the Spanish Inquisition. Although subsequently released, he clearly had become disenchanted with the Spanish government and Spanish elite society and began to think more of Venezuelan independence. Alerted by friends that he was being considered for arrest by the Inquisition yet again, he fled to the new United States of America, where he discussed independence with veterans of the American independence movement such as Jefferson, the Adamses, Paine, Knox, Hamilton, and Livingston. Miranda would return to Europe before Franklin departed for America, in 1785.[539]

After extensive travels in Europe, Miranda insisted upon meeting with Thomas Pownall in Everton. They discussed the Enlightenment and its meaning for the colonies of Latin America. While at face value the choice of Pownall might seem odd, he had come highly recommended by Thomas Paine for unclear reasons (the public was unaware that these two were even aware of the other's existence). Pownall was philosophically supportive but no longer had the physical energy or Parliamentary connections to press Miranda's cause. There was in 1789 some interest on the part of Great Britain to suppress the rich trade of the Spanish in the Caribbean, despite their European alliance against France. But then, unfortunately for Miranda, the Nootka Sound crisis broke that consideration. Originating in the absolute most remote corner of the world at that time in the waters between British Columbia and Alaska, the Spanish fleet asserted its territorial authority against British fur traders, confiscating British ships. In the ensuing dustup, it would be Spain that would ultimately get the worst of the negotiations, with the waters from Alaska to present-day Washington declared internationally open for commerce. And with that, Great Britain's interest in suppression of international trade against its European rivals rapidly faded away.

While Pownall urged British support of Miranda in pursuit of Venezuelan independence, Prime Minister William Pitt the Younger advised him that his government would support no war against Spain while their alliance against France endured, and further advised Pownall to drop the matter. Miranda would then become involved in the various intrigues of the French Revolution of the 1790s and barely escaped with his life. He made one final trip to Great Britain in 1801, and Miranda and Pownall would meet at Everton, and at Bath, where Pownall maintained a home close to the mineral waters that had restored his health over the last fifteen years of his life. But while Miranda found in Pownall a sympathetic ear at a personal level, Miranda would never be well received in his goal to create a Venezuelan aristocracy, a concept that flew in the face of all that the United States patriots had fought against in their revolution. What he was seeking was, in the philosophy of Paine and Hume, simply substituting one corrupt system for another. So in the end, Miranda and Pownall would part friends but would accomplish nothing for Miranda's goals for Venezuela.

At that time, Pownall wrote one last treatise about the politics of the Enlightenment, *Memorial Addressed to the Sovereigns of Europe and the Atlantic*, advising that a coalition between Great Britain and the United States of America would create a world trade center through which commerce could be directed globally. Published in 1803, the treatise argued that this coalition of powers would usher in a global free market and an era of peaceful commerce.[540] While generally considered far too visionary, and not practical, it afforded Pownall his final day in the sun politically. Later that year, he would develop another in a long line of attacks of heart failure, and despite his return to Bath, he would not survive this time. While convalescing over the ensuing year, he realized that there would be no recovery. He died at his home in Bath on February 25, 1805.

The life of Thomas Paine after 1785 was far more peripatetic than that of any others of the inner circle and would encompass all three principal nations directly involved in the American Revolution.[541] He had yet two major works to publish, *The Rights of Man* and *The Age of Reason*. Both these treatises would sway nations every bit as much as did *Common Sense*. From their sequential publications, one would nearly cost Paine his life, while the other would tarnish his patriotic reputation in perpetuity. Paine left the United States in 1787 from his home in New Rochelle, New York (a gift from the New York State legislature for his service to American independence) to travel back to Great Britain. It would not take long for him to become embroiled in bitter arguments with Edmund Burke over the role of the aristocracy in government and to publish *The Rights of Man* in part as a response to Burke's criticism of the populist revolt against the French monarchy in Paris. During 1790–92, the political situation in Paris was rapidly deteriorating into political chaos relative to the French aristocracy and the corruption inherent in their government. The British government became naturally sensitive about publication of works that would encourage popular revolt against any monarchy and took significant steps to suppress Paine's writings.

Warned by friends that he was treading preciously close to charges of seditious libel, punishable by death, Paine fled to…Paris. In Great Britain, he would be tried *in absentia*, convicted, and sentenced to death were he to return. On that note, he elected to stay in Paris, where he had been enthusiastically welcomed by one of the populist parties there, the Girondins. Unfortunately for Paine, they were by 1793 in a bloody power struggle with the Montagnards ("Mountain men") and Jean-Paul Marat. During the early summer of that year, Paine would see several French colleagues arrested for conduct in opposition to the revolution and executed. At one point in June, he would become the only surviving Girondist seated in the National Convention. And in that setting came a call to execute or banish any members who were not native-born French. Due to Charlotte Corday's assassination of Marat, Paine managed to survive that threat. But in December he would be jailed by Robespierre as a suspected British spy.

Slated for execution the following summer, Paine would be rescued by diplomatic officer James Monroe. And still he inexplicably remained in Paris, where he felt that he was providing a valued voice of reason in the development of a national constitution for the French people.

In 1796, Paine wrote a treatise roundly critical of the American (lack of) response to the French Revolution and singled out John Adams and George Washington for personal criticism of their conduct in the American Revolution. Now, without the oversight of Franklin to curb his zealotry and lack of social filter, he wrote that Washington was a failed military leader, lacking in character. This opinion was likely due in part to Washington's inability to secure a pension for Paine from the American government, as well as Washington's awareness of and refusal to attempt intervention in Paine's short sojourn on "death row" in Paris. Adams was accused of betraying the French people who had played such a critical role in the success of the American Revolution. Struggling to find an American printer for this, he approached Franklin's younger grandson, Benny Bache, who accepted the work for publication. The response from the American people was one of outrage and ultimately would culminate in the burning of Paine's home in New Rochelle.

But it would be Paine's treatise *The Age of Reason* that would damage his legacy most severely and most permanently. Written in part as a response to Burke's stance as a devout Christian, but more as a counterargument by a devout deist against the atheism of Robespierre at the height of the "Reign of Terror," Paine chose to advance his deism at the expense of traditional Christian doctrine to a point not previously examined by a popular author. And in so doing, Paine would alienate the Christian world of Western Civilization in the waning years of the eighteenth century. Even a hundred years later, Theodore

301

Roosevelt would refer to Paine as "that filthy little atheist" (despite the fact that Paine was neither filthy, nor little, nor an atheist).[542]

In 1800, Paine would engage with Napoleon Bonaparte in devising a plot to invade Great Britain. Paine then published a treatise encouraging the common people of Great Britain to aid Napoleon in this endeavor against the British aristocracy. By 1802, he was in poor health and ready to return to America. Locating with the Bonneville family, whose passage to America he had paid in France, he settled once more in the New York area. He would die in Greenwich Village in 1809 in lonely circumstances. Six persons would attend his funeral, and the Quaker Meeting of New York refused to allow his burial in their cemetery; he was buried under a tree on his farm in New Rochelle with a simple marker. His body was later exhumed to be taken to his hometown of Thetford, England. But before this could take place, the person who had his body exhumed, William Cobbett, likewise passed away, and the whereabouts of Paine's remains are unknown to this day.

Thomas Paine had defied Franklin's directive to the inner circle to destroy their correspondence and had scrupulously and carefully preserved all of it. In the close of the eighteenth century, he began an autobiography that ultimately ran to over two thousand pages, including all of his efforts during the American Revolution and the French Revolution. An acquaintance of Paine, Redman Yorke, independently attested to the existence of this library including extensive correspondence between Paine, Franklin, and "other persons in London." These documents were carefully transported to New York by Nicolas and Margaret Bonneville and stored in New Rochelle at Paine's home. Upon his death, Paine bequeathed this library of documents to Margaret, urging publication of any and all of it. Madame de Bonneville began the formidable process of editing and cataloging this library about 1829 in St. Louis, Missouri, at the home of her son, Benjamin (!). Whether the process was completed or not will forever remain unknown. This final repository of the story of Benjamin Franklin and his inner circle in London was lost in a fire at the Bonneville storage house in about 1843, in St. Louis.

Charles Guillaume Frédéric Dumas would continue to live at the America

House in The Hague, where Adams was still the Minister/Ambassador to the United Provinces. But political upheaval was ubiquitous in the United Provinces in that time frame: the Patriot party, sympathetic to Dumas and the United States, would publish constitutional proposals based upon Adams's Constitution of the State of Massachusetts, 1783. These would appear in the press at The Hague from 1782 to 1787, but in that year, due to fresh alliances between Great Britain, Prussia, and the United States, the old "Anglomanes" party of the Stadtholder, opposed to Dumas and the United States, returned to power. Riots broke out in The Hague, and at one point, the America House became a target of vandalism. Dumas sent word to the United States Congress requesting funds to repair and renovate the embassy. Funds would arrive delivered by the new ambassador to the United Provinces in 1794, John Quincy Adams. Dumas was naturally thrilled to greet the son of his previous superior and now vice-president. Over that year, the situation in The Hague stabilized temporarily, but by 1795, proximity to revolutionary France proved the undoing of the old United Provinces federation. The new Patriot party seized control, heavily supported by the French, and renamed the old provinces "The Batavian Republic." In reality, it was nothing more than a puppet state for the French. Adams fled The Hague in favor of London, where he would make the acquaintance of, propose to, and ultimately marry Louisa Johnson. The couple would never return to the Batavian Republic and would relocate to Berlin, where in 1797 Adams was appointed ambassador by his father. Dumas, seventy-four and no longer in good health, left America House and The Hague, returning to Amsterdam in 1796. With his wife and daughter at hand, he would die from complications of heart disease that same year.

James Somersett would indeed carry the message of his freedom to Granville Sharp by the evening of June 22, 1772.[543] From there he would find a living space, such as were available to free Blacks in London, likely in the East End. Three weeks later, a friend of George Steuart would advise Steuart that Somersett had been spreading the news, however inaccurate, to the Black African slaves of London that they too were now free men. Indeed, during the remainder of that year, thousands of Black African slaves throughout Great

Britain were voluntarily manumitted by their owners, based upon an inaccurate press interpretation of the Mansfield decision. Interestingly, Mansfield himself would, almost from the outset, attempt to "walk back" his decision, advising learned counsel in the matter of abolition that the only issue addressed in *Somersett v. Steuart* was the debarment of sending slaves out of Great Britain for resale elsewhere.[544] But the decision had been made, and the impact on America in the short term was real, and in the long term would be the first step in many that would culminate in the 13th amendment to the United States Constitution. For two hundred years after *Somersett v. Steuart*, the press, the public, and the legal minds of the world would adopt Franklin's interpretation, rather than Mansfield's, as to what the decision had generally meant to slavery. As to James Somersett, by the fall of 1772, he was lost to history; the remainder of his life remains unknown and unknowable.

William Murray, First Earl Mansfield, was at the time of *Somersett* a slave owner, having assumed the care, housing, and education of his illegitimate great-niece given the name Elizabeth Dido Belle, but known to one and all as Dido.[545] In his will he directed her manumission with a lifelong annuity for her support, thus finally affirming the basis of his interest in, and support for, the efforts of Granville Sharp to manumit an African slave so many years previously. The library of Mansfield would be destroyed by fire during the Gordon Riots of 1780 in London; this library held Mansfield's personal notes regarding the cases brought before him at the Court of King's Bench, among other cases, and were of course forever lost. While Mansfield was a loyal member of the British judiciary, he was Roman Catholic by birth, and the targets of the Gordon Riots were wealthy Roman Catholics, along with Catholic churches and public buildings. He would remain chief justice until 1788 and would modernize the British legal system on the eve of the Industrial Revolution, providing a smooth transition into the nineteenth century for British industrial and mercantile law. He would die quietly at his estate, Kenwood House, Hampstead Heath, London, March 18, 1793.

Granville Sharp moved on from pursuing legal manumission of individual slaves after *Somersett v. Steuart*, feeling that 1) it had, rightly or wrongly, produced the voluntary manumission of several thousand African slaves in Great Britain in the months following the decision, and 2) it was not terribly cost-effective from a pragmatic standpoint but had served its symbolic purpose. In 1781 he would become embroiled in the *Zong* affair, as he was yet recognized as the British authority on issues of the slave trade and abolition.[546] Through the encouragement of manumitted slave and author Olaudah Equiano, Sharp pursued legal redress against the crew of the ship for the unlawful drowning of 133 African slaves when water supplies ran low on the slave ship *Zong*, threatening the survival of all. Although ultimately the case would stagnate in appeals, and no criminal charges would ever be pressed against the crew, the case garnered enough attention among abolitionists worldwide, and among philanthropists in London, to spark the creation of The Society for Effecting the Abolition of the Slave Trade in 1787.

Granville Sharp strategically dodged being awarded chair of this organization but attended and contributed to every meeting for the ensuing twenty years, always pressing for full abolition of slavery and not simply the "slave trade."[547] In that same year, he was approached by free Black Africans in London who were destitute and bereft of occupations in a city that would no longer support them. Sharp and others hit upon the idea of repatriation of free Blacks in Sierra Leone and set up the "Province of Freedom" and its modest capital of Granville Town. Plagued by poor to nonexistent advance planning, undercapitalization, and illnesses, the project proved disastrous, but in 1790, Freetown, Sierra Leone replaced this approach and was further reinforced with the resettlement of Blacks from Nova Scotia and creoles from Jamaica. That same year, Granville Town burned and was destroyed. Late in Sharp's life, his abolitionism was overshadowed by the more energetic work of William Wilberforce and Thomas Clarkson, but he left a legacy of strong advocacy against slavery, dating back to the 1760s. He too would pass away quietly, on July 6, 1813.

Most of Franklin's acquaintances in France would successfully navigate the treacherous waters of their own revolution. Julien Achard de Bonvouloir, the original envoy to America in December 1775, would be arrested twice as a spy by British agents, once in 1776, and after being freed, again arrested in 1778. Aided by Franklin in arranging his second release, he would enter the French navy and die in India while deployed there in 1783. Charles Gravier, known as Vergennes, would continue to serve Louis XVI as foreign secretary through the American Revolution, and in the fallout of a dispute with Necker in 1781, he would assume the role of director of the Council of Finance. By 1787, Vergennes was essentially running the French government, and during that year he would collapse with chest pain. He would be sent home to recover, but his heart failed and he died abruptly. Louis XVI sobbed inconsolably upon hearing the news; there was, quite simply, no one else who could handle the reins of French government. By 1789, the French Revolution ensued, and on January 21, 1793, Louis XVI would be executed by guillotine.

Jacques Necker was more fortunate than his king. Embroiled in the politics of the revolution, he would protest the financial policies of the bankrupt French court leading into the 1790s. By September 1790, radicals in the French government were threatening, and Necker would flee from Paris with ₶400,00, headed for the eastern border. He was apprehended before he could leave the country and imprisoned. After some discussion with his captors, he was able to convince them that he was indeed a commoner, the only commoner in the French ministry, and was released. He went directly to Coppe, Switzerland, where he would safely weather the Reign of Terror. Exonerated officially in 1798, he would remain in Switzerland, where he died in April 1804.

Beaumarchais, the con man and courier of the French gifts to the American patriots, would never stop moving after the American Revolution, going from intrigue to intrigue, never slowing down. He too would narrowly escape the Reign of Terror, but after his status was reinstated in 1796, he would return to a quieter Paris, where he would live out his life until 1799.

Franklin's landlord, Le Ray de Chaumont, would more sagely look to America for the safety of his family after the conclusion of the American Revolution. With storm clouds brewing across France, Le Ray would send his son Jacques ("James") Le Ray to New York for asylum. James would acquire land in New York (now Le Ray and Chaumont, New York) and there arrange a home for his father and their families. Le Ray would withdraw and would live out his life in America, passing away quietly in 1803.

And yes, Lafayette would, as a minor French aristocrat, have some difficulties during the French Revolution and would be imprisoned in Austria during the Reign of Terror. But "Le Garçon Guerrier" would triumph over the Reign of Napoleon and the fallout of Waterloo and would return for a victorious tour of the United States of America in 1824–25. He would pass away quietly in 1834 and would be hailed as a hero of two nations, France and the United States.

The Boston loyalists did not fare well. More tragic figures in a melodrama than true antagonists, Andrew Oliver would die before the revolution, in 1774, of a stroke, following the events of the Boston Tea Party. Thomas Hutchinson, following his recall to London, would lose his daughter in 1777, and after writing a history of colonial Massachusetts in four volumes, would himself pass away before the end of the Revolution, in 1780.

The most central loyalist to our story, William Franklin, would remain in the colonies through most of the American Revolution, where he would create problems for his father, himself, and his son. The relationship among the three generations of Franklin men can best be termed "difficult," although some experts would say "troubling" or "dysfunctional." Benjamin had brought William with him during his second sojourn to Great Britain in the 1750s, and before their return to America, William would directly solicit Lord Bute, a friend of Benjamin, for the appointment as Royal Governor of New Jersey. Bute would make this appointment as a personal favor to Benjamin. William would then serve in that role from 1763 until January 1776, when, ignoring advice from fellow Loyalists in New York and New Jersey to flee to London, he was taken from the statehouse into custody by a local patriot militia and held until that summer. In the wake of the Declaration of Independence, he was transferred to a prison in Connecticut and held in that state until exchanged in a prisoner exchange in 1778.

At that point, he would become involved with Loyalist militias in New York and New Jersey; during that time, local militias on both sides of the revolution were carrying out acts of terrorism and retaliation across the borders and the harbors.[548] William apparently became a primary instigator in these skirmishes, and in 1782, the Associated Loyalists, a New York militia, possibly at the direction of William, seized control of a small fort at Toms River, New Jersey, and took the captain, Joshua "Jack" Huddy, into custody. Huddy had a reputation as a ne'er-do-well patriot and had himself been involved in intrigue against loyalists throughout the revolution. On April 12, 1782, about six months after Yorktown, he was allowed by a Captain Lippincott of the Associated Loyalists to write out his will and then was summarily hanged.

Amid cries of outrage along the Atlantic seaboard, a clamor arose directed toward Washington to avenge this vigilante justice. Washington, holding various British officers since the siege of Yorktown, drew lots over them, and the lot fell to Sir Charles Asgill. Washington had him imprisoned, suing for the delivery of Richard Lippincott to stand trial for murder. This was refused by the loyalists of New York, including William Franklin, whereupon Washington threatened a retaliatory hanging of Asgill. It was at that point that the French stepped in: their support in the revolution generally and at Yorktown specifically gave them a self-assurance of interposing their influence in what was now an international affair. The Court of Louis XVI prayed for mercy for Asgill, especially as execution of British prisoners from the Yorktown siege stood as a specific violation of the surrender terms agreed to by Cornwallis and the French. Now Washington, angered and frustrated, turned the decision over to the Second Continental Congress. After delaying a decision at the request of Benjamin Franklin, the Congress, with the Peace of Paris in the final stages of agreement over American independence, ordered the release of Asgill on November 7, 1782. Lippincott would never be turned over to the American government and was subsequently sent to Canada.

For Washington, William Franklin had instigated this mess and would never be forgiven. William withdrew to London during the international appeals over Asgill and would never return to America. In 1784, he approached his father in an overture toward reconciliation; Benjamin would reject this olive branch. In 1785, during Benjamin's brief stop at Southampton, William would try one last time; Benjamin directed him to finalize his estate holdings in America in favor of Temple.[549] William did this, and then William and Benjamin departed. They would never see each other again. William would apply for, and receive, compensation from the British government over losses in New Jersey and would spend the rest of his life in comfortable circumstances in London. He died in 1813 and was buried in the churchyard of St. Pancras Old Church in London. His marker has been misplaced.

Temple Franklin returned with his grandfather to America in 1785, and Benjamin directed him to apply to the Second Continental Congress for a ministerial position (hoping that Temple would receive a diplomatic post in France) or a secretarial position for a Congressional committee. But by that point, Washington made it quite clear that as long as he was president of the Congress (or, for that matter, president of the new nation), the son of a loyalist murderer of a patriot militia captain would *never* serve in the United States government in any capacity. Frustrated, Temple advised his grandfather that he was leaving America; Benjamin begged him to stay in his household. In 1790, after the death of his grandfather, Temple moved to London as an agent of Robert Morris in land speculation and investment.[550] He would, in the family tradition, sire two illegitimate children. In 1800, he relocated to Paris, where he would live out his life in progressively impoverished circumstances. He would die penniless in 1823. He is interred at Père LaChaise Cemetery in Paris, alongside his common-law wife.

So what, then, of Benjamin? His quest completed, his life's goal achieved, he returned to America in 1785, as noted, arriving in September. He was almost startled by the welcome awaiting him; after years of criticism by Arthur Lee, Ralph Izard, and John Adams over his incompetence as minister to France, Franklin had every reason to expect a quiet return. But if indeed that was what he anticipated, he could not have been more incorrect: he was literally mobbed at the Philadelphia wharf, by his family, including four new grandchildren, and by the general population.[551] At age seventy-nine, Franklin was the undisputed patriarch of the nation, and the nation could not have been more proud. In the election at the close of 1785, without so much as a solicitation for political office, Franklin found himself atop the slate for "President" (Governor) of Pennsylvania...for *both parties*!! And so, by near-unanimous vote, he won election to that office as 1786 dawned. The United States had been governed since 1781 by a document known universally as the Articles of Confederation, and by 1786 it was clear that something different had to be done. Daniel Shays had led a rebellion in western Massachusetts against the imposition of any form of taxes, advising Congress that they had no status to pursue taxation. And at that time, he was quite correct. The various states were in dispute with borders, debts, and currency.[552] Two territories, the New Hampshire Stakes, now referring to itself as "Vermont," and the State of Franklin, now referring to itself as "Tennessee," had no idea how to join this agglomerated mess, or, in reality, whether they really wanted to.

When Maryland and Virginia nearly came to warfare over trade in the Chesapeake Bay, Hamilton and Madison knew it was time for "something else."[553] They called for a special convention for the summer of 1787, in... Philadelphia. Franklin wrote to his replacement as minister to France, Thomas Jefferson, that *our federal constitution is generally thought defective and a convention...is to meet here next month to...propose amendments. If it does not do good....it will show that we have not the wisdom enough among us to govern ourselves.* At age eighty-one, Franklin was fifteen years older than the next oldest member. On the first day of the convention, he would arrive on his sedan chair, that old gift from Marie Antoinette, carried by four prisoners from the local gaol.

In his role as one delegate from Pennsylvania (he had scrupulously avoided being drafted to chair the convention, ceding that role to Washington), he brought a nuance to the general meetings. He was there with Thomas Pownall and David Hume now firmly seated on his shoulders. With Hume he would denounce any trace of aristocratic corruption the delegates might propose: suffrage for the elite alone, representation by the elite alone, no role for the common man in the new government. Franklin would hear none of this and would quell in his quiet, aging manner, any effort to deprive the American commoner of his voice in his government.[554] With Pownall, he would treat with each and every state, demonstrating a unique oversight of the many assemblies and statehouses and understanding the needs and wants of New England, the Atlantic states, and the South. And always, as Lord Kames had taught him so many years ago, always in a spirit of compromise and *not* confrontation. "None of us will receive everything we wish; we are here to consult, and not to contend." Franklin would press for the old Albany Plan of Union; he and Pownall were the only two remaining who had witnessed the original discussions. But its basis remained sound: a federal government empowered to protect all the states by a mobile defense, provided by federal funds derived from taxation of the voters, and subordinate to the assembly.

He would likewise reveal his overarching contempt for the House of Lords, ever since that day of infamy in the Cockpit. America needed but *one* house of assembly, based on Commons, and most assuredly did *not* need anything remotely like the House of Lords. (With some irony, the Americans would deny Franklin this initiative by creating a senate (from the Latin: old men) as an upper house of Congress, while in Great Britain, the *Parliament Act* of 1911 fully agreed with Franklin and did away with any authority by the House of Lords). Furthermore, Franklin lobbied against excessive compensation for elected officials, which accomplished nothing more than the creation of shameless electioneering. In the eyes of Franklin, Kames, and Hume this practice had no part in effective government and was to be avoided.

In the end, none of the delegates would get everything he wanted.[555] But Franklin, who appropriately offered the closing speech to encourage the delegates to agree to and sign the document, spoke with an eloquence and persuasiveness that moved the vast majority of the delegates to form a line, quills in hand. And on that day, September 17, 1787, Franklin would become the *only* person on the planet ever to scrawl a signature on the Declaration of Independence of 1776, the Treaty of Versailles with France of 1778, the Peace of Paris with Great Britain of 1782, and now the Constitution of the United States of America. It was not only coincidental; it was not only appropriate. It was preordained in meetings with three, and then four, other champions of liberty in private rooms in London so many years before. And Franklin was signing for each one of them: Fothergill, Pownall, Barclay, and Paine. He briefly wiped his eyes as he stepped away from the document, with the realization that of all the inner circle he and he alone would ever receive recognition for this remarkable achievement.

Over the winter of 1790, Franklin would make his final amends and fulfill his final obligations to Benezet, Sharp, Fothergill, Barclay, and Paine, as he wrote out a petition to Congress for the abolition of slavery: he reminded them that their newly-printed Constitution called for them to secure the blessings of liberty for "ourselves and our posterity," and then gently chided them that the blessings of liberty were not color-blind and belonged to the enslaved of America along with every other man.[556] After a stinging rebuttal in Congress to this petition from James Jackson of Georgia, Franklin was moved to write his final op-ed for the *Federal Gazette,* March 23, 1790.

Playing off Jackson's idiotic question, "If we lose our slaves, who will do the hard work in the heat?" he wrote "Sidi Mehemet Ibrahim on the Slave Trade" and with tongue held firmly in cheek, his fictitious Algerian slave owner posed, *If we free our infidel Christian slaves, who will cultivate our hot arid lands? Who will do the common labor in our cities?*[557] Knowing that this issue would have to be addressed ultimately and knowing that it would not be addressed in his lifetime, Franklin laid down his pen for the last time.

In March of 1790, having responded in dictated correspondence to a specific inquiry by Jefferson in Paris regarding the river boundaries on the western border of the United States as agreed to in the Peace of Paris, Franklin felt pressure in his chest, and his breathing quickened.[558] Over the next ten days, he would take to his bed almost constantly, allowing only for changes of bedclothes by his daughter Sally. By April, his status was deteriorating progressively, and his grandchildren, his daughter, his son-in-law, and Polly Stevenson, the daughter of his landlady in Craven Street so many years ago, took spells at his bedside, reading to him, talking softly. At one point, Sally suggested, "Perhaps you'll get better and still have some years left."[559]

Franklin flatly responded, "I hope not." On the morning of April 17, an aneurysm ruptured in one lung, and he began coughing up blood. He lay quietly after that, no longer speaking, holding the hand of the younger grandson who was with him in Passy, Benjamin Franklin Bache.[560] Late in that same evening of April 17, 1790, he drew his final breath. Franklin was buried in the Christ Church cemetery, after a funeral attended by twenty thousand in Philadelphia, alongside Deborah Read Rogers Franklin.

Acknowledgments

This book has been a labor of love for me for the past two years, and would never have arrived to the eyes of its readership without a lot of help along the path. In some ways it was born of an abiding interest in history generally, and American history in particular, that was nourished throughout my life by family. My parents insisted on my getting a quality education from elementary school on through post-graduate school, and never wavered in their support and encouragement. My three brothers, Roland, Steve, and Chris, have been a periodic sounding board and ongoing source of moral support throughout my life; my only regret is that time and careers have sent us to all corners of the country, so thanks, guys, for being brothers in the best definition of the term.

The Bibliography of this book is replete (and yes, I *do* know how to spell it!) with authors far more talented and thorough than I could hope to be, who have allowed me to stand upon their shoulders to tell a story that otherwise could not have been told. Please read about them in the Bibliography; my notes regarding the significance of their work is quite sincere. For all the cited works here, thanks to all for your contributions.

This book was spawned over the course of about four weeks while I was at work with two surgical technologists, Nicole Gauert and Niki McCush, who because of interest or expediency, encouraged me daily to keep searching for answers to my many questions. You are holding the result of their encouragement. Thanks to both of you for keeping me on track during the project.

My family has been, and continues to be, a source of joy and inspiration. Eight children and seventeen grandchildren have been a source of entertainment, encouragement, some worry, but many rewards. Thanks to all of you: you know who you are.

My son-in-law advised me during the late stages of bringing this story to fruition that the writing process today is about 50% putting words on a page, and 50% formatting those words on a page to make them reproducible in an electronic world. As a professional academic, he knows full well what this effort requires. Only after the story was completed, did I realize that I had written a 20th century book in the 21st century, and that this simply was not going to make it to print. So special thanks are due to Allister Thompson, my book editor, who transformed my hieroglyphics into legible English, and to my book cover and interior designer, Mark Thomas (who knew that a designer was needed to make the inside of a book look great rather than like an eighth-grade term paper?). Thanks to both of you, and to reedsy.com, who directed me down the long and winding road.

Finally, thanks to my wife Melodee for ceding so many of her long-suffering evenings with a distracted husband, her invaluable assistance with navigating the electronic nuts and bolts of the writing process, and her unflagging support despite my frustrations and irritability.

About The Author

Phillip Goodrich is a practicing surgeon, and has been active on physician forums for the past fifteen years, but this is his first foray into the realm of narrative history. An amateur American history buff and graduate of Northwestern University and the University of Southern California, he has spent countless hours studying early American history. He lives with his wife Melodee and their geriatric dog and cat in Platte City, Missouri.

To learn more about Phillip and this book, please visit his website:
www.philgoodrichauthor.com

You can also connect with Phillip on Instagram:
www.instagram.com/philgoodrichauthor

Bibliography

Ackrill, Margaret, and Hannah, Leslie, *Barclays: The Business of Banking, 1690–1996*, New York: Cambridge University Press, 2001. The authors, under the auspices of Barclays Bank, provide the closest thing to a "biography" that David Barclay would authorize, two hundred years after his death.

Alexander, John K., *Samuel Adams: America's Revolutionary Politician*, Lanham, Maryland: Rowman & Littlefield, 2002.

Anderson, M.S., *The War of the Austrian Succession, 1740–1748,* Abingdon, UK: Routledge, 2000.

Ayer, A.J., *Thomas Paine,* Chicago: The University of Chicago Press, 1988. This text evaluates the major works from the pen of Thomas Paine, with a quite scholarly look at the man behind the essays.

Bailyn, Bernard, *The Ordeal of Thomas Hutchinson,* Cambridge, Massachusetts: Harvard University Press, 1974.

Blakemore, Erin, *Smithsonian.com,* "George Washington Used Legal Loopholes to Avoid Freeing His Slaves," February 16, 2015.

Barclay, David, *An Account of the Emancipation of the Slaves of Unity Valley Pen, in Jamaica,* London: William Phillips, 1801. This remarkable monograph conveys the entire story of the freeing of the slaves, which Barclay, to his horror, came to own through acquisition of the security for a failed bank loan.

Bowen, Catherine Drinker, *Miracle at Philadelphia,* New York: Little, Brown and Co., 1966. The definitive story of the writing of the American Constitution in 1787, with an almost day-by-day narration, exhaustively researched by the author.

Brands, H.W., *The First American,* New York: Anchor Books, 2002. Brands's choice of title speaks volumes about his subject, and this is perhaps the most exhaustive recent retelling of Franklin's incredible life. Interestingly, Brands chooses to open this massive work with the "Cockpit Incident." How apropos!

Breig, James, "Dear Eighteenth Century," in *Colonial Williamsburg Journal,* Winter 2011.

Buach, Allan J., Jr., "Charles William Frederick Dumas and the American Revolution (1775–1783)", Omaha: University of Nebraska, Omaha, 1966. This master's thesis is oddly the most extensive biography of Dumas in print, despite its relatively obscure origin.

Calhoun, Jeanne A., "Thomas Lee of Stratford, 1690–1750: Founder of a Virginia Dynasty," *Northern Neck of Virginia Historical Magazine,* vol. XLI, no. 1 (1991).

Center for the Study of Intelligence, "Beaumarchais and the American Revolution," *Central Intelligence Agency Documents Approved for Release,* 22 September 1993.

Charles Steuart Papers, Colonial Williamsburg Foundation, Williamsburg, Virginia, "Narrative of the 'Spanish Affair,' Charles Steuart, August 26, 1789."

Chisholm, Hugh, ed., "Rosslyn, Alexander Wedderburn, First Earl of," *Encyclopedia Britannica, 1911,* Cambridge: Cambridge University Press, 11th edition.

--------, "The Cistercian Order: Medieval and Early Modern Challenges," Cistercian Abbey/Our Lady of Dallas, cistercian.org.

Conway, Moncure Daniel, *The Life of Thomas Paine,* London: Watts & Co., 1909. This remains a well-documented, thorough assessment of the life of Thomas Paine, with excellent citations throughout.

Covart, Elizabeth M., "Silas Deane: Forgotten Patriot," *Journal of the American Revolution,* July 30, 2014.

Currey, Cecil B., *Code Number 72 Ben Franklin: Patriot or Spy?* Englewood Cliffs, NJ: Prentice-Hall, Inc., 1972. A fascinating look at Franklin and the men surrounding his life in France during the American Revolution. The author does a credible job in recalling the evidence at hand about intrigue from the American ministry to France but stops short of providing a theory for the behavior of these men.

Dumas, Charles Frederic Guillaume, *Historical Account of Bouquet's Expedition against the Ohio Indians, in 1764*, Cincinnati, OH: The Robert Clarke Co., 1907. This little treatise, translated from the French by Francis Parkman originally in 1867, gives a nice memoir of a little-known military figure in the life of Franklin prior to the American Revolution. The author is, of course, Franklin's ministry secretary to the United Provinces during the Revolution.

Ellis, Joseph J., *His Excellency, George Washington,* New York: Alfred E. Knopf, 2004.

Ferling, John E., *John Adams: A Life*, Knoxville, Tennessee: The University of Tennessee Press, 1992.

Finkelman, Paul, *An Imperfect Union: Slavery, Federalism, and Comity*, Chapel Hill, NC: University of North Carolina Press, 1981. An exhaustive legal evaluation of the implications of the *Somersett* decision in the United States, along with a host of other legal precedents and the reaction of the various states to the decisions over manumission and abolition handed down from various courts. This book provides a definitive discussion of the legalities regarding slavery that would develop in the decades between the revolution and the civil war.

Founders Online, *The Final Hearing before the Privy Council...29 January 1774*, New Haven, Connecticut: Yale University Press, 1978.

Fox, Richard Hingston, *Dr. John Fothergill and His Friends,* London: MacMillan and Co., 1919. The "Friends" in the title is a double entendre, recalling the Quaker (officially the "Society of Friends") roots of Fothergill and most of the other persons discussed in this review of a now nearly forgotten pioneering physician of the late eighteenth century. The brief overview of David Barclay, as well as the discussion of the relationship between Fothergill and Franklin, are uniquely presented here.

Franklin, Benjamin, *The Autobiography of Benjamin Franklin*, New York: G.P. Putnam's Sons, 1887, extensively reprinted thereafter. Before the reader becomes apoplectically excited about hearing of the existence of this volume, be assured that it is a *most* incomplete work, with which Franklin dabbled only intermittently throughout his long, eventful life. I relied upon a 2015 reprint edition that required but 116 pages. While he provided us some interesting narratives about his early life, there is truly precious little here to address the intrigues of his political career. Read it for the enjoyment, but do not seek any new answers to the enigma of Franklin; they will not be found here.

"From Alexander Hamilton to Lieutenant Colonel John Laurens" [April 1779], National Archives: Founders Online, founders.archives.gov/documents/Hamilton/01-02-02-0100).

Gallegos, Jeremy, "Hume on Revolution," Boston, Massachusetts, Twentieth World Congress of Philosophy, 1998, archived online.

Hannah, Leslie, *Oxford Dictionary of National Biography*, Oxford: University Press, online edition, 2019, see "Barclay, David (1729–1809)."

Heward, Edmund, *Lord Mansfield: A Biography of William Murray 1st Earl of Mansfield 1705–1793 Lord Chief Justice for 32 Years*, Chichester: Barry Rose Ltd., 1979. This remains perhaps the most definitive biography of Mansfield yet compiled.

Higginbotham, A. Leon, Jr., *In the Matter of Color: Race & The American Legal Process: The Colonial Period*, Oxford: Oxford University Press, 1978. This remarkably thorough evaluation of the slavery issue in the American colonies provides an excellent framework for understanding the day-to-day lives of Americans living under the long shadow of this institution in the eighteenth century. This volume, the first of an intended five-volume set, takes us from the inception of American slavery in 1619 in Virginia all the way through the American Revolution, looking at each colony individually.

Hoare, Prince, *Memoirs of Granville Sharp, Esq.*, London: Henry Colburn and Co., 1820. This remarkable biography is based upon the extensive written material left by Granville Sharp to posterity. Sharp provides an extensive narrative of his efforts culminating in *Somersett v. Steuart* in 1772, but his labors on behalf of American independency (sic) and abolition of slavery went on for another forty years after *Somersett*.

Holbrook, Sabra, *Lafayette: Man in the Middle*, New York: Atheneum Books, 1977.

Hosmer, John K., *The Life of Thomas Hutchinson,* Boston, Massachusetts: Houghton Mifflin Co., 1896.

Hunter, Robert, *The Imperial Encyclopaedic Dictionary,* London, 1901, volume 4.

Independence Hall Association, *Virtual Marching Tour of the American Revolutionary War, The Philadelphia Campaign, 1777,* Philadelphia, Pennsylvania: ushistory.org, 1999.

Ingrao, Charles, *The Habsburg Monarchy, 1618–1815 (New Approaches to European History),* Cambridge: Cambridge University Press, 2000.

Isaacson, Walter, *Benjamin Franklin: An American Life,* New York: Simon & Schuster, 2003. Here is a definitive biography of Franklin for our generation in America. A rich trove of facts and character studies, Isaacson provides a definitive timeline for the life of Franklin from birth to death. He takes full advantage of the extensive manuscripts by Franklin and for Franklin, which have been meticulously preserved in various archives throughout the world. Following him chronologically through the eighteenth century, Isaacson provides an answer for where Franklin was located, and what he was doing, throughout his long life.

Jackson, Maurice, *Let This Voice Be Heard: Anthony Benezet, Father of Atlantic Abolitionism,* Philadelphia: University of Pennsylvania Press, 2009. The author introduces us to a most remarkable American colonist whose efforts on behalf of abolition of Black African slavery in America, *as well as* black equality, have for too long passed unnoticed. Long before Douglass, long before Garrison, long before Beecher, there was Benezet, toiling quietly in Philadelphia to promote the novel idea that all people are capable of learning, and therefore all people are deserving of freedom.

Jenkins, Howard, "The Family of William Penn (continued). IX. Thomas Penn," *The Pennsylvania Magazine of History and Biography,* vol. 21, no. 3, 1897.

Ketchum, Richard, *Saratoga: Turning Point of America's Revolutionary War,* New York: Henry Holt, 1997.

Labaree, Benjamin Woods, *The Boston Tea Party,* Boston: Northeastern University Press, 1964, p. 78–79.

Leepson, Marc, *Lafayette: Lessons in Leadership from the Idealist General,* London: Palgrave MacMillan, 2011.

Middlekauff, Robert, *Benjamin Franklin and His Enemies,* Berkeley, CA: University of California Press, 1996. The author reaches deep into the early life of Franklin to support the concept of Franklin's personal motive for ultimate pursuit of American liberty through revolution.

Morgan, Edmund S., *Benjamin Franklin,* New Haven, CT: Yale University Press, 2002. This author delves deeply into the personal correspondence of Franklin in an effort to provide an accurate psychological profile of his subject, in order to explain his actions on behalf of American liberty. The result is a great success that provided much valuable insight; Morgan comes exquisitely close to uncovering the covert plot of Franklin and his inner circle to liberate the American colonies from the British, but at every turn, coyly turns away.

O'Meara, Walter, *Guns at the Forks,* Pittsburgh: University of Pittsburgh Press, 2005.

Packard Humanities Institute, *The Papers of Benjamin Franklin.* This most extraordinary collection of papers and correspondence written by Franklin and to Franklin is an invaluable resource to the serious researcher for understanding Franklin's relationships with literally hundreds of correspondents all over the world, for essentially his entire life. Just as an example, it is clear that Franklin and Dumas, based on the sheer volume of their correspondence, were swapping letters weekly throughout the entire American Revolution. The papers are filed in alphabetical and chronological order and are easily accessed. And if any readers here have original Franklin correspondence or published material, please alert this organization as they are continuing to compile their collection and always eager for new acquisitions to this collection.

Penegar, Kenneth, *The Political Trial of Benjamin Franklin,* New York: Algora Publishing, 2011,

Pownall, Thomas, *The Administration of the British Colonies,* London: J. Walter, at Homer's Head, 1777 (sixth edition). I cited this edition for the necessity of a second volume to elaborate on the crucial fracturing of the interrelationship between Great Britain and her North American colonies. The book is all Pownall, some awkward descriptions and complex sentences, a ready cure for insomnia. But it provides a nice introduction of the author to an American public that has long forgotten this tireless British patriot on behalf of American independence.

Proceedings of the Court of King's Bench, George III, multiple sessions. These are readily available online and provide a fascinating first-hand account of all cases, famous and obscure, adjudicated in the Royal Courts of London in the eighteenth century.

Proud, Robert, *The History of Pennsylvania in North America*, Philadelphia: Zachariah Poulson, Jr., 1797. This ancient text provides a history of the Pennsylvania that Franklin would have recognized as a young man in Philadelphia, from the perspective of an author who would have known Franklin in his dotage.

Pulling, Alexander, *The Order of the Coif*, London: 1884, William Clows & Sons, Ltd.

Raphael, Ray, *Founding Myths: Stories that Hide Our Patriotic Past,* New York: MJF Books, 2004. This author lays the groundwork for righteous skepticism over the propagandist narratives of the first hundred years following the American Revolution, and invites the reader to look deeper, especially through the eyes of the contemporary authors of the eighteenth century, into the causes which precipitated the war. He points out, for instance, that it was indeed *all* the "Intolerable Acts" of 1774, and not simply the *Boston Port Act*, which led directly to revolution in Massachusetts. Indeed, we are only now, over two hundred years later, beginning to understand the true motivators of the Revolution.

Roider, Karl A., "William Lee: Our First Envoy in Vienna," *The Virginia Magazine of History and Biography*, Vol. 86, no. 2 (1978).

Schaeffer, Thomas J., *Edward Bancroft, Scientist, Author, Spy*, New Haven, CT: Yale University Press, 2011. This author provides a far more coherent argument and exposition about the conspiracies taking place in Franklin's Passy during the American Revolution, accounting for the realities of the eighteenth century, including what a "secret agent" could and, more importantly, *could not* accomplish through the simple agency of providing information available in plain sight. It further gives a more credible sketch of the complicated relationships between Franklin, Deane, Lee, Adams, and the subject himself, Bancroft.

Schutz, John A., *Thomas Pownall: British Defender of American Liberty*, Glendale, CA: The Arthur H. Clark Co., 1951. This author made a noble effort to reintroduce Thomas Pownall, 150 years after his death, to an American audience unaware of his existence. The book is well-researched and documented and brutally honest about Pownall and his political abilities in Parliament. It also points repeatedly to the close relationship between Pownall and Franklin in the years leading to revolution.

Stephen, Sir James, *A History of the Criminal Law of England,* London: MacMillan and Co., 1883, volume 1.

Trinity Writers, *Oliver Goldsmith,* Dublin, Ireland: Trinity College, Dublin, updated 2016.

Waldstreicher, David, *Runaway America: Benjamin Franklin, Slavery, and the American Revolution,* New York: Hill and Wang, 2004. Here we have yet another author who had ascertained the fine points of the reasons for revolution developed by Franklin during the run-up to the American Revolution. He points out the gyrations needed by Franklin and others to keep the northern colonies focused upon freedom issues, and the southern colonies focused upon states' rights issues, such as the right to own Black Africans. And while waxing philosophical on Franklin's walking this fine line, he stops short of theorizing conspiracy to foment revolution.

Wallace, David D., *The Life of Henry Laurens, with a Sketch of the Life of Lieutenant-Colonel John Laurens,* New York: G.P. Putnam's Sons, 1915. This interesting biography of the father and son Laurens by a faculty member at the University of Virginia, is clearly a latter-day attempt to repair the legacy of both. With what is known about Henry Laurens from other sources, this effort is a failure. But the sources are well-documented, and the book gives invaluable information regarding the short life of John Laurens in the Appendix.

Weber, Ralph E., *Masked Dispatches: Cryptograms and Cryptology in American History, 1775–1900,* Washington, DC: Center for Cryptologic History, National Security Agency, 2002. This encryption expert traces the experience among the American revolutionaries in comparison with Dumas and Franklin in Europe and points out the facile nature of the Dumas approach, which was used successfully by the Franklins, grandfather and grandson in Passy, and Dumas at The Hague; while at the same time, the far more complex and error-prone codes of James Lovell of Massachusetts, which left the colonists more frustrated than informed, and of course left John Adams...outraged. Abigail wrote to her husband, in Lovell code, that she had *no* difficulty in translating the code herself, which only left Adams *more outraged.*

Wise, Steven M., *Though the Heavens May Fall,* Cambridge, MA: Da Capo Press, 2005. This outstanding explanation of the complexities of the law leading to the *Somerset v. Steuart* decision brings eighteenth century British legal proceedings within the range of understanding for the lay reader. It is a slow, deliberate read but affords the reader the ability to sort through the proceedings and up to Mansfield's inevitable and monumental decision. The title is a direct quote from Mansfield espousing his own concern about the implications of the decision.

I am also indebted to the various online sources provided by historical societies and historical sites, all throughout the thirteen original states, and in the United Kingdom.

Endnotes

1   Anderson, MS, *The War of the Austrian Succession 1740–1748*, Abingdon, UK: Routledge, 2000, p. 7-9.

2   Ingrao, Charles, *The Habsburg Monarchy, 1618–1815 (New Approaches to European History)*, Cambridge: Cambridge University Press, 2000, p. 113.

3   Ingrao, op.cit., p. 129.

4   Ingrao, op.cit., p. 149.

5   Franklin, Benjamin, *The Autobiography of Benjamin Franklin,* 1791 edition reproduced New York, 2015, p. 15.

6   Waldstreicher, David, *Runaway America*, New York: Hill & Wang, 2004, p. 4.

7   Franklin op.cit., p. 17.

8   Franklin op.cit., p. 17.

9   Jackson, Maurice, *Let This Voice Be Heard*, Philadelphia: University of Pennsylvania Press, 2009., pp. 7-8.

10   Franklin op.cit. pp. 18-21.

11   Franklin, op.cit., pp. 21-22.

12   Franklin, op.cit., pp. 30-32.

13   Franklin, op.cit., p. 36.

14   Franklin, op.cit., pp. 38-44.

15   Franklin, op.cit., p. 64.

16   Franklin, op.cit., pp. 38-44.

17   Franklin, op.cit. p. 41.

18   Middlekauff, Robert, *Benjamin Franklin and His Enemies,* Berkeley: University of California Press, 1998, p. 34.

19   Proud, Robert, *The History of Pennsylvania in North America from the Original Institution and Settlement of that Province . . . ,* Philadelphia: Zachariah Poulson, Junior, 1798, pp. 208-209.

20   Isaacson, *Benjamin Franklin: An American Life,* New York: Simon and Schuster, 2003, p. 156. See also Waldstreicher, op.cit., p. 151 for a more critical viewpoint of how this deception led directly to threatening the safety of the Pennsylvania settlers.

21   Middlekauff, op.cit., p. 71.

22   Middlekauff, op.cit., p. 35.

23   Ingrao, op.cit., p. 157.

24   Middlekauff, op.cit., p. 35.

25   The Packard Humanities Institute *Papers of Benjamin Franklin*, 1988, Los Altos, California, Tuesday, November 17, 1747.

26   Middlekauff, op.cit., p. 36.

27   Middlekauff, op.cit., p. 36.

28   Franklin, op.cit, p.73. For full manuscript: The Packard Humanities Institute, ibid.

29   Middlekauff, op.cit., p.37.

30   Middlekauff, op.cit., p. 38.

31   Middlekauff, op.cit., p. 39.

32   Isaacson, op.cit., p. 158

33   Chernow, Ron, *Washington: A Life,* London: Penguin Press, 2010, pp. 41-45.

34   Morgan, Edmund S., Benjamin Franklin, New Haven, CT: Yale University Press, 2002, p. 91.

35   Franklin, op.cit., pp. 90-93.

36   Middlekauff, op.cit., p.47.

37   Franklin, op.cit., p. 93.

38   Chernow, op.cit., pp. 57-58.

39   Middlekauff, op.cit., p. 41.

40   Middlekauff, op.cit., pp. 40-41.

41   Middlekauff, op.cit., p. 51.

42   Morgan, Edmund S., *Benjamin Franklin*, New Haven, CT: Yale University Press, 2002, pp. 82-85.

43   Schutz, John, *Thomas Pownall, British Defender of American Liberty*, Glendale, California: The Arthur H. Clark Company, 1951, pp. 37-38.

44   Schutz, op.cit., pp. 41-42.

45   Morgan, op.cit., p. 88.

46   Waldstreicher, op.cit., pp. 176-177, Morgan, op.cit., p. 85.

47   Waldstreicher, op.cit., p. 152, Middlekauff, op.cit., p. 55.

48   Morgan, op.cit., p. 103.

49   Isaacson, op.cit., p. 175, Morgan, op.cit., p. 105.

50   Isaacson, op.cit., p. 176.

51   Morgan, op.cit., pp. 109-110.

52   Fox, Richard Hingston, *Dr. John Fothergill and His Friends,* London: MacMillan and Company, Ltd., 1919, p. 314.

53   Middlekauff, op.cit., pp. 64-65.

54   Isaacson, op.cit., pp. 184-185.

55   Isaacson, op.cit., p. 185.

56   The Packard Humanities Institute, *PBF,* [Isaac Norris] January 14, 1758.

57   Middlekauff, op.cit., p. 71.

58   Fox, op.cit., p. 317, Morgan, op.cit., p. 113.

59   Schutz, op.cit., pp. 19-29, for the biographical sketch leading up to his emigration to the British colonies in 1753.

60   Schutz, op.cit., pp. 15-16.

61   Schutz, op.cit., pp. 31-35.

62   Schutz, op.cit., pp. 50-51.

63   Schutz, op.cit., p. 55.

64   Schutz, op.cit., pp. 58-63.

65   Schutz, op.cit., pp. 68-69.

66   Schutz, op.cit., pp. 70-71. During this time, suspicion was rampant in the colonies, and especially in Philadelphia, that Pownall was conspiring with Franklin about a variety of topics including politics and colonial defense, see also Schutz, pp. 49-50, 74-75.

67   Schutz, op.cit., pp. 70-71..

68   Schutz, op.cit., p. 83.

69   Schutz, op.cit., pp. 105-107.

70   Schutz, op.cit., pp. 169-173.

71   Schutz, op.cit., p. 175.

72   Schutz, op.cit., p. 180.

73   Franklin, op.cit., pp. 110-111. For the close friendship of Franklin and Fothergill which was developing in this time, see also Fox, op.cit., p. 315.

74   Isaacson, op.cit., p. 183-184, Morgan, op.cit., p. 114.

75   Isaacson, op.cit., p. 195. Franklin, op.cit., pp. 112-113. This incident would essentially end Franklin's autobiography; he never returned to the project.

76   Isaacson, op.cit., pp. 192-194. For a summary of Franklin's likely thought processes in this difficult time of his life, see also Middlekauff, op.cit., pp. 110-114.

77   Isaacson, op.cit., pp. 195-198, Morgan, op.cit., p. 107. After that trip, he would be known to one and all as "Dr. Franklin".

78   Isaacson, ibid.

79   Isaacson, op.cit., pp. 55-60.

80   See for example, Gallegos, Jeremy, "Hume on Revolution", Boston, Massachusetts, Twentieth World Congress of Philosophy, 1998, archived on-line.

81   Middlekauff, op.cit., p. 77.

82   Morgan, op.cit., p. 129.

83   Dumas, Charles G. F., *Historical Account of Bouquet's Expedition Against the Ohio Indians, in 1764,* Cincinnati, Ohio: The Robert Clarke Company, 1907, pp. 3-6.

84   Dumas, op.cit., pp. 8-9.

85   Dumas, op.cit., pp. 9-14.

86   Dumas, op.cit., pp. 14-21.

87   Dumas, op.cit., p. 22.

88   Dumas, op.cit, p. 67.

89   Isaacson, op.cit., p. 210.

90   Isaacson, ibid.

91   Isaacson, op.cit., p. 212.

92   Isaacson, op.cit., p. 213.

93   Isaacson, op.cit., pp. 216-218.

94   Dumas, op.cit., p. 72.

95   Morgan, op.cit., p. 145.

96   Morgan, op.cit., p. 149.

97   Morgan, op.cit., p. 157, Isaacson, op.cit., p. 222.

98   Isaacson, op.cit., p. 247.

99   Middlekauff, op.cit., pp. 106-107, Schutz, op.cit., pp. 203-204.

100   Schutz, op.cit., p. 204-205.

101   Schutz, op.cit., p. 183-184.

102   Schutz, op.cit., pp. 208-214.

103   Schutz, op.cit., p. 197.

104   Schutz, op.cit., pp. 199-200.

105   Schutz, op.cit., pp. 204-208.

106   Schutz, op.cit., p. 209.

107   Schutz, op.cit., p. 210.

108   Schutz., op.cit., pp. 205-206.

109   Schutz, op.cit., pp. 190-191, 207.

110   Morgan, op.cit., p. 150.

111   for the varied reception of this edition, see Schutz, op.cit., pp. 207-213.

112   Schutz, op.cit., p. 208.

113   Schutz., op.cit., p.205.

114   Schutz, op.cit., p. 213.

115   Schutz, op.cit., p. 212. Franklin had, by this time, come to agree with Pownall regarding Pownall's stance that *all* the colonies had to be freed from the Crown, rather than simply trying to free Pennsylvania from the Penn family. But in this public notice, Franklin acknowledged to London, and to *us*, that it was indeed Pownall who had led him to this realization, rather than the other way around.

116   Schutz, op.cit., p. 213. Already Pownall was drawing undue attention to himself with his discrete evening meetings with the Americans.

117   Schaeper, Thomas J., *Edward Bancroft,* New Haven, Connecticut: Yale University Press, 2011, p. 14.

118   Schaeper, ibid. Schaeper provides a clear-eyed discussion of this controversy, pp. 14-21, that betrays Bancroft as an acolyte of Pownall and Franklin, right down to the "solution" that Bancroft advances in his treatise: federation of the Empire with an international Parliament.

119   Schutz, op.cit., pp. 215-217.

120   Schutz, op.cit., pp. 218-220.

121   Schutz, op.cit., pp. 224-225.

122   Schutz, op.cit,, p. 222.

123   Schutze, op.cit., pp. 225-226.

124   Hosmer, John K., *The Life of Thomas Hutchinson,* Boston, Massachusetts: Houghton Mifflin Co., 1896, pp. 1, 2.

125   Hosmer, op.cit., p. 4.

126   Hosmer, op.cit., pp. 27-30.

127   Bailyn, Bernard, *The Ordeal of Thomas Hutchinson,* Cambridge, Massachusetts: Harvard University Press, 1974, p. 54.

128   Hosmer, op.cit., pp. 72-73. James Otis would coin the term here, but variations would be heard throughout the American colonies for the ensuing twenty years.

129   Bailyn, op.cit., p. 65.

130   Bailyn, op.cit., pp. 68-69.

131   Fox, op.cit., p. 319, which also accords great credit to William Pitt the Elder, and of course, John Fothergill.

132   Bailyn, op.cit., p. 157.

133   Schutz, op.cit., p. 228.

134   Middlekauff, op.cit., pp. 108-114. Middlekauff is more or less certain that at this point in his life, Franklin was willing to risk revolution to wrest Pennsylvania from the Penn grip, if that was the only remaining solution.

135   Fox, op.cit., pp. 320-321, where Fothergill is already lamenting the potential loss of Franklin as an agent for the colonies in London.

136   Fox, op.cit., p. 271, p. 326.

137   Fox, op.cit., p. 24. By this time, Fothergill and Barclay were nearly inseparable, with a deep father/son relationship.

138   Fox, op.cit., pp. 263-267.

139   The Packard Humanities Institute, *PBF,* letter to John Fothergill, March 14, 1764 for Franklin's assessment of the daily life of John Fothergill, presumably in jest.

140   Schutz, op.cit., p.226 for a discussion of Pownall's concerns of the inevitability, by spring 1770, of colonial revolution.

141   Schutz, op.cit., pp. 227-229 for the efforts by the Whigs generally, and Pownall in particular, to mollify both Parliament and Massachusetts following the Boston Massacre.

142   Schutz, op.cit., p. 228. David Barclay, grandson of Robert Barclay, the author of *An Apology for the true Christian Divinity,* 1676, remained a devout Quaker throughout his life, and his speech was always punctuated with the "Quaker pronouns".

143   Hoare, Prince, *Memoirs [of Granville Sharp]*: London, Ellerton and Henson, 1820, p.69. Fothergill was a devout abolitionist in ongoing correspondence with Benezet, and here enlists Franklin in a promise of joining in abolitionism as a condition of Fothergill's devotion to his cause.

144   Fox, op.cit., p. 271.

145   Fox, op.cit., p. 315, p. 321, for an observation of the tender relationship between Franklin and Fothergill during this time.

146   Isaacson, op.cit., p. 259.

147   Isaacson, op.cit., pp. 260-261.

148   Schutz, op.cit., p. 229.

149   Currey, Cecil B., *Code Number 72--Ben Franklin: Patriot or Spy,* Englewood Cliffs, NJ: Prentice-Hall, Inc., 1972, p. 38.

150   Wallace, David D., *The Life of Henry Laurens, with a Sketch of the Life of Lieutenant-Colonel John Laurens,* New York: G.P. Putnam's Sons, 1915, pp. 13-15.

151   Wallace, op.cit., pp. 16-18.

152   Wallace, op.cit., pp. 44-56.

153   Wallace, op.cit., p. 47, for example reveals Laurens selling 17 Scottish indentured servants for profit. Not *all* unfree persons in 18th century America were black Africans.

154   Wallace, op.cit., p. 191 Curiously, Laurens was in London when *Somersett* was decided, and spoke only of Mansfield making a decision "suitable to the times." With the moral blindness of the 18th century plantation owner, Laurens is outspokenly critical of the "low morals" rampant in London at that time.

155   Wise, Steven M. *Though the Heavens May Fall,* Cambridge, MA: Da Capo Press, 2005, pp. 1 ff. The sketch about the early life of James Somersett is based in part on the conjectures regarding slaves in similar circumstances in mid-18th century Virginia. We do know that he was taken to the Caribbean from Sierra Leone in 1748.

156   Wise, op.cit., p. 129.

157   *Charles Steuart Papers,* Colonial Williamsburg Foundation, Williamsburg, Virginia, "Narrative of the 'Spanish Affair', Charles Steuart, August 26, 1789".

158   *The Magazine of History with Notes and Queries,* Indiana University Press, v. 3, 1906, p. 151.

159   Wise, op.cit., p.10.

160   Wise, op.cit., p. 53.

161   Wise, op.cit., p.10.

162   Jackson, op.cit., biographical information, pp. 2-7.

163   Jackson, op.cit., p. 8.

164   Jackson, op.cit., p. 8. Clearly, Franklin would be well-acquainted with the entire Benezet family from 1743 until the end of Anthony's life.

165   Jackson, op.cit., pp. 11 ff.

166   Jackson, op.cit., pp. 18-20.

167   Jackson, op.cit., pp. 18-20.

168   Jackson, op.cit., pp. 21-22. This seemingly simple statement was in fact ground-breaking in that era, and flew in the face of "relative learning" espoused by Hume, Jefferson, and even Sharp, that blacks had to be offered lesser accommodations based upon their "lesser abilities." To that, Benezet, who had clearly demonstrated quite the opposite, would loudly, roundly, and correctly, object.

169   Jackson, op.cit., p. 27.

170   Jackson, op.cit., p. 28. Benezet in his later life, in the years leading up to the American Revolution, and throughout the conflict, about 1770-1783, was clearly revered throughout Philadelphia as something of a "holy man", and was accorded due deference by Americans, French, indigenous peoples, and British alike. He was, in that era and in that place, something akin to Mother Teresa of Kolkata.

171   Hoare, op.cit. p. 27 ff., for biographical sketch information.

172   Hoare, op.cit., p. 30.

173   Hoare, op.cit., p. 30.

174   Hoare, op.cit., p. 31.

175   Hoare, op.cit., p. 32.

176   Wise, op.cit., p. 21.

177   Hoare, op.cit., p. 32.

178   Hoare, op.cit., p. 33.

179   Hoare, op.cit., p. 34.

180   Hoare, op.cit., p. 36.

181   Wise, op.cit., pp. 34-35. "Plagiarism" of pamphlets among abolitionists throughout the British Empire in the 18th-19th century was not considered a tort; on the contrary, it was perceived throughout the Empire as the sincerest form of flattery. The editing and interchange of treatises between Sharp and Benezet was no exception.

182   Hoare, op.cit., p.41.

183   Hoare, op.cit., p. 47.

184   Hoare, op.cit., p. 47 with footnote.

185   For a discussion of Mansfield's thought process on this issue, see Wise, op.cit., p. 71 ff., Hoare, op.cit., pp. 69-70.

186   Hoare, op.cit., pp. 69-70.

187   Higginbotham, A. Leon, Jr., *In the Matter of Color,* New York: Oxford University Press, 1978, pp. 392-395.

188   Waldstreicher, op.cit., p. 20.

189   Waldstreicher, op.cit., pp. 20, 23.

190   Waldstreicher, op.cit., pp. 3-4.

191   Hoare, op.cit., p. 53.

192   Hoare, op.cit., pp. 54 ff. (this is a relatively prolonged retelling of the extremes which Stapylton put Mrs. Banks and Granville Sharp through, for uncertain reasons).

193   Wise, op.cit., pp. 40-43 (a brutally honest discussion of John Dunning as he presented himself in the days leading up to 1772). As to the running feud between Dunning and Mansfield, see also Wise, op.cit., pp. 64-67.

194   Wise, op.cit., p. 85.

195   extensively retold by Wise, op.cit., pp. 87-92.

196   Stephen, Sir James, *A History of the Criminal Law of England,* London: MacMillan and Co., 1883, vol 1, p. 311.

197   Hunter, Robert, *The Imperial Encyclopaedic Dictionary,* London, 1901, v. 4, p. 1481, for a legal definition of "dither", from Northumberland "didder", to tremble, quake, waver.

198   Hoare, op.cit., p. 60.

199   Hoare, op.cit., p. 60-61.

200   Heward, Edmund, *Lord Mansfield: A Biography of William Murray 1st Earl of Mansfield 1705-1793 Lord Chief Justice for 32 Years,* Chichester: Barry Rose Ltd., 1979, pp 2-10.

201   Wise, op.cit., 117-120, for a carefully researched and thorough expository of the shortcomings of Sharp's legal background, which led him to conclude that Dunning's actions were "abominable and insufferable".

202   Hoare, op.cit., p. 70.

203   Hoare, op.cit., p. 70.

204   Hoare, op.cit., pp. 71-75, for the fascinating exchange of correspondence regarding the nature of slavery in the British Empire.

205   Hoare, op.cit., p. 83.

206   Hoare, op.cit., p. 75.

207   Wise, op.cit., p. 124.

208   Hoare, op.cit., pp. 49-51.

209   Wise, op.cit., p. 155.

210   Pulling, Alexander, *The Order of the Coif*, London: 1884, William Clows & Sons, Ltd., for much of the history of the Serjeants at law in the Inns of Court, London.

211   Wise, op.cit., p. 133. For a discussion of the implication of the return, and the deception about the residence of Somersett and Steuart in Virginia, rather than Massachusetts, prior to their emigration to London, see Wise, op.cit., pp. 129-133.

212   Hoare, op.cit, pp. 75-77.

213   Wise, op.cit., p. 140.

214   Hoare, op.cit., p. 77.

215   Hoare, op.cit., pp. 77-78.

216   Hoare, op.cit., p.81.

217   Wise, op.cit., p. 153.

218   The Packard Humanities Institute, *PBF*, [Tuesday], February 11, 1772.

219   Hoare, op.cit., pp. 83-84.

220   Hoare, op.cit., p. 84.

221   Wise, op.cit., p. 149.

222   Wise, op.cit., pp. 149-150.

223   Wise, op.cit., p. 151.

224   Wise, op.cit., pp. 151-152.

225   Wise, op.cit., p. 153.

226   Wise, op.cit., p. 153.

227   Wise, op.cit., p. 153.

228   Wise, op.cit., pp. 157-158.

229   Hoare, op.cit., p. 89., Wise, op.cit., p. 155.

230   Wise, op.cit., pp. 156-157.

231   Wise, op.cit., pp. 158-159.

232   Wise, op.cit., pp.159-161.

233   Hoare, op.cit., p. 88.

234   Wise, op.cit., pp. 160-162.

235   for a thorough breakdown on the Dunning defense, and its clear futility in the eyes of its original audience, see Wise, op.cit., pp. 162-167.

236   Wise, op.cit., p. 168.

237   Hoare, op.cit., p. 88.

238   Wise, op.cit., pp. 169-173.

239   Wise, op.cit., p. 173.

240   Hoare, op.cit., pp. 89-91, Wise, op.cit., pp. 179-182. This judgment, so critical to the American Revolution, to the cause of abolition, and to history, is far too important to simply annotate here. Wise affords it the thorough dissection it so richly deserves, op.cit., pp. 179-191, while carefully noting that there were no recordings, no concurrent annotations of that day in court, no "court reporters", etc., and therefore the best we can do is rely upon such authors as Capel Lofft, who provided timely court summaries in that era.

241   Dumas, Charles, *Historical Account of Bouquet's Expedition Against the Ohio Indians, in 1764*, Cincinnati, Ohio: The Robert Clarke Company, 1907, publisher's preface, p. V.

242   The Packard Institute, *PBF*, "To Charles Dumas, Monday, July 25, 1768".

243   Hoare, op.cit., pp. 97 ff., for a discussion of the correspondence between Franklin, Fothergill, and Benezet from the 1760's regarding abolition.

244   Hoare, op.cit., pp. 49-51. Sharp and Fothergill had been in confidential correspondence for almost two years at this point, on the topic of legal manumission of a slave.

245   Hoare, op.cit., pp. 41-43, where Sharp attributes his information in pursuit of abolition to an essay from Benezet, 1762.

246   Hoare, op.cit., pp. 69-70.

247   Alexander, John K., *Samuel Adams: America's Revolutionary Politician*, Lanham, Maryland: Rowman & Littlefield, 2002. For biographical sketch, see pp. 1 ff.

248   Alexander, op.cit., p. 58.

249   Alexander, op.cit., see pp. 14, 27, 53-54 for the traditional issue of collecting local taxes in Boston.

250   Alexander, op.cit., pp. 30-33.

251   Alexander, op.cit., pp. 55-60.

252   Ferling, John E., *John Adams: A Life*, Knoxville, Tennessee: The University of Tennessee Press, 1992, pp. 11-20 for biographical sketch.

253   Ferling, op.cit., pp. 36-39.

254   Ferling, op.cit., pp. 47-49.

255   Alexander, op.cit., p. 97.

256   Hoare, op.cit., pp. 92-94 for the public impact of this decision in London.

257   The Packard Humanities Institute, *PBF,* editorial in *London Chronicle,* June 18-
20. There is a significant, and apparently previously unrevealed, problem of significance
regarding the dates of the decision from King's Bench, and the date of Franklin's editorial
in the *London Chronicle.* The one group most likely to have been given forewarning of
this decision would be the London meeting of the Society of Friends ("Quakers"), from the
Roman Catholic Lord Mansfield in a chambers discussion with Granville Sharp, and then
from Sharp to Fothergill and perhaps Barclay as well. The wording of the editorial may be
telling: Franklin hedges as to whether the court, or a prior settlement by the British plantation
owners, had actually "freed" Somersett. And remember that the publisher of the *London
Chronicle* is one of Franklin's closest lifelong friends, William Strahan, who could well have
been a confederate in this part of the conspiracy to publicize the *Somersett* decision.

258   Wise, op.cit., pp. 209-210.

259   Wise, op.cit., pp. 202-203.

260   Shakespeare, William, *MacBeth,* Act. I, Scene 7.

261   Alexander, op.cit., p. 97., Schutz, op.cit., p. 229.

262   Schutz, ibid.

263   Bailyn, op.cit., p. 227.

264   Penegar, Kenneth, *The Political Trial of Benjamin Franklin,* New York: Algora
Publishing, 2011, pp. 23-24.

265   Bailyn, op.cit., p. 227.

266   Morgan, Edmund, *Benjamin Franklin,* New Haven, Connecticut: Yale University
Press, 2003, p. 187.

267   Morgan, op.cit., p. 196.

268   Morgan, op.cit., p. 197.

269   Morgan, op.cit., p.196.

270   Labaree, Benjamin Woods, *The Boston Tea Party,* Boston: Northeastern University
Press, 1964, p. 78-79.

271   The behavior of Adams during his exhortation at the Old South Meeting House on December 16, 1773, will forever remain a source of conjecture. While his family and historians of the past fifty years have held firmly to the stance that Adams was in fact trying to suppress the shipboard riots of that evening, he most assuredly did not thereafter condemn the behavior. Rather, he publicly condoned it as the appropriate response to the "illegal" tax on British tea levied upon the colonists, Alexander, op.cit., p. 126 and p. 129.

272   Morgan, op.cit., p. 199.

273   Morgan, op.cit., pp. 205-208.

274   Penegar, op.cit., pp. 23-24.

275   Morgan, op.cit., p. 196. But Franklin knew *precisely* "what he was doing", in direct contradiction to Morgan's conjecture.

276   Morgan, op.cit., p. 199.

277   Morgan, ibid.

278   Morgan, ibid.

279   Morgan, op.cit., p. 197.

280   Morgan, op.cit., p. 202.

281   Isaacson, op.cit., p. 277.

282   for one of the most thorough reviews of the famous "Cockpit Hearing", see the overview from Founders Online, *The Final Hearing before the Privy Council . . .29 January 1774,* New Haven, Connecticut: Yale University Press, 1978, pp. 37-70.

283   all biographical information from Chisholm, Hugh, ed., "Rosslyn, Alexander Wedderburn, First Earl of", *Encyclopedia Britannica, 1911,* Cambridge: Cambridge University Press, 11th edition.

284   Isaacson, op.cit., p 278.

285   Isaacson, ibid.

286   Schutz, op.cit.,

287   Conway, Moncure D., *The Life of Thomas Paine,* London: Watts & Co., 1909, pp. 1-6.

288   Conway, op.cit., p. 7.

289   Conway, op.cit., p. 7-8.

290   Conway, op.cit., p. 9.

291   Conway, op.cit., pp. 11-12.

292   Conway, op.cit., p. 13.

293   Conway, op.cit., p. 15.

294   Conway, op.cit., p. 16.

295   Trinity Writers, *Oliver Goldsmith,* Dublin, Ireland: Trinity College, Dublin, updated 2016.

296   The life of Thomas Paine between June and October, 1774, remains an historical cipher, even for his most definitive biographer, Conway. The only remaining historical record of this time is the coverage of the cost of his emigration to America, borne by Franklin, and the introductory letter penned by Franklin, to Franklin's son-in-law, Richard Bache, written in September, 1774, Conway op.cit., p. 16., v.i.

297   The Packard Humanities Institute, *PBF,* Letter of Charles Dumas, sent after January 28, 1774.

298   Isaacson, op.cit., p. 278.

299   Isaacson, op.cit., pp. 279-280.

300   Isaacson, p. 279.

301   Conway, op.cit., p. 16.

302   Conway, op.cit., p. 20.

303   Morgan, op.cit., p. 65.

304   Hannah, Leslie, *Oxford Dictionary of National Biography,* Oxford: University Press, online edition, 2019, see "Barclay, David (1729-1809)". It is regrettable that at the present time, no definitive biography has yet been written of this most influential 18th century British banker, political figure, and religious leader, v.i., especially in the Epilogue.

305   Ackrill, Margaret and Hannah, Leslie, *Barclays: The Business of Banking 1690-1996,* Cambridge: University Press, 2007, pp. 8-14.

306   Ackrill and Hannah, op.cit., p. 16.

307   Ackrill and Hannah, op.cit., p. 18.

308   Currey, op.cit., pp. 75-76.

309   Isaacson, pp. 325-326.

310   Isaacson, op.cit., pp. 320-321.

311   The Packard Humanities Institute, *PBF,* to Dumas, Saturday, December 9, 1775: Franklin writes in response to Dumas to encrypt all further correspondence to Arthur Lee in London due to concerns re: intercepted correspondence by British agents overseas.

312   --------, "The Cistercian Order: Medieval and Early Modern Challenges", Cistercian Abbey/Our Lady of Dallas, cistercian.org.

313   Ellis, Joseph J., *His Excellency, George Washington,* New York: Alfred E. Knopf, 2004, pp. 92-109.

314   James, James Alton, "Oliver Pollock: The Life and Times of an Unknown Patriot", New York: -----, 1937, p. 1 ff.

315   O'Meara, Walter, *Guns at the Forks,* Pittsburgh: University of Pittsburgh Press, 2005, p. 249.

316   Conway, op.cit., p. 16.

317   Conway, op.cit., p. 18.

318   Isaacson, op.cit., p. 282.

319   Isaacson, op.cit., p. 285, Morgan, op.cit., p. 212.

320 Isaacson, op.cit., p. 284.

321 Isaacson, op.cit., p. 286.

322 Isaacson, op.cit., p. 287, Morgan, op.cit., pp. 215-217.

323 The Packard Humanities Institute, *PBF,* return correspondence from Dumas [original apparently destroyed], May 17, 1775.

324 Isaacson, op.cit., pp. 287-288.

325 Isaacson, op.cit., p. 288.

326 Jenkins, Howard, "The Family of William Penn (continued). IX. Thomas Penn", *The Pennsylvania Magazine of History and Biography,* vol. 21, no. 3, 1897, pp. 343-344.

327 Isaacson, op.cit., p. 205.

328 Morgan, op.cit., p. 218. The essay by Franklin cited here, sums up in a few words, Franklin's anger and dejection over the absolutely deplorable state of corruption in Parliament as he saw it, in March, 1775.

329 Isaacson, op.cit., p. 288.

330 Fox, op.cit., p. 378, regarding Fothergill's progressive loss of spirit at this point in his life.

331 Fox, op.cit., p. 336. This author's point of view is purely that of Barclay and Fothergill, and affirms their stance at that point in time, that the American colonies were the *only remaining hope* for English-speaking peoples of all demographics to secure an honest, free, and democratic form of government. Far from rejecting the demands of the American patriots, they were at this time expressing their disapproval of their own government, and wished Franklin ultimate success.

332 Isaacson, op.cit., pp. 290-291.

333 Isaacson, op.cit., pp. 291-292, Morgan, op.cit., pp. 224-225.

334 Morgan, op.cit., p. 225.

335 Isaacson, op.cit., p. 292.

336   Isaacson, op.cit., pp. 293-294.

337   Isaacson, op.cit., p. 296, Morgan, op.cit., p. 225.

338   Buach, Jr., Allan J., *Charles William Frederick Dumas and the American Revolution (1775-1783)*, Omaha, Nebraska: University of Nebraska, 1966, pp. 4-5. The Secret Committee of Correspondence, with Harrison, Franklin, Jefferson, Dickinson, and Jay, was already being formulated when the "Olive Branch Petition" was sent to King George III.

339   Isaacson, op.cit., p. 298.

340   Isaacson, op.cit., p. 299.

341   Isaacson, op.cit., pp. 301-302, Currey, op.cit., p. 60.

342   Isaacson, op.cit., pp. 302-304, Currey, op.cit., pp. 60-61.

343   Isaacson, ibid.

344   Morgan, op.cit., pp. 228-229.

345   Currey, op.cit., p. 73.

346   Morgan, op.cit., pp. 229-230, Buach, op.cit., pp. 5-6.

347   Conway, op.cit., p. 25.

348   Buach, op.cit., p. 11.

349   Buach, op.cit., pp. 16-17.

350   Isaacson, op.cit., pp. 307-308, Morgan, op.cit., 230-231. The massive impact of this effort, and the mistaken attribution to Franklin, is thoroughly discussed in Conway, op.cit., pp. 25-32.

351   Isaacson, op.cit., pp. 305-307, Morgan, op.cit., pp. 230-231.

352   Isaacson, op.cit., p. 308, Morgan, op.cit., p. 231.

353   Isaacson, op.cit., pp. 310-312.

354   Isaacson, p. 312.

355   Calhoun, Jeanne A., "Thomas Lee of Stratford, 1690-1750: Founder of a Virginia Dynasty", *Northern Neck of Virginia Historical Magazine,* vol. XLI, no. 1 (1991), recovered on-line September 27, 2007, for biographical information on the Lee family.

356   Isaacson, op.cit., pp. 316-320, Morgan, op.cit., pp. 231-236.

357   Isaacson, op.cit., pp. 320-322, Morgan, op.cit., pp. 240-241.

358   Chisholm, Hugh, ed., "Arthur Lee", *Encyclopaedia Britannica,* Cambridge: Cambridge University Press, 1911, for biographical information.

359   Isaacson, op.cit., p. 321.

360   Morgan, op.cit., p.256.

361   Center for the Study of Intelligence, "Beaumarchais and the American Revolution", *Central Intelligence Agency Documents Approved for Release*, 22 September, 1993, for the most exhaustive retelling of the entire, extremely convoluted "Beaumarchais affair". The legitimacy and lack thereof, by Arthur Lee and by Silas Deane, can be left to the reader of this document.

362   Schaeper, op.cit., pp. 1-3.

363   Schaeper, op.cit., p. 5.

364   Schaeper, op.cit., pp. 13-14.

365   Schaeper, op.cit., p. 42.

366   Schaper, op.cit., pp. 263-272, for an extensive discussion of the ongoing controversy regarding the complicated relationship between Franklin, Bancroft, and the British government during the American Revolution.

367   Currey, op.cit., p. 84.

368   Schaeper, op.cit., p. 69.

369   Currey, op.cit., p. 85.

370   Schaeper, op.cit., p. 143.

371 Covart, Elizabeth M., "Silas Deane: Forgotten Patriot" *Journal of the American Revolution,* July 30, 2014, on-line, for biographical information.

372 Schaeper, op.cit., p. 48-49.

373 Schaeper, op.cit., p. 49

374 Buach, op.cit., pp. 27-28.

375 Center for the Study of Intelligence, ibid.

376 Currey, op.cit., pp. 97-98. This ruse was set up to last through the Revolution, and Jefferson in Paris after the war, was shown thousands of similar worthless firearms which had been gathered, had the British blockade proven efficient, to continue to use as decoys.

377 Schaeper, op.cit., p. 53.

378 Isaacson, op.cit., p. 324, Morgan, op.cit., pp. 240-241.

379 Schaeper, op.cit., p. 72.

380 Isaacson, op.cit., pp. 305-306.

381 Schaeper, ibid.

382 Buach, op.cit., p. 30. Deane, it would appear, never really pursued encryption aggressively, and this would be yet another factor in Franklin's ultimate decision to sever all ties with Deane.

383 Buach, op.cit., p. 31.

384 Schaeper, op.cit., p. 85.

385 Isaacson, op.cit., p. 331, Schaeper, op.cit., pp. 86-87.

386 Isaacson, op.cit., p. 329.

387 Currey, op.cit., p. 116.

388 Schaeper, op.cit., p. 86., Currey, op.cit., p. 117.

389 Schaeper, op.cit., pp. 49-50, Currey, loc.cit.

390   Currey, op.cit., pp. 126-127.

391   Schaeper, op.cit., pp. 85-87. Schaeper is but one of many authors, including future president John Adams, who immediately picked up on the concept that Lee's presence in Passy was neither needed, nor wanted, nor requested, nor accepted.

392   Schaeper, op.cit., p. 89.

393   Schaeper, op.cit., p. 91.

394   Currey, op.cit., p. 127-128.

395   Currey, op.cit., p. 128.

396   Currey, ibid.

397   Currey, op.cit., pp. 128-129.

398   Currey, op.cit., p. 129.

399   Currey, op.cit., p. 130.

400   Currey, op.cit., pp. 130-131.

401   Buach, op.cit., pp. 34-36.

402   Buach, op.cit., p. 37.

403   Conway, op.cit., p. 34.

404   Conway, op.cit., p. 35.

405   Conway, op.cit., p. 36.

406   Conway, op.cit., pp. 37-48.

407   Conway, op.cit. p. 36.

408   Conway, ibid.

409   Conway, op.cit., p. 38.

410   Conway, p. 37.

411   Morgan, op.cit., p. 196. Franklin had recognized this issue by 1770, and by 1775 was far more comfortable with the vicissitudes of distance in the decision-making issues between Europe and its colonies, than most of his contemporaries.

412   Schaeper, op.cit., pp. 161-162, for just a few examples. Generally, the time delay factor proved not only insurmountable for the British government, but a major contributor to its overall defeat in the American Revolution.

413   Buach, op.cit., p. 38.

414   New York State Division of Military and Naval Affairs: Military History, February 21, 2006.

415   Ketchum, Richard, *Saratoga: Turning Point of America's Revolutionary War,* New York: Henry Holt, 1997, pp. 82-85.

416   Ketchum, op.cit., p. 335.

417   Independence Hall Association, *Virtual Marching Tour of the American Revolutionary War, The Philadelphia Campaign, 1777,* Philadelphia, Pennsylvania: ushistory.org, 1999, for a detailed examination of Howe's relatively inept campaign against Washington, while Burgoyne was marching into a mousetrap.

418   Ketchum, op.cit., p. 171.

419   The Packard Humanities Institute, *PBF,* Dumas to the American Commissioners, 23 January 1778. The loss of this German commander and German army would have disastrous consequences in Prussia and Saxony, where civil war was threatening, and thereafter the King of Prussia was extremely reluctant to continue to facilitate the British practice of hiring German soldiers to fight the British wars.

420   Nickerson, Hoffman, *The Turning Point of the Revolution,* Port Washington, NY: Kennicat, 1967 edition, pp. 180, 216.

421   Ketchum,op.cit., pp. 347-348.

422   Nickerson, op.cit., p. 309; Ketchum, op.cit., p. 362.

423   Schutz, op.cit., p. 236.

424   Schutz, op.cit., p. 237.

425   Schutz, op.cit., pp. 237-238.

426   Schutz, op.cit., pp. 238-239.

427   Schutz, op.cit., p. 240.

428   Schutz, op.cit., p. 241.

429   Schutz, op.cit., p. 247.

430   The Packard Humanities Institute, *PBF,* before February 1, 1778, for an example of the cryptic notes to Franklin from Grand during this critical time, in regard to the laundering of French currency through Amsterdam, and the subtle latitude of dates and places in the transfers to expedite their transmission to the Americans.

431   Isaacson, pp. 343-344.

432   Weber, Ralph, *Masked Dispatches: Cryptograms and Cryptology in American History, 1775-1900,* Washington, D.C.: Center for Cryptologic History, National Security Agency, 2nd edition, 2002, pp. 18-20.

433   Conway, op.cit., pp. 39-40.

434   Conway, op.cit., p. 41.

435   Conway, op.cit., pp. 41-42.

436   Isaacson, pp. 345-346.

437   See the Prologue for the financial and political significance of this statement. Also, Isaacson, op.cit., p. 344.

438   Isaacson, op.cit., p. 347.

439   Isaacson, op.cit., p. 349.

440   Buach, op.cit., p. 33.

441   Currey, op.cit., p. 226.

442   Roider, Karl A., "William Lee: Our First Envoy in Vienna", *The Virginia Magazine of History and Biography*, Vol. 86, no. 2 (1978), pp. 163-168. This is perhaps the most "positively" biased account of the William and Arthur Lee experience in Europe, and still comes across as little more than a "Laurel and Hardy" short subject.

443   Roider, op.cit., p. 167.

444   Buach, op.cit., p. 57.

445   Isaacson, op.cit., pp. 350-353. Lest the reader presume that the 'outrage of Adams' is my peculiar invention, this passage of Isaacson reveals the nature of Adams's perception of Franklin, and of Franklin's idolization in Europe. Adams looked at all of this, and his response was . . . outrage. The personality of John Adams may well have served as the inspiration for the personality of Donald Duck.

446   Conway, op.cit., p. 51.

447   Conway, op.cit., p. 58.

448   Conway, op.cit., pp. 49-51.

449   Middlekauff, op.cit., p. 157.

450   Conway, op.cit., p. 51.

451   Conway, op.cit., p. 52.

452   Conway, op.cit., pp. 55-59, for a thorough retelling of this entire sordid affair, and its fallout in the lives of Deane and Beaumarchais. Deane's gambling against the survival of the United States as a political entity is exposed, and Paine's steadfast assertion of the true source of the 'gift' is affirmed.

453   Schutz, op.cit., pp. 251-252.

454   Schutz, op.cit., pp. 255-256.

455   Schutz, op.cit., p. 256.

456   Schutz, op.cit., pp. 261-262.

457   Schutz, op.cit., p. 262.

458   Morgan, op.cit., p. 262.

459   Isaacson, op.cit., pp. 350-351.

460   Isaacson, op.cit., pp. 382-383.

461   Middlekauff, op.cit., p. 173. Middlekauff's chapter on Adams, pp. 171-202, provides some incisive commentary on the difficult personality of this complicated American diplomat and future president.

462   Middlekauff, op.cit., pp. 167-170, for a thorough discussion of the grief these two inflicted upon the overworked Dr. Franklin, and his unique response to their behavior.

463   Buach, op.cit., p. 60.

464   Isaacson, op.cit., p. 396.

465   Wallace, op.cit., p. 349.

466   Wallace, op.cit., p. 358.

467   Wallace, op.cit., p. 359.

468   Wallace, op.cit., pp. 359-360.

469   Buach, op.cit., pp. 69-70

470   Buach, op.cit., pp. 70-71. The Rule of 1756, by which the British ruled the seas worldwide, was that ports closed to trade with any but a single trading partner during peace-time, could not trade with foreign partners during war-time. This of course applied directly and explicitly to their colonies in North America.

471   Buach, op.cit., pp. 72-76.

472   Buach, op.cit., p. 78.

473   Buach, op.cit., pp. 83-84.

474   Brands, op.cit., p. 577 for biographical information.

475   Brands, ibid.

476   Brands, op.cit., p. 578.

477   Brands, op.cit., p. 579.

478   Buach, op.cit., p. 84.

479   Brands, op.cit., p. 580.

480   Buach, op.cit., p. 85.

481   Buach, op.cit., p. 88.

482   Buach, op.cit., pp. 101-102.

483   Buach, op.cit., p. 105.

484   Buach, op.cit., p. 114. This overview of the "Texel affair" is reviewed by Buach exhaustively in his remarkable thesis, and was politically complex. Franklin, Dumas, and Jones were shamelessly manipulating *three* European governments (France, Great Britain, and the United Provinces) for a simple end: recognition of the United States of America by the United Provinces, to afford Barclay and Dumas the ability to negotiate financial support for the Revolution. They were triumphant in this mission to an extraordinary degree, and *this* would prove John Paul Jones's greatest political victory, far exceeding anything he accomplished on the high seas.

485   Currey, op.cit., p. 185.

486   The Packard Humanities Institute, *PBF,* Monday, October 9, 1780.

487   Isaacson, op.cit., p. 396.

488   Conway, op.cit., pp. 68-69.

489   for biographical information on Lafayette, see especially Leepson, Marc, *Lafayette: Lessons in Leadership from the Idealist General,* London: Palgrave MacMillan, 2011. pp 8-26.

490   Holbrook, Sabra, *Lafayette, Man in the Middle,* New York: Atheneum Books, 1977, pp. 19-20.

491   Brands, H.W., *The First American,* New York: Anchor Books, 2002, p. 594.

492   Brands, ibid.

493   Conway, op.cit., pp. 70-71. The relationship between Paine and Laurens is most assuredly problematic. Laurens was the recipient of the now-famous "I love you" letter from Hamilton (see for example, "From Alexander Hamilton to Lieutenant Colonel John Laurens" [April 1779], National Archives: Founders Online, founders.archives.gov/documents/Hamilton/01-02-02-0100), which creates an enigma to this day as to the sexual proclivities of the sender and recipient. John Laurens was somewhat evasive regarding the reason for his untimely marriage to Martha Manning following her announcement to him of her pregnancy (father? Or empathetic gay suitor seeing a ready family?). For further exposition of this dilemma, see Wallace, op.cit., pp. 464-468. As for Paine, he was married twice, his first marriage ending within one year with the death of his wife. His second marriage ended in annulment presumably for lack of consummation, three *years* after its inception. Conway goes to great lengths to describe this situation (Conway, op.cit., see especially pp. 13-15) and Paine's undying financial devotion to this ex-wife. After that, Paine would never again be described in the company of women by his biographer. I will simply leave conclusions to the reader, but will advise the reader that the sexual proclivities of persons in the 18th century were seldom explicitly described, as homosexuality at that time was a capital offense in the British Empire, and perhaps the majority of homosexual men and women of that era engaged in heterosexual (and not infrequently platonic and childless) marriages due to societal pressures.

494   Conway, op.cit., p. 70. For a completely different, and clearly fanciful, telling of this encounter, see Wallace, op.cit., pp. 481-485. This version is based on the recollection of William Jackson, John Lauren's secretary, from 1832, 50 *years* after the fact, and fails to recall the presence of Paine altogether, making Laurens's impertinence into a *tour de force* that left the French Crown in awe. As if. Indeed, much of Wallace's efforts here are clearly intended to "whitewash" the Laurens family 130 years too late.

495   Isaacson, op.cit., p. 396.

496   Conway, op.cit., p. 70.

497   Isaacson, loc.cit.

498   Isaacson, op.cit., p. 397.

499   Brands, op.cit., pp. 595-596.

500   Davis, Burke, *The Campaign That Won America,* New York: HarperCollins, 2007, p. 225.

501   Ibid.

502   Davis, op.cit., pp. 229-230.

503   Davis, op.cit., p. 265.

504   Schutz, op.cit., p. 262-263.

505   Schaeper, op.cit., p. 165, Brands, op.cit., p. 601.

506   Brands, op.cit., p. 602.

507   Schutz, op.cit., p. 247.

508   Raphael, Ray, *Founding Myths,* New York: MJF Books, 2004, pp. 211-215 for a thorough discussion of the common misconception that Yorktown equaled the end of hostilities.

509   Wallace, op.cit., pp. 463-494.

510   Wallace, op.cit., pp. 369-370.

511   Wallace, op.cit., pp. 488-490.

512   Isaacson, op.cit., p. 408.

513   Isaacson, op.cit., pp. 415-417.

514   Morgan, op.cit., p. 292, Isaacson, op.cit., p. 417.

515   Conway, op.cit., pp. 72-73.

516   Conway, op.cit., pp. 80-86 for an account of the efforts directed toward Paine to stabilize his pension for life, in tribute to his work on behalf of Franklin and the United States of America (including the mercenary vote of Arthur Lee in the Virginia Legislature).

517   The Packard Humanities Institute, *PBF,* Monday, October 6, 1783.

518   Buach, op.cit., p. 153.

519   Buach, op.cit., pp. 153-156.

520   Buach, op.cit., pp. 176-177.

521   Buach, op.cit., p. 178.

522   Buach, op.cit., p. 186.

523   Currey, op.cit., pp. 14-17.

524   Breig, James, "Dear Eighteenth Century", in *Colonial Williamsburg Journal*, Winter, 2011, on-line.

525   Wise, op.cit., pp. 180-181.

526   Schutz, op.cit., a recounting of all the remarkable roles held by Pownall during the Colonial Era is thoroughly discussed in this biography.

527   Schutz, op.cit., pp. 199-201, and p. 265.

528   Morgan, op.cit., p. 304.

529   Fox, op.cit., p. 275.

530   The Packard Humanities Institute, *PBF*, Monday, April 7, 1783, also quoted in Franklin, op.cit., p. 51. The profound significance of this letter, especially with Franklin including it in his autobiography, has apparently eluded historians to the present time. Benjamin Vaughan credits Franklin here as *the author of American independence*, contemporaneously with the signing of the Treaty of Paris, and with Vaughan in possession of access to the deepest of British intelligence over the previous ten years. The "last seventeen years of your life" statement is most telling.

531   Morgan, op.cit., p. 298.

532   Schutz, op.cit., pp. 268-271.

533   Fox, op.cit., pp. 379-382.

534   Isaacson, op.cit., p. 435.

535   Higginbotham, op.cit., pp. 91-99.

536   Higginbotham, op.cit., pp. 306-310.

537   Blakemore, Erin, *Smithsonian.com,* "George Washington Used Legal Loopholes to Avoid Freeing His Slaves", February 16, 2015.

538   Barclay, David, *An Account of the Emancipation of the Slaves of Unity Valley Pen, in Jamaica,* London: William Phillips, 1801.

539   Schutz, op.cit., pp. 279-284 for this remarkable tale of early Latin American pursuit of independence from Spain.

540   Schutz, op.cit., pp. 284-287.

541   Conway, op.cit. The entire Thomas Paine saga is told in great detail by Conway, and could be a miniseries of books or cinema by itself. I simply commit to the serious history student of Thomas Paine, that remarkable biography.

542   Roosevelt, Theodore, *Gouverneur Morris,* New York: Houghton Mifflin & Co., 1888, p. 289.

543   Wise, op.cit., p. 223.

544   Wise, op.cit. See esp. p. 214. Wise devotes an entire chapter of his *Somerset* (sic) account to this issue, pp. 205-215.

545   Wise, op.cit., pp. 78-79, 183-184.

546   Wise, op.cit., pp. 205-207.

547   Wise, op.cit., pp. 218-219.

548   for the entire discussion of the Charles Asgill affair, see Isaacson, op.cit., p. 413, Conway, op.cit., pp. 75-76.

549   Isaacson, op.cit., pp. 434-435.

550   Isaacson, op.cit., pp. 471-472 for a more exhaustive epilogue of the conclusion of Temple Franklin's life.

551   Isaacson, op.cit., pp. 437-438.

552   Bowen, Catherine, *Miracle at Philadelphia,* New York: Little, Brown & Co., 1966, pp. 169-170.

553   Bowen, op.cit., p. 9.

554   Isaacson, op.cit., p. 455.

555   Isaacson, op.cit., pp. 458-459.

556   Isaacson, op.cit., p. 465.

557   Isaacson, op.cit., pp. 466-467.

558   Isaacson, op.cit., p. 469.

559   Isaacson, ibid.

560   Isaacson, op.cit., pp. 469-470.

Made in the USA
Monee, IL
30 June 2020